The Entrepreneur

Research: James Miller, Helen Sykes, Melanie Jarvis-Vaughan, Peter Guthridge, Mark Gregory and Shawn Willis

Edited By Kizzi Nkwocha (c)

Published with love, respect and admiration by Mithra Publishing 2015

The Entrepreneur is sponsored by My Entrepreneur Magazine.
Visit the magazine at www.myentrepreneurmagazine.com

www.mithrapublishing.com

All rights reserved. No part of this work may be reproduced or transmitted in any form or by any means, electronic or mechanical, including photocopying, recording, or by any information storage or retrieval system, without the prior written permission of the copyright owner and the publisher.

This book is presented solely for educational and entertainment purposes. The author and publisher are not offering it as legal, accounting, or other professional services advice. While best efforts have been used in preparing this book, the author and publisher make no representations or warranties of any kind and assume no liabilities of any kind with respect to the accuracy or completeness of the contents and specifically disclaim any implied warranties of merchantability or fitness of use for a particular purpose.

Neither the author nor the publisher shall be held liable or responsible to any person or entity with respect to any loss or incidental or consequential damages caused, or alleged to have been caused, directly or indirectly, by the information or programs contained herein. No warranty may be created or extended by sales representatives or written sales materials. Every company is different and the advice and strategies contained herein may not be suitable for your situation. You should always seek the services of a competent professional.

Also by Mithra Publishing

Escape Your 9-5 And Do Something Amazing
Customer Service
SocMed: Social Media For Business
How To Start A Business With Little Or No Cash
Facebook For Business
Social Media Marketing: Write Up your Tweet
Getting Your Business LinkedIn
It's That Easy! Online Marketing 3.0
Business, Business, Business!
Mind Your Own Business
Insiders Know-how: Running A PR Agency
Insiders Know-how: Caring For Your Horse
Energy Efficiency
Social PR

Visit us at www.mithrapublishing.com

"Success is walking from failure to failure with no loss of enthusiasm."
Kizzi Nkwocha

"Stop chasing the money and start chasing the passion."
Tony Hsieh

"Take up one idea. Make that one idea your life--think of it, dream of it, live on that idea. Let the brain, muscles, nerves, every part of your body, be full of that idea, and just leave every other idea alone. This is the way to success."

Swami Vivekananda

"All our dreams can come true if we have the courage to pursue them."
Walt Disney

The Inspiring thought leaders profiled in this book:

Garrett Kenny - The Feltrim Group
Jack Barmby - Felicitas Media and Creator of Gnatta
Kemi Egan - The Freedom Group
Michelle Wright – Cause4
Ben and Michael Dyer - The Ryman National Enterprise Challenge
Jensen Wheeler Wolfe – The Little Yoga Mat
Alex Hunn - freemarketFX
Robert Gavin – NDD Group
Luke Goodwin - GripSox
Erika Clegg – Spring
Catherine Broughton - holidaychateaufrance.com
Heidy Rehman - Rose & Willard
Charli Morgan - The Cult PR
Mike O'Hagan – MiniMovers
Melissa Reed - Packable Pails
Jessica Nazarali - Devine living coach
Nicky Leonti - Clarity Consultant & Dream Business Builder
Marcus Orme - Medialab Group
Amber Daines - Bespoke Communications
David J. Bradley - Primal Digital Marketing
Kevin May - Sticks
Fleur Sexton - PET-Xi Training
John Stapleton - Little Dish
Raeleen Hooper – Snap Franchising
Ben Hutchinson - Ginger Sport
Manel Daetz - Henry Corbett & Co

The Entrepreneur is sponsored by My Entrepreneur Magazine.
Visit the magazine at www.myentrepreneurmagazine.com

Inside The Entrepreneur

About Kizzi Nkwocha	15
Welcome To The Entrepreneur	17
The Entrepreneur's Mindset	18
Installing A Winning Mentality	29
Homeless To Real Estate Millionaire In 12 Months	40
Understanding Clarity And Focus	53
The Journey To Cause4	64
Creating An Enterprising Young Britain	77
Helping Young People Make A Change And Get On In Life	85
An Insight Into Entrepreneurship	93
Am I An Entrepreneur?	112
Happiness Is The New Black (And White)	121
Creating Beautiful Environmentally Friendly Yoga Mats	135
From Idea To Reality	140

Creating Solutions For Problems	149
Striving For Success – From Physiotherapist To Sock Entrepreneur	162
Creating A Business Full Of Energy And Positivity	172
An English Entrepreneur In France	188
Creating Something Of Your Own And Seeing It Come To Life	197
A PR Agency Success Story	205
The Making Of A True Entrepreneur: From Scratch To Success	216
Houston We Have A Product	229
Success Coach For New Coaches	236
Clarity Consultant & Dream Business Builder	245
Small Beginnings – Big Ambitions	256
The Secret To Being A Great Entrepreneur? Love What You Do	265
A Leap of Faith	278
Lessons From Sticks	292

About Kizzi Nkwocha

Kizzi Nkwocha made his mark in the UK as publicist, journalist and social media pioneer.

As a widely respected and successful media consultant Nkwocha has represented a diverse range of clients including the King of Uganda, mistresses of President Clinton, Amnesty International, Pakistani cricket captain Wasim Akram, campaign group Jubilee 2000, Dragons Den businessman, Levi Roots and world record teenage sailor, Michael Perham.

Nkwocha has also become a well-known personality on both radio and television. He has been the focus of a Channel 4 documentary on publicity and has hosted his own talk show, London Line, on Sky TV.

He also co-presented a weekly current affairs program in Spain on Radio Onda Cero International and both radio and TV shows in Cyprus.

His books have included the fiction novel, Heavens Fire, the business guide books: Business, Business, Business!, Mind Your Own Business, Insiders Know-How: Public Relations and the international bestseller SocMed: Social Media For Business.

Nkwocha publishes the online marketing magazines,
My Entrepreneur Magazine (www.myentrepreneurmagazine.com)
Social Biz Magazine (www.socialbizmagazine.com),
My Logistics Magazine (www.mylogisticsmagazine.com)
and My Well-being Magazine (www.mywellbeingmagazine.com).
He also runs a successful agency called Social Biz Training which trains people to use social media for business. His agency site is at www.socialbiztraining.com

Follow Kizzi on Twitter: https://twitter.com/kizzinkwocha

Welcome to The Entrepreneur

The very nature of being an entrepreneur and an innovator means that you fully embrace ambiguity and are comfortable with being challenged regularly. Choosing this career path is completely irrational because the odds of succeeding are dismal, but most succeed because of their unwavering belief, laser focus on delivering and persistence.
Starting a company, or managing a company through a period of transition and growth, can be a riveting roller coaster of emotions with tremendous highs and at times, difficult lows. But despite the challenges, many men and women have risen to become leaders and influential figures in their respective areas. The Entrepreneur recognizes and celebrates the outstanding contribution made by individual men and women to their businesses and, in many cases, their local communities.
The business leaders profiled in this book are of various ages, social backgrounds and industries. However, the one common thread which unites them is that they dared to believe. And, in believing, they made the seemingly impossible a reality.
Their individual stories tell of the challenges we all face: uncertainty, fear, discouragement, hope, commitment and yes, that indefinable, illogical and yet all-consuming belief that we will succeed against all odds. These are real-life individual stories of success that I hope will also encourage you to believe - and to make that difference.

Kizzi Nkwocha, Editor of My Entrepreneur Magazine

The Entrepreneur's Mindset
Garrett Kenny - Feltrim Group

In 2008 in the midst of perhaps the greatest crisis the real estate industry faced in a generation, our company was facing a moment of truth. I had just opened my biggest project up to that point; a $100 million condo resort near Disney World in Orlando, but we had opened at the worst possible time. Bear Sterns and Lehman Brothers had collapsed. The mortgage market had dried up and the bottom fell out of the real estate industry. We became seriously exposed and were facing a takeover or worse.

The bank from whom I raised the finance to build our new project had sent an investor down to us from New York in order to buy the loan we had taken out to build the project. He was a tough individual and was adamant that we would repay all the money and that he would own all of our companies - as they were used as collateral. So he essentially would 'own me'. My Chief Financial Advisor was getting very worried during the discussions that we would end up working for this individual forever in order to pay off the debt. This was definitely our darkest hour.

So facing possible collapse I tried to ask myself what were this guy's hot buttons, what made him tick. Often when you're doing a deal you need to look at things from the other side, to understand what is driving him or her. When the investor came down to see us, on the first day he made it known that he paid for his own flights and accommodation; something the bank apparently should have done. He was a very wealthy individual and had significant resources behind him, and made no secret of the fact, and had a especially healthy ego. He told us he would always buy at the right price and that would never pay what a bank was asking. So in this instance I listened a lot. I phoned the bank that evening and said that the investor they sent was pretty tough to deal with, has a lot of money, but that he was buying the project very cheaply. They responded that they had told him what the deal was, and told me that if he tried to change it then the deal was off. So on one side I had someone who wanted to buy back the loan cheaply, and I had the bank on the other side who wanted a certain price. So the next day when meeting the investor I told him he was paying too much for these units, and I drilled this in to him all day. He got back on the plane and flew back to New York. When he was back he phoned the bank and told them he was going to pay a lot less than what they wanted. The bank told him to get lost, and I lived to fight another day.

When approached to write this chapter I started to think about what has it been that has allowed us to be as successful as we have become in business, and this story I think sums up a lot of it. Firstly money is always a challenge, and trying to raise and manage finances responsibly is hard work. Secondly dealing with people and being able to think on your feet is essential. Its often a battle of wits, but I've always had a good ability to look at any deal a few moves down the chess board, and this is crucial in doing business at any level. Determination not to give up regardless of what challenge you face - and I've faced many - means there is always a solution as long as you believe in what you are doing. You need to also go with your instincts, learn from lessons and naturally have a bit of luck. So in this chapter I'd like to talk about what I think makes an entrepreneur, then I go through my own career and try to relate these themes to what I have done, giving a few tips at the end, and hope that this can provide some useful tidbits of advice for others who have a dream or a goal.

The Entrepreneurial Mindset

I think entrepreneurship is a mindset. You can give people advice, tell them what to watch out for, and, some advice is very useful and can stay with you, but you can't teach entrepreneurship. Its something that is innate, its really about belief and determination, about creativity, about being able to spot opportunities and going for them. You don't need to be intellectual, but you do need to be intelligent. Now there are different levels of entrepreneurship; some people set up a small business, they stick with it, maybe earn a decent living, enough to get by and life goes on. There's nothing wrong with this. But what I'm talking about though is almost every waking hour you're trying to move forward, you're thinking about the business, you're thinking about doing a deal, you're on the phone, you're emailing in your sleep and you're constantly spotting opportunities, no minute is wasted. If someone has the ability to do something for you, you ask them, the worst they can say is no. Now, it doesn't mean you don't enjoy the other things in life, you do, but your reason for being here is the business and to do the deal. You want to make money and be rewarded for your work, and that's important, but its the deal, or achieving something worthwhile that drives you.

This mindset has no use for faulty logic, especially from people you rely on. I am the first to admit I don't know everything, but everything can be explained. I don't let things slide, if I don't understand something or why something has happened, I'll press the issue until I do. I want to understand how something works whether its a bill of lading or a Google ad campaign. If I have the information I can make informed decisions. It also means you have your house in order, you pay bills on time, you pay your staff, you fulfill your end of the agreement. This way you're straight to deal with and you build and protect a good reputation. It all makes sense when you read it, but so many people don't do business this way and they are at a disadvantage.

Now I'm not a literature buff but something that the Irish writer George Bernard Shaw said has stayed in my mind. He said that the reasonable man tries to adapt to the world around him, and that the unreasonable man makes the world adapt to him, so history is determined by the unreasonable man. So you try to make things adapt to what you need. This doesn't mean you have to be arrogant. Well, maybe to an extent. You do need to have a dogged determination to get something done, to not give up, to not take no for an answer, and if you're too reasonable maybe you won't fight for your idea. While you need to understand the other side, you can't empathize too much or you'll never get anywhere, and in that case you'd be better off working for someone else. Though having said that, if you get information that tells you that you're wrong, then you go with the information. Facts are facts, so don't be too stubborn either.

Everyone is different and I don't want to compare myself to people who have become household names, but if I look at Steve Jobs, or to take an Irish example Michael O'Leary who runs the world's most profitable airline, I think they have all these things in common. They work hard, they live for the business and they succeed. Now, not everyone can be Steve Jobs, but you can succeed, you can do well and you can get to places you never imagined possible.

It's a Cliché but What Can I do?
I suppose its a familiar story, you start by sweeping the floors and before you know it you have a fleet of trucks in Ireland or you're building a multi million dollar resort in Florida. I don't mean to be clichéd but that's how it happened. I left school in my native Dublin about three months before graduating high school or what in Ireland we called secondary school. This was the late seventies and Ireland was not in a good state, so jobs were few and far between. So when I had the opportunity to work I left school and took a job sweeping floors and looking after a warehouse. I was 16 but told them I was 17 in order to get the job.

After about one year on the job I approached my boss. I would see how transport companies or truck drivers would let him down by arriving late or by not turning up, or by getting stuck in traffic or by delivering a baby on the side of the road or who knows what. So I asked him that if I were to get my own truck would he give me some work. He said he wouldn't like to let me go but that yes he could give me some work. It wouldn't be enough to keep me going he said, but I said that's ok, that I would try to get work from others as well. I managed to get a loan from the bank for a truck, though not the truck I wanted, it didn't have a lift at the back, so I'd have to bend my knees a lot, but it was a start. I soon got busy and had more than enough work for a second truck. Though of course I didn't have the money, so I went back to my former boss and asked him to lend me some. He did and I paid him back within the year. So finance was an issue, but I knew what I was doing was working so found a way.

By the time I was in my late twenties we had a successful business with over 20 trucks on the road. Now Ireland is about the size of New Jersey in the US, so for Ireland and in the 80s, in the midst of continuing recession, that was a decent sized business. I also became trusted to transport concert equipment and worked with U2, Meat Loaf, Bob Geldof and others.

During that early period I tried to keep my nose clean, I only owned a second hand car, for a few years I also drove a truck myself, I didn't overstretch, made sure everyone was paid on time and we delivered on promises. People were happy to do business with us and our business grew as a result.

When we're playing football we play to win

So how do you move from trucks to building resorts? Well it didn't happen over night. My interest in property was born out of necessity at first. I needed a warehouse to store goods, as renting space was proving to be more of a pain than anything else. So I bought my own warehouse. Soon I needed more space, and I sold that warehouse, made a profit, and bought a second more than twice the size. I wondered how I would fill this one, but then within a year it was full, so I sold that one, made a profit again, and next time I bought one with some land adjacent, so that if I ran out of space I could build more. With this new space I had three warehouses, and since I had all this space I ended up building commercial space to rent out. This was in the Feltrim part of North Dublin; it became my first development and gave the name to my group. So I started to think. When I bought a truck, the moment I took it off the lot for the first time it began depreciating in value, yet here was this real estate, fully leased, appreciating in value, and what's more it never complained, and it never showed up late. So I began look at this more seriously and to branch into other industrial developments. I also started by buy, sell and rent residential properties, and on some I managed to make a sizable profit when sold on. So when the development and real estate business began taking off and started to overtake the logistics business in terms of revenue I sold it and dedicated myself full time to property.

What made me make the switch to real estate was seeing the opportunity. It wasn't an opportunity that I was detached from, it was working for me already before I had made the switch in my mind, and so I slowly moved things in that direction. People say don't give up your bread and butter business, your core business and they can be right. But it was already working and my philosophy is that it doesn't matter what the nature of the business is, you can understand any business if you try, and the same principles and approach to work apply. For me property development seemed to have proven advantages over what I had been doing to that point, so I took my determination to that and it worked.

While I was in one of my larger industrial projects at that time, there was an issue getting the land I owned re-zoned for industrial purposes. It took six years but we got there in the end. During the time one of my main investor partners was getting worried that the land would not be re-zoned. In the meeting when he started to seriously worry, and I had no answer for him, and didn't have anything that could re-assure him, but one of my managers said to him straight; "When we're playing football we play to win. This land will be re-zoned." That diffused the situation, and the determination in that statement got us through that period, it did end up getting rezoned thankfully. Its a lesson I've taken with me; you play to win, you're in business to do deals, you're not in it for the good of your health. You don't hope that maybe you will do a deal….no, you do them, and you find a way.

Building on Success

I started to visit Orlando on vacation in the mid 80's and stayed in the Disney resorts. I liked the place from the start. For me America was the best place for service, I liked the scale and ambition in everything. Nowhere did it like America. After a few years of visiting I decided to buy a house in Orlando. I had seen that people were buying vacation homes and renting them out while they were not visiting, so I looked in to it. That first house was 4 bedrooms, a nice resort and cost $160,000. Exceptional value and I managed to buy with a mortgage. I went back to Ireland told some of my colleagues and friends about the value, and then they wanted to do the same. (In fact I sold the house at a profit later on.) So I was now starting to send people over to the broker I had been dealing with, and I was now starting to earn money on this. There was a property management company looking after the homes, but they were letting us down and causing problems. So as I was the one who got everyone in to this I decided to set up my own property management firm to look after these properties more efficiently, this was 1998, and at this point we opened our first office in Florida. From there the business began to expand; we branched into development both commercial and residential and it grew quickly becoming the main business. I finally moved over to Florida and dedicated myself full time to business in the US. You might think that moving to the US was a big step, and moving into the unknown a little. But I found the US to be a great environment for business, and if an idea doesn't work you try again and people give you a second chance. As of this writing we have built and sold over $600 million worth of property in the United States. We have staff now in Florida, Ireland, the UK, Brazil and China.

It hasn't always been easy of course; I mentioned in the introduction when things came to a head during the recession. We kept ourselves going through the recession, again by determination. When property development went down, we started buying and refurbishing foreclosed or cheaper properties and either selling them on at a profit or renting them out. When no-one was buying I flew to China and found clients willing to buy when no-one else was, and built a successful network of agents there.

People sometimes look at our business and see how successful we've become and wonder why we haven't made the leap to something more corporate. Its a good question, perhaps a corporate joint venture could be a way to grow the firm further. I tried it for a short period but it wasn't me. I need to be able to make quick decisions, to go with my instinct. People say I should delegate more and not be so involved in the minutiae of the business. For me delegation or responsibility is earned.

At times I've stepped back and been more democratic only to find that I need to get back in embrace the Napoleon in me and get more hands on, especially in periods like the recession. We're not one of these so called learning businesses or I'm not Google, people don't sit on beanbags, but there is a flexibility in the organization that many others don't have. I'm fortunate that the continued success of the business has allowed me to provide my family with a good life, and I am very ambitious for the business. Perhaps the corporate side will be for the next generation. We'll see. In the meantime I have a trade show to prepare for and a new development to launch.

5 Tips on Being Successful as an Entrepreneur

I thought I would try to list a few personal tips that I think can be important in being successful in business. I said earlier that an entrepreneur is not made, instead born. I believe that's true but it doesn't mean you can't take some advice. The below isn't a definitive list by any means but its what has been important in how I have done business over the years

1. **Be Determined**

This is one of those things that you have it or you don't. You're someone who is energetic or you're not. If you have an idea then you make it work and you reap the rewards. There is always a way to do something, there is always a solution. Whether its getting started, or branching in to a new venture, or solving a problem; it can be done. Don't put up barriers or objections, let others have the objections. You need to be optimistic and positive.

2. **Believe in what you're Doing**

You need to know that you're idea will work, that belief or passion will carry you much of the way. But if you're wrong then you're wrong, if you get information that means you need to change something then go with it. Your belief will also inspire passion and confidence in others, whether its a potential partner, a banker or an employee.

3. Build and Protect a Good Reputation
Get a reputation as someone who delivers, who is straight to deal with. I'm very pleased to have developed good working relationships with many people in different kinds of organizations including local government. If people see you as someone of integrity they will be happy to do business and will help you. Reputation is sacrosanct. Get back to people, and never be afraid to take a call.

4. Delegate but Be in Charge
I said above that responsibility is earned. Through both loyalty and through delivering people earn trust. Loyalty is important. I may not be a literature buff, but I like movies. In one scene in the original Godfather movie, Al Pacino's character Michael turns to his brother Fredo, who had just been taking the side of Michael's adversary in a heated discussion, and says "Fredo you're my older brother and I love you, but don't ever take sides against the Family, ever". Pay your staff, be fair, reward them, tell them they've done a good job, be an example, command (not demand), respect and loyalty, but be in charge.

5. Never Give Up
This is somewhat related to the first point. No matter what is thrown at you, whether the economy has tanked, whether you have made a mistake, whether it's financing issues, and if no-one will listen to your idea, you don't give up. You keep pushing, persevering and you'll succeed. That's what an entrepreneur does.

Garrett Kenny

Garrett Kenny is the founder, owner and CEO of the Feltrim Group; a group of companies located near Orlando in Florida that specializes in resort and property development. The firm has become recognized as one of the premier developers in Central Florida and was recently commended by Governor Rick Scott as making a significant contribution to the local economy. Feltrim has built and sold over USD $600 million worth of property in Florida with many new projects in the pipeline.

A true self made man, Garrett, born in 1962, left school in his native Ireland at an early age in order to take any work he could get, and within a few short years had built a successful nationwide logistics company, transporting various goods including concert equipment for well known international acts such as U2 and others. He diversified into property development and investment and eventually made the move to Florida in the late 90's. Garrett is a classic entrepreneur and continues to run his business that way. He is proof that no matter where you are, or no matter what industry you're in, if you're dedicated and put your mind to it you can be successful.

Installing a winning mentality

Marcus Orme is the CEO of Medialab Group

My journey to becoming an entrepreneur wasn't one that will go down in history. I didn't start a company aged 14 using a telephone box and a yellow pages. Neither did I start a tech company while still at University. My journey started in a way that tens of thousands of graduates start their careers. I joined the world of work as an eager graduate looking to make my impact on the business world. 18 years later I still work for the same company. However that company is now my company and has moved from being a one product company to a leading London agency that plans media for many of the UK's leading brands.

Back in 1997 when I graduated with my History and Politics Degree, Marketing seemed like an interesting career to get into. Iconic adverts such as the famous Guinness surfers 'Good things come to those who wait' were making headlines and becoming forms of entertainment rather than just adverts. However, past my fascination with marketing on a basic level, I had little understanding of the channels involved or the granular level techniques that could be applied. So when a job came up at Fleet Street Publications, to work in their data admin support team (SDMS). I jumped at the chance to get on the ladder - it was an excellent chance to learn a trade.

Suddenly the world of marketing opened up to me. Marketing wasn't just about entertaining people during the commercial break on TV, it was about reaching an audience, the right audience and it was about using varied techniques to convince an audience to buy what you were offering. Quickly I realised that data was at the core everything that we did and I became fascinated by the insight that data could deliver such as understanding a customer's lifetime value. I loved working through the mechanics of how to run a successful direct response direct mail campaigns from start to completion, and it became clear to me that my OCD was going to serve me well in this line of business as marketing, and especially response driven marketing, requires a rigorous scientific approach and an unfaltering attention to detail.

Looking back I was fortunate to start working in an industry about to experience seismic change. Being in the right place at the right time certainly helped, but for me, success came from seeing an opportunity on the horizon, having the confidence to grasp that opportunity and working hard, very hard, to make it into a success. We are all familiar with the Mark Twain quote "if you keep doing what you have always done, you will get the same result". Well in my opinion, this couldn't be more relevant to business. I believe success comes from constantly changing and evolving to stay relevant to your clients' needs. Real success comes from pre-empting the change and delivering a product or service before a client knows they have that need. Of course it depends on the industry you are in – the pace of change in some industries such as technology cannot be compared to less dynamic industries such as shipping but the sentiment can be applied regardless.

Another quote that resonates with me is from golfer, Gary Player who once famously said "the harder I work the luckier I get" and I couldn't agree more. I know of very few successful business people who haven't busted a gut to get to where they are today. People have said to me in the past that I'm lucky to be in the position that I am in, but they usually don't realise it is the result of working through many weekends, constant late nights and the occasional cancelled holidays – I' m afraid it goes with the territory. If you are truly passionate about your business you never really switch off.

After spending 7 years working my way through the ranks from Sales Executive to Director of the Media Sales division which was renting the newsletter mailing lists to third party advertisers, my real entrepreneurial journey started. By 2004, and at the tender age of 30, I was the Managing Director, responsible for a company that had a successful but limited product offering. However, I was convinced there was a greater opportunity and had diversified outside of our core area. This had proved a great success for the business as it had increased our revenues and also established the company as a leading supplier in the area of list management and broking. The problem was that our parent company didn't really want to diversify outside of their core business of publishing and marketing newsletters. It was what they did and they did it exceptionally well and for them it wasn't in line with their strategy. For me this presented a significant opportunity – the chance to initiate a management buy-out and maximise on the opportunities that were starting to present themselves within the rapidly changing marketing industry.

In 2004 the marketing industry was a significantly different beast to what it had been when I had started out as a fresh-faced graduate. Internet usage had increased exponentially with 70% of households having access to the internet. New channels were emerging such as the launch of Facebook that entered onto the market in 2004 and marketing budgets were under increased scrutiny as boards wanted to understand the link between spend and results. This all pointed to one thing – marketing channels that were measurable and direct were winning greater and greater shares of budgets. Traditional marketing channels such as TV that had typically 'owned' marketing budgets were securing a smaller share of advertisers' budgets and their effectiveness was starting to be questioned. For me – this was my epiphany moment. What if we could create a leading marketing agency that could capitalise on this growth in response marketing? With our current limited but successful product offering we had the foundations of what could be a strong proposition.

So in 2004 I and 2 other members of the management team, Ben Ennis and Alex Kirk conducted a management buy-out of the business. Having never gone through the process of a management buyout before, it was a steep learning curve but we took it step by step and made sure that we carried out thorough due diligence. Of course we had the benefit of having worked inside the business so we knew how secure the client base was, we knew the team that was working within the business and importantly we know the potential that the business had. However we needed to get an in-depth understanding of the costs associated with the business post-buy-out and we needed to ensure we could turn the business into the type of business that we wanted. So 18 months after I initiated the buy-out, I along with 2 Directors became the owner of a successful business but only offering a small number of direct marketing services to organisations. Our immediate challenges were three-fold; to keep the business profitable and retain our existing client-base. Secondly to build revenues in our core business area and thirdly, to diversify outside our core business to build the long-term business that we wanted.

The first thing that we did was to put in place solid account management function that focussed on delivering an undisturbed service to our existing clients. We were acutely aware that without this revenue stream our other plans wouldn't get off the ground. So to secure existing client revenues, a reward structure was put in place to incentivise account management team to deliver the highest level of service and results for this important client base. Our second focus was to continue building revenues in our core business. By now we were well established and respected in this area and had gained a reputation for high service levels and delivering results for clients. Our existing team were targeted with building revenues in this core area so that we could continue to take advantage of this area of expertise.

So with our core business protected and growing, we turned our attention to building a successful integrated media agency. By now channel changes were gathering pace and the momentum for change within the marketing industry was unstoppable. In 2006 digital spend was starting to increase as new channels such as email, search engine marketing and even social media were producing valuable returns for companies. 2006 saw the launch of Twitter which had yet to make an impact on marketing plans, but was already on the radar of forward-thinking agencies and marketers. In short, the market was changing and fast. This presented both an opportunity and a threat to our business as the number of opportunities to diversify into new areas was huge, however the competition for budget on our core business was growing under the pressure from new channels.

In my opinion we only had one route – to diversify our business, build revenue streams in new and emerging areas that would allow us to build an integrated media agency with a diverse product offering and also spread our risk away from a narrow product offering. We needed to embrace change within the industry and be at the forefront of this change. We didn't want to be playing catch-up on the changes happening within the industry so it was critical for us to create an environment that would encourage rather than inhibit innovation. So in 2006 we set about transforming our business. For me it was clear that there were 3 things that we needed – the right skill base, the right environment that could incubate innovation and the right business structure and processes that could allow change to happen.

Getting the right team
Getting and keeping the right team is undoubtedly the most important factor in the success of any business. Back in 2006 we had a good foundation, with a strong management team and a team of people that were strong in our core area. However the key is to be honest about where you are and what you are lacking. I knew that we had gaps in certain areas, especially those areas that we wanted to diversify into, so I set about recruiting talent to fill the holes in our expertise and really kick-start change in key areas. For me, the old adage that you should always recruit people better than yourself really rings true. In our business we never let our ego's rule our decisions, especially when it comes to recruitment. Our aim is to always recruit people who can move the business forward and who will thrive in the environment that we have worked hard to create. Finding and successfully recruiting the right talent is an ongoing challenge. Getting the right balance of skills, personality and importantly, finding people that bring different qualities is key to success. I am always surprised how many businesses underestimate the value of emotional intelligence when recruiting. People deal with people they like so I always look for people with rounded personalities. It's not just about what's on their CV, you really have to trust your gut instinct when it comes to recruitment.

I also strongly believe that it's important to have a soundboard and surround yourself with people who will bring a different perspective and challenge your ideas whether that's at a management team level or across the company. As a business owner, you have to be open to criticism and also be able to give criticism that is constructive and delivered in such a way that will improve the person not just demotivate them. I am not a particularly religious person, but there is one mantra that I have stuck to throughout my life, both at work and personally and that is 'Do unto others as you would be done by'. I only speak to people in a way that I'm willing to be spoken to myself! This has consistently served me well and I have always tried to impart this onto my team.

Of course, salary and monetary benefits have a significant impact on performance and motivation. Incentives for the team are important. Your team need to see that their hard work is not just to the benefit of the senior team and that they see a direct monetary impact. It also nurtures team spirit and bonding between our team which helps when your al working hard together. But of equal importance is the ability to feel part of something where there is the opportunity to grow and make an impact. As the business grows this is harder to achieve, and will no doubt become one of our biggest challenges in the future, but we believe that financial rewards alone are only part of the solution.

Getting the right environment
I knew that if we were going to achieve our goals there was going to be a lot of change in the business. One thing I was certain of was that if we were going to be successful, change needed to be initiated by everyone in the business. A top-down approach where everyone feels like change is forced onto them just wasn't going to cut it. Creating a culture of innovation was critical to our vision. The market was changing fast and we needed the business to keep pace with this change. This meant that we needed everyone on board and able to not only work in an environment that was constantly evolving, but also be instrumental in initiating and effecting that change. Today we achieve this through not only sharing the company vision, but also encouraging staff to help create the vision. It's all very well saying that you want your staff to feel part of something but you have to put your money where your mouth is and allow participation, not only in the implementation of the plan but also the creation of the vision. At the end of the day, management don't have the monopoly on good ideas so it would be short-sighted to exclude views of team members, especially in

our industry where younger members of the team are often better placed to make suggestions on channels such as social media. And it's not only creating the vision that is important. We go to great lengths to ensure progress is reported regularly so the team can contribute in a meaningful way. We work hard through annual company presentations and weekly team meetings to ensure a joined up approach. No one in the team should ever be in the dark about the company's common goals, objectives and its trading position.

Installing a winning mentality was also key to our success. Being competitive is good and we celebrate success whether that's through monetary reward or just through recognition which can be more powerful. We are careful to do this in a gracious way, but never the less we do celebrate success and I was keen to ensure that we never lost sight of this important business ethic. Whilst we wanted to encourage healthy competition I also wanted to ensure our long-term business interests were protected. For this reason I have always instilled in the team that we are not interested in quick wins, we don't over promise and under-deliver and we NEVER take existing business for granted. This has served us well and our client retention rates are testament to this.

Facilitating change
Encouraging the whole team to contribute to the strategy is great, but this falls down as soon as you don't have the structure and process in place to allow innovative ideas to happen. Our aim is to encourage everyone within the business to be an entrepreneur. Everyone from Chief Executive Officer to Account Executive is encouraged to generate innovative ideas, develop business cases and champion those ideas within the business. Of course there has to be a system in place to assess ideas and establish if they are right for the business, but having the ability to impact on the business in this was is extremely motivating for the team and provides an invaluable stream of product development for the business. Some of our most profitable business divisions have started out as an idea by a member of staff who has gone on to develop it into a revenue generating business division. For me this is one of the businesses biggest successes. There's

nothing more rewarding than seeing an idea being transformed into a real business division by a member of the team who has taken ownership and made it a success.

However, if you are going to give your team the freedom to pursue their own ideas and projects, it's vitally important to recognise that some of those projects won't get off the ground. Obviously I want every project to succeed but that's not realistic so you just have to stand back and look at the projects that didn't work out and say that's ok, let's move on. It sounds strange but I want people to be motivated by a failed project – I encourage them to think about what they learned and how can they use the experience to improve the result next time. For me failure is an essential experience on the path to success. I always encourage the team to assume they can improve – no matter what. It's extremely dangerous to sit back and think you have reached your destination – that's when others will pass you by.

Managing change
Creating the environment and culture for change was great and whilst we were incubating lots of ideas and potential new business areas, I needed to ensure that we stayed true to our core strengths and founding principles. I wanted to encourage innovation and move the company forward however I didn't want to end up with a disparate set of products that were not connected by a set of common principles. With this is mind, we established a set of guiding principles that allowed us to evaluate new product ideas and guide product and service development.

At the heart of everything we did was a focus on delivering measurable results for our clients and providing a transparent service that allowed clients to see exactly where their spend was going. Our guiding principles remain in place today and influence everything we do from our contact with clients to our public relations and marketing.

Along with getting the right culture, environment and process we knew that market perception was critical to our success. Listlab (as a business was known) had built up considerable brand equity within that niche however the brand name itself limited our business. For this reason we took the decision to re-brand to Medialab which we felt better reflected our long-term focus of becoming an integrated media agency.

We were also aware that the market was busy. There was a lot of noise but little in the way of differentiation so we had to be careful to present ourselves through our three principles of innovation, insight and transparency. Our aim was, and still is, to build and reinforce a brand that secures us a strong position in the market that makes us front of mind with our target market.

I always believe that it's very dangerous to become too inward looking as a business. Keeping one eye on competition and market changes is essential. In my experience those companies who haven't done this have left themselves being out maneuvered or caught out by market changes, often with catastrophic consequences.

For this reason we always make sure we are on the pulse of legislative changes, market developments and keep a keen eye on our competitors for any strategic shifts. This not only allows us to protect our business but also allows us to deliver a better service to our clients.

So where has this led us? Today, 10 years on from the management buy-out, we are a leading integrated media agency. We are a very profitable company that has achieved double digit growth through a recession and have built a client list that we are proud of including Post Office, Amex, National Trust, Macmillan Cancer Support, Alzheimer's Society and many more. More importantly, we have a client referral rate of 78%, which we think is testament to the quality of work that our team do and the commitment that we have to our clients.

Looking back an immense amount has been achieved but I see this as a continuous journey rather than a destination. It has been a journey with many peaks and troughs and a lot of lessons learnt along the way. I certainly can't begin to claim I have all the answers, but if I was to pass on any words of wisdom I would say that the biggest lessons I have learnt is to have a clear vision that everyone buys into, get the right team in place to help you achieve your vision and be prepared to work very hard to get where you are going.

Most successful businesses I see come from equal measures of innovative thinking, a winning mentality and lots of blood, sweat and tears to make it happen.

Marcus Orme

Marcus Orme is the CEO of Medialab Group, a leading integrated direct response media agency. After starting his career as a graduate in the direct response marketing industry, Marcus went on to become Managing Director of a list management and broking businesses. In 2005 Marcus successfully initiated and navigated a management buy-out and subsequently built a leading direct response media agency that includes many leading UK brands as its clients. With a business that has seen double digit growth throughout the recession and boasts a client referral rate of 78% Marcus gives an innovative viewpoint on the vital ingredients for building a successful business.

Homeless to Real Estate Millionaire In 12 Months

Kemi Egan - Co founder of The Freedom Group

If you've seen me speak or have been to any of my trainings, you might know me as a real estate investor and wealth coach sharing my experiences in creating multiple high six-figure businesses, creating financial security and training others how to do the same.

You might not know that it hasn't always been the case.

If you had been with me in late December a few years back, you would have seen me at my mum's house, curled up in an armchair, rocking back and forth and sobbing uncontrollably in between bouts of violent vomiting. It was around 6 am, and the fog was heavy. Wind and rain hammered our small house. I'd only been in from a night out dancing for a couple of hours, but I was wide awake.

You see, I'd just been told that one of my best friends had been murdered by her boyfriend. We had dropped her off on the way to our respective homes, and within an hour, she was dead.

I was only in my late teens, but this wasn't the first person I'd lost to violence. The year before, a classmate had been stabbed to death in the street, and in that same year, another friend had died in a street fight.

In the world in which I grew up, violence and addiction was prevalent. It ran through my family, my friends and my schooling. You see, I'm mixed race and from a single parent family that polite company likes to call 'of modest means'. I was a statistical failure waiting to happen. A particularly 'motivating' teacher once told me I would either be a criminal or a cleaner—if I was lucky!

In addition to the carnage that went on around me, I never quite fit in. I always knew that if I fought hard enough, I could change things for myself and my family, but I had no idea how to do that. Traditional advice pointed to education and getting a degree, so that's what I set about doing. I had a vision—I wanted to support my family financially and build a rehabilitation center for victims of domestic violence.

Fast-forward a couple of years, and I was the first person in my family to go to college. I worked night shifts in supermarkets to pay my way through, and I graduated with honors as a physical therapist.

I subsequently worked very hard to get to the top of my profession as quickly as I possibly could. I completed my master's degree and was soon traveling internationally and working with top sports teams. Although I enjoyed it, I had made a commitment to making a difference and helping people. Traditionally, healthcare was either extortionate or of poor quality. I wanted to change that, so I opened a private health care practice with an allowance of free treatments for children and people on welfare.

In the first year, it was awesome. I had hundreds of happy clients, cash was flowing, and my shoe collection was growing. I was on top of the world, but it was definitely the pride before the fall. I had moved away and started my business in a blaze of glory, denounced my former life, changed my life completely. But my master plan hadn't quite worked out as I had expected.

I was homeless.

Businesses need leaders, strategic thinkers, and great planning. In the middle of a global economic crisis, they need this more than ever, and back then, I didn't have any of that. My paying patients quickly dried up. After all, when a country is in a recession, who can really afford a back massage, right? Things spiraled out of control, and before I could blink, I was selling my cars, my shoes, my books, my CDs. I was selling everything I had just to pay my rent, bills, and taxes and put food on the table. It got so bad that because of personal guarantees to close the business would have cost around $25,000 on top of around $100,000 personal debt. I felt like the only person in the world too broke to fail!

Eventually I had nothing left to sell, and I was forced to move into the office to keep a roof over my head. I snuck in one night with the single bag of clothes I had left and a blow-up bed, praying I wouldn't be seen.

The next few months were ugly. I cried constantly, ate garbage comfort food, and drank way too much alcohol. About four months into my meltdown, my next lightbulb moment happened. I realized that right then, in that very moment, there were successful people in the world who were making money, creating wealth, and living a great lifestyle. Recession or not, people were making money, and I decided that I was going to figure out how.

Over the next few months, I read literally hundreds of books, listened to just as many audio programs, attended seminars and conferences, and put thousands of dollars on credit cards I couldn't afford to pay—all this in order to educate myself. And I quickly noticed a trend—a whole lot of people had made a whole heap of cash investing in real estate, and in doing so, they had created passive, leveraged income, long-term sustainable wealth, and a future legacy. They had created the time, the lifestyle, and the wealth necessary to pursue their ambitions, start charities, and provide for their families.

This was everything I had ever dreamed of. Almost immediately, I could imagine my future. It was so vivid I could almost touch my future home and the home I would buy for my mum. I could see the rehabilitation center I had dreamed of—I could even picture its name and the floor plan. For the first time ever, I had absolute clarity.

But I had no interest in reinventing the wheel. I knew real estate could give me everything I had ever dreamed of, and I made the decision to pursue it with 100% commitment.

The obvious elephant in the room was that I had no money and no experience, there was no way I was going to let that stop me. I continued to read everything possible in and around investing and began attending evening networking events on the subject of business and real estate.

I learned two of the most important factors to success during this period. 1) Your network is your net worth and 2) Build your network before you need it. I started building relationships with as many different people in as many different stages of business and investing as I could. Wherever I could, I added value and did anything I could to help them, expecting nothing in return.

Most of us have heard the phrase "You are the average of the five people you spend the most time with." We often don't realize why. The reality is we all love to be liked, and so we gradually morph into a person similar to those around us in order to fit in with them. If we spend time with people who eat huge meals, our portions will gradually increase. If we spend time with people who like to exercise, we will become more active. Likewise, if we spend time with people who take their wealth seriously and work to educate themselves, to invest, and to plan strategically, then so will we.

Most of us can remember a friend our parents asked us not to associate with for fear they'd 'rub off' on us, but sometime later in life, we forget how powerful associates can be.

Without hesitation, I can say that most of the best investing opportunities I have had have come through my network. I became known initially for real estate and for a smaller niche—rentals. I bought properties, rehabilitated them, and rented them out. Therefore whenever the possibility of a great project or joint venture came up, I was contacted. Eventually this spread to the multimillion dollar investments, but the same principle applies. I have a reputation for high quality, ethical, and profitable investments, and when a project comes up, it will find its way through my network to me.

I spent the early few months adding value to as many people as I could in as many creative ways as possible. The reality was I didn't have any money or much experience to offer, but I could recommend a good book or training video or reach out to my network and find a reliable contractor or realtor for someone. Whenever possible, I did anything I could to help others in the hope that I would gain some knowledge and start building a network of people who were on the same journey as I was. At the time, I didn't realize how powerful the law of reciprocity is. As Zig Ziglar says, "Help enough people get what they want, and you can have anything you want."

By doing this, by helping as many people as I could, I was inadvertently building my network before I needed it. I was setting the wheels in motion for the law of reciprocity to start working for me so when I needed advice or an investment, I had a network of friends and peers that I had previously helped and supported. It felt natural then to pick up the phone to ask if they had five minutes to spare for some advice.

Before I decided on my initial strategy—rentals—I began researching many real estate strategies. I looked at everything from 'flips', where you buy a run-down property, rehabilitate it, and then sell it for a profit, to lease options, a strategy you use to control property without buying it. After doing all the research, I settled on buying run-down property, refurbishing it, and leasing it because it's one of the fastest ways to increase your monthly cash flow—and that is what I desperately needed.

The next stage was to research investment areas. It's always advisable when possible to buy property within an hour of your home. The proximity makes managing the property and the tenants much easier, even if you have a leasing agent. But I lived in London, England where the returns on rental property are terrible and, in a lot of cases, they don't even cover the expenses on the property. There was no profit there, so the only option I had was to go further afield. I spent days in my car researching different locations.

The challenge was finding a balance between areas that would give me a good income really quickly and areas that would go up in value. In real estate, the properties that provide you with the best monthly income tend to be those that don't increase in value as much. I settled on an area in the northeast midlands for a variety of reasons. 1) The property prices were so low they could only go up! 2) The rental income was enormous in comparison to most of the UK. To put it in perspective, rental yields in England at the time averaged around 8% for a single family unit, but I achieved 16%. 3) It also happened to be an area of high enterprise, and there was a lot of external investment from governments and large organizations, which is usually a good sign that an area is on the rise. 4) It was 3 ½ hours from home, and that was about as far as I could drive in one stretch.

The early stage was exhausting. I was putting in hours upon hours driving and talking on the phone—spending even more money. It seemed endless. Remember that during this time I was living in a 70 square foot windowless room, sleeping on an inflatable bed. The only thing that got me through was remembering my goal of financial security for my family and the dream of building a rehabilitation center for sufferers of domestic violence. If you are merely chasing money, you will soon burn out. You need a goal bigger than yourself to keep driving you forward. Of course in the early days, your initial concern will be paying the bills, but there are easier ways to do that than being an entrepreneur. If you find yourself following this path, more than likely something is burning inside you that is much bigger than you are. That is what you will need to access while you are building a long-term, successful, profitable, and ethical business.

During the early days and the challenging times, it's tempting to give up and decide that something else is easier or quicker. The reality is that building massive wealth is possible. Is it easy? Yes! But is it difficult? Yes again! You don't have to be a rocket scientist or a genius, but you do have to work hard and commit. Just when it seems too difficult to continue and you feel like you are going nowhere, that's when you are closer than ever. This is when most people quit. DON'T! When you learn any new skill, you front load your mistakes. The first six months of learning a new language or sport are always the hardest. You make all the mistakes, take all the knocks, and have your confidence dashed time and time again. But if you quit every time you experienced a hardship, you would never make it through to mastery—and eventually to success. Just remember that 99% of people will give up and quit, but you want to be the 1% that perseveres.

"Go the extra mile, it's never crowded" ~ Dr. Wayne Dyer

I spent four months putting in below market value offers, negotiating with vendors (poorly), and making mistakes before I had my first offer accepted. Once that happened, I had eight accepted in the next two months. I had front loaded my mistakes, and I had learned from each one. I earned a reputation with local realtors for being consistent and persistent and as a result earned their trust and respect. They believed that I would do what I said. If I had quit after the first three months and chased the next shiny penny that came along, my learning experience and time to success would have started all over again. Instead, I had the compound effect on my side. You need to do the same.

Once I had some offers accepted, I began sharing the discounts, planned projects, and profits with my network using a technique called 'through not to'. This technique is something we train investors to use to soft sell to potential investors. Within a few days, I had offers of investment and joint ventures. The first investment was for $200,000. I'll never forget the feeling of pride when I realized that of all the places he could have chosen to invest, he chose me. I had paid my dues and earned my stripes, and along with that, I had developed credibility and respect. The investment opportunities I'd found were good but not amazing, but that didn't matter to him—he'd bought into me, and he believed in me. I'd heard the phrase 'people buy from people', but until that point, I didn't truly understand what it meant. But in that moment—and from that point on—I was educated, smart, hardworking, and worthy of investment. The investors then, and the investors now, buy into me. They trust me. I have a reputation for being honest, hardworking, reliable, and ethical, so whether or not they know (or care) much about the specific investment, they are happy to invest their money with me. Guard your reputation above all else.

From that point, my investments and portfolio snowballed. Within twelve months, I'd raised $1m in investments and bought a portfolio worth $2m. At the time, I wasn't sure what it was that had caused investors to believe in me, made realtors want to work with me, and encouraged vendors to sell their houses to me, but now I get it because I get to see it in others. I was hungry for success and security, I had educated myself and taken action, but most importantly, I was authentic and acted with integrity.

I believe rentals form the basis of a sustainable and profitable portfolio. The premise is that tenants pay your expenses, including paying the mortgage (in essence buying a house for you), while the property value increases over time. Meanwhile you earn a nice monthly profit. For that reason, although I do much bigger developments and flips these days, I still continue to grow and nurture my rental portfolio. As the mortgage for each property is paid off, it is placed into the most tax-efficient model available to ensure it forms a part of my legacy and will be passed down to future generations.

Real estate laws and developments change constantly, and staying current enables you to take advantage before the rest of the market catches on. It really is true that the early bird catches the worm. While I invest in lots of different places, in the UK at the moment there is a short-term change in planning law which enables developers to convert offices into flats without planning permissions or most of the usual taxes that would normally go along with that. The opportunity has never been around before and may not last forever, so we are focusing most of our efforts in this area for the time being. For example, we are in the process of buying a 15,000 square foot office block which will be converted to eighteen flats and three shops on the ground floor. Utilizing the recent changes, there is an opportunity to earn around $1m profit along with my joint venture partners, but before the changes there would have been no profit projected, which is exactly why it's important to stay abreast of changes and take advantage while you can. Whatever the market, there will always be opportunity for educated, strategic investors.

When you begin your journey into wealth creation, you will start to notice opportunities everywhere! As the laws change and different loopholes and techniques open up, it's tempting to jump from one thing to another. It's easy to spread yourself too thinly and end up starting a lot of things—and finishing few. As entrepreneurs, we are more inclined than most to have this personality type, but we have to guard against it.

If you begin hopping from one thing to another, it's easy to develop a reputation as a 'get rich quick' scammer. By focusing on one strategy—be it real estate or stocks—you develop a reputation as the 'go-to expert' much quicker, you front load your mistakes, and you achieve the financial rewards much faster than you would otherwise. Once you achieve a level of success, then absolutely diversify and add an extra income stream to your portfolio.

I teach the 80:20 set and forget principle to decide when it's best to add another strategy. In wealth creation, as in all other areas of life, Pareto's principle is king. Pareto was a mathematician who first coined the 80/20 principle. That principle says that in any area of your life, 80% of the results will come from 20% of the effort. This has been shown to be true in so many areas.

To break it down further, the principle says that 80% of your profits will come from 20% of your clients, and 80% of your hassles will also come from 20% of the people in your life. It's an incredibly powerful principle. Imagine for a second that 80% of your income comes from 20% of your activities. When you decide which real estate strategy you will use to create your wealth, remember that 80% of your results will come from 20% of your activities.

Once your strategy is decided, commit yourself wholeheartedly to it for 80% of your time. Don't waiver on this. Take your time to learn the strategy, and then test it. Test different procedures, different avenues, and tweak your marketing and systems. Maximize the revenue, and then test it

again. Once you have gotten it down in a system that is profitable, ethical, and scalable, begin to delegate and outsource everything. Train your team, outsource, and then train some more.
Your first income stream is set up.

During that period, you were focusing 80% of your time on it. Why 80%? Because the other 20% of the time was spent researching and taking the first steps to begin your next income stream.

Real estate is a fantastic vehicle for creating wealth through multiple income streams because it gives you have the opportunity to leverage the skill, knowledge base, and resources you already have built up to reduce the learning curve and the time it takes to get results. If your first income stream is a portfolio of rental properties, and you have a team managing them, it is simple to expand that to managing other people's properties and owning a leasing agency.

Once you have set that up and extracted yourself from the day-to-day running, you rinse and repeat. A great extension to your portfolio and leasing agency could then be adding an income stream by helping cash-rich, time-poor investors to build a hands-free portfolio using the team you already have in place. These slight deviations use all the tools and materials you already have at your disposal, but they gently move you into having an income stream in another sector.

This is exactly how we structure our business development, and it works well for our clients and for us. Eighty percent of our time, we focus on one income stream/business. We use this time to maximize the profit potential in that revenue stream. Once we have tried and tested different things and know what works, we create systems based on that. These systems include everything—from the day-to- day running of the business, telephone scripts, and customer query responses to business growth processes. We then produce guides, staff handbooks, and videos to allow our team to continue to do great work without my personal day-to-day input. And that is called 'Set'—you have set the business up. During this time, the other

20% of my time is spent researching a maximum of two other opportunities or income streams. You may have one or two ideas that you are considering pursuing. Spend that 20% testing the market, doing research, getting some more education, reading up on things, and then beginning a new venture.

Once the first business is set up, and the systems are working and have been tested, you can then 'forget' it. The second business then moves in to take center stage and takes up 80% of the time with a third business becoming the next 20%. Following this system will allow you to quickly and efficiently add income streams and create wealth and security for your family while reducing the risk of becoming overwhelmed and avoiding the confusion that often follows the magpie syndrome.

Whatever situation you are in, chances are you're better off than I was. I had no money, no confidence, and no clue. Of course, there have been challenges, and it wasn't all smooth sailing, but if you are willing to work for it, financial freedom and security is possible. I have gone from being homeless to having a multimillion dollar real estate portfolio and developing $4m upwards projects. I have multiple six figure businesses. I get to spend my time sharing everything I have learned—the mistakes and the successes. I am honored to share the shortcut to wealth and help people avoid the mistakes and pitfalls. I am living my dream, and you can too.

Kemi Egan

Kemi Egan is an entrepreneur, real estate investor, Wealth Coach and Author of 35 time #1 International Bestseller The Power of Real Estate Investing'. She is a personal finance, entrepreneurial expert and thought leader, sought after speaker and bestselling author.

The CEO and Founder of innovative and ethical multi-national organizations Freedom Academies and Freedom Investment – Kemi is set apart from other wealth experts by her uncommon honesty in sharing exactly the exact steps that helped her create wealth and her innate ability to draw those talents out of any person that wants to change their life whilst inspiring and supporting them in creating wealth through wealth building education keynotes, workshops, products, events, programs and coaching services.

Kemi has succeeded in creating a community of entrepreneurs building wealth using ethical, sustainable and highly profitable strategies that anyone can employ and has created a manual described by Brian Tracy as

"This powerful, practical book gives you a proven step-by-step process to start with nothing and become financially independent in real estate investing".

Kemi electrifies and inspires audiences live form the stage, on television and in the media with her straight talking, no nonsense approach and unquestionable candor to wealth creation, her willingness to authentically share her own personal journey and the entrepreneurial journey.

She is regularly featured in wide ranging platforms such as; the BBC, Business Insider, IdeasMensch, Yahoo News, Elite Business, Female Entrepreneurs Inc & many more.

Find Out More at: www.freedomacademies.com
www.thepowerofrealestateinvesting.com

Connect with Kemi at: www.facebook.com/kemieganfreedomacademies
http://twitter.com/kemiegan

Understanding clarity and focus

Jack Barmby, CEO, Felicitas Media and Creator of Gnatta

I would love to write about how the business I have built has come from careful planning, identifying a gap in the market and analysing the route to market, generating strong growth through careful planning and organisation. The reality however is much different; the company comes from a happy accident. Today, it has teams in three countries and clients ranging from small sports teams to FTSE 100 companies, all coming from finding a niche in a market and focusing relentlessly on it. Coming from what was at first a University project, I know all too well the difficulties of setting up the processes and systems to make your business successful and scalable.

During my second year at University, I was gaining work experience from a company wanting to dabble in social media. The problem I faced would turn into the business I have today, the problem that I could not find a piece of software that would let multiple people collaborate effectively on Twitter. Over the next two years, I worked on a web application with an ever growing team of developers that spawned Gnatta, our answer to large scale collaboration of not only social channels, but also traditional marketplace and review platforms. We license this out to companies, as well as providing an outsource solution for companies preferring that route. This was a real challenge while still at University, with a growing team and a growing client base, juggling studies and a business proved difficult.

We all know the importance of effective time management and to call upon the well known phrase 'don't work hard, work smart' I can speak from experience and vouch that it's not only about putting in all the hours you can, but finding a way that allows you to work 'smart'. At one point, I found myself working 16 hours a day every day of the week. I had an idea of what I aspired to and focused on it restlessly. Of course, as with the entrepreneurial spirit that hasn't changed today, it is commitment to your goal that is important above everything else. However, the challenges I have faced in the last few years will help contextualize ways in which you can manage your time more effectively and lay down the building blocks for having a business that can grow quickly without losing control. As a business still growing at pace, I continue to face some of the problems I will discuss in this chapter, and hope that the traps I fell into can be duly avoided by you.

Focus

Undoubtedly, without question, the most important part of your business is focus. If someone walks up to you in a bar and says, 'what do you do?' what would you reply? If you can't answer in one sentence, you're not focused enough. For some, this is clear. For others, me included, it took a long time to be able to define it in one sentence, so don't worry right now if you can't as you may be just starting out or evolving. For us at Felicitas, our software evolved from being a social media add-on to a tool that manages all forms of communication, and so the 'what do you do' question changed dramatically. Now ask yourself another question, 'what do you want the business to become?'. Jim Collins coined the term BHAG (big, hairy, audacious goal), and having yours is essential. A BHAG, or BHAG's should be outlandish; they should overstretch your expectations and aims. BHAG's give you the drive and focus to move towards a set goal. It is far too easy to get caught up in the day-to-day tasks of cash flow, employee management and so on, but whenever you lift your head from the day-to-day, you should have your BHAG's to keep you focused. Jim Collins speaks in depth about this, and it's worth learning more about to set your own.

All that being said, focus and clarity on what you do and what makes you differ from your competitors is the most important thing to understand. It will form your business strategy, your sales pitches and will be the basis of why your employees come to work every morning. As a start up, it is so very easy to take on work that people ask of you, things that are similar to, but not true to your original focus; because let's face it, you want to impress the client, and you want to grow, so why would you not take the work? Making the decision to diverge from your original focus may seem like the logical thing to do, but you will find yourself backtracking in the long run. Diverging from the original focus has downsides for a couple of reasons. Firstly and most importantly, if it isn't your number one focus, it is someone else's. Someone will be devoting all their time to the thing you're doing on the side, and you'll find yourself delivering a product or service that can be rivaled by competitors. Secondly, every day, every minute you're not spending focused on your original idea, someone else is. If you think you're 6 months ahead of anyone else, in reality they're a lot closer than you think. Look at every successful business you can think of, you know exactly what they do and what's special about them and you can describe it in layman's terms.

As difficult as it is, don't be afraid to say no; don't be afraid to turn away work that isn't profitable or attractive. Having made this mistake, it's very difficult to make a U-turn and get back to your original focus, but it is so very important you don't become a Jack-of-all-trades. Saying no will ultimately give you a better return, as you can really wow the clients by delivering only what you know you can excel at and can grow and develop in the way you want to most, without spending time playing catch up with the aspects of your business you were never passionate about in the first place. Try this: walk into the office, into your home and ask your employees or loved ones two questions; what do we do, and how are we different from our competitors? If you're getting the same answers, good job, if not then you need to work with them in defining exactly what the answers to those questions are. They are the most frequently asked questions in business and will form the backbone of everything else.

Shape Your Culture Around Your Business Goals

Every day when I wake up and head to work I ask myself, 'what kind of business do you want to be perceived as?' From the roots of Felicitas

Media and Gnatta, we have family at our core, so I do my best to imbue family values into the day-to-day work and into the lives of my co-workers. Deciding early about your cultural stance is important, and thankfully, this is never a problem I have suffered but have seen it all too often: businesses fall into the trap of not having a strong and defined culture.

When you take on a new employee they will spend 37.5 hours per week sat in the office, minus breaks. On average, they will see you and their coworkers more than their family, children or pets, so what kind of work environment do you want to provide? Culture gives a business intangible value and endless assets; you only need look as far as AO.com to see what culture can do for the value of a business. There are endless studies to enforce how cultural strength in business creates hard working, loyal, positively charged and motivated employees.

But it requires thinking out of the box. For example at Felicitas, we have introduced a house system, where every employee has a house, a house captain and a set of activities they carry out within their house. It gives a sense of community, of loyalty, and not only that but we also link to charities and get each house contributing to our chosen charity, thus creating an atmosphere people are proud to work in.

As you grow and expand, culture becomes even more important. Every aspiring entrepreneur is faced with the same dilemma; you want to be involved in every decision. It's a blessing and a curse that will ultimately cause you a headache as you grow, because it becomes practically impossible to be involved in every decision.

By giving focus as previously discussed as well as engraining a healthy culture into your business, you effectively get everyone pushing towards the same goal; everyone knows what is required and are harmoniously linked through the business culture. This shouldn't be underestimated, as it gives you the ability to scale out much faster and have the confidence in your people to let them independently make decisions and collaborate effectively.

Product Before All

Felicitas Media and Gnatta have grown through word of mouth since their birth. Being in the business of software, it is so very important to always innovate, however this is true of any industry regardless of your vertical. As you sit here reading this book, someone, somewhere is trying to innovate in your sector, doing something outside the box and pushing to be the next best solution. Knowing this, we made sure we put the product at the core of our business. All our functions, our meetings and our expenditure would be to the benefit of the development of our application either directly, through growing the development team, or indirectly by creating friendly working environments. Having your product or service at the heart of your function is vital as it is what ultimately drives growth. To get to the stage Felicitas Media is at today has come from the back of almost no sales team. All growth has come almost solely from word of mouth and recommendations, because the offering is not based around a gimmicky sales pitch; it defines a user need and fulfills that need better than anything else in the market (or so I like to think!). This of course cannot remain forever; sales teams are the lifeblood of your business however, take a moment to sit back and think about how you spend your time. Is it all spent on sales, or on developing your product? If the answer leans towards the former it is worth thinking about whether your product is developing at a pace that is sustainable in the long run, because you can develop your product first and your sales team later, but will struggle to do it the other way around.

Today's Challenges

Now that the focus is clear and we have a strong culture to help us grow at scale, we're facing new challenges. As every aspiring entrepreneur will know, as your business becomes successful you will find a whole plethora of new issues arise, even things as simple as cash flow and HR. Issues as they may be, these are problems every business runs into, and I won't divulge into the many ways and means in which you can get around these problems. One of the biggest current problems, and as with most of the issues I have faced, and one that could have been avoided with forward thinking from the outset, is future proofing. Not future proofing your business from the outset can be a death blow in the long run, and at every stage you need to ask yourself, 'will this be okay in a one or two years time?'

With many decisions, this is impossible, but have the future in your mind at all times. What if that big client comes along? How do you deal with their acquisition? Personally, as Gnatta began life as a University project it was done by University students who often did not apply the most efficient and well practiced coding principles. Once we began liaising with big clients, it became apparent that we needed to redo a lot of the things we already had in place. It's a huge pain, even in decisions such as what cloud storage solution you'll use, the accounting software, the employee on boarding scheme, it all needs future proofing to protect you from breaking in the future, because as you grow it becomes harder and harder to make these changes.

As the business continues to develop in the coming months and years, new problems always arise and for me, that is the thrill of business. The experiences I have outlined in this chapter are only to name a few, however if I could go back and do it again, these are the things I would focus on most of all. To put it briefly:
- Focus, relentlessly and restlessly
- Product at the heart
- Culture is your lifeblood

Following these principles has served me well, and I hope you take something from them too. Get these principles right and growth will follow; more importantly, sustainable and manageable growth will follow. Growth is a byproduct of a strong base of operation that stems largely from the principles outlined above, so move away if you have been focusing previously on growth as the core of your business and move to the areas that fuel growth. Strip it back to basics, your offering should be simple to comprehend and communicate, your goals clear and your focus sharp. Work smart and get your team behind you, and success should follow.

Jack Barmby

Jack Barmby is the founder and CEO of Felicitas Media. Having cut his teeth as a social media consultant at Parcels2Go during his summer holidays, he was inspired to start Felicitas Media in 2011 while sill at University. Since its conception there has been a strong focus on the business's growth and expansion.

Having graduated in 2014, Felicitas is now a business with over 100 employees. Jack continues to focus on growth and market disruption, and believes that what Felicitas does can change the way businesses communicate with their customers.

Now focusing on Gnatta, the software developed by Jack which is currently used by Felicitas in-house, the next stage of business growth will be marketing out the software as a stand alone product through the selling of licenses to businesses who wish to centralise their communications.

He's reading My Making Money Magazine... Are you?
www.mymaking
moneymagazine.com

The journey to *Cause4*

Michelle Wright – *Cause4*

In the back of my mind I always thought that I might want to start a business.

Up to that point my career journey had been slightly unusual. I had trained as a violinist at one of the UK's leading conservatoires - London's Guildhall School of Music & Drama - and then had a five-year career as a professional violinist playing in London orchestras. Then completely by chance, I found my way into the charitable sector where I worked in a variety of communications and marketing roles and eventually became a Chartered Marketer.

I loved the charity sector, and immersing myself in the world of arts and social charities I eventually accepted a role in 2005 as the Marketing Director of a socially-driven theatre company in the East End of London. The job turned out to be both a baptism of fire and fortuitous in equal measure. On my first day, one of the Directors said *'forget marketing, we need you to raise £1m this year just to keep the charity going,'* and on that note….and quite by accident, I found myself plunged into the world of charitable fundraising. For a year I had to learn quickly to try and raise the money that would keep the charity afloat. With no track record to speak of, I could only work on instinct and to be as creative as I could in positioning the charity to be as attractive as possible to a wide variety of funders and supporters.

Fundraising can be a brilliant career – challenging, entrepreneurial and developmental all rolled into one. After having learned on the job, made mistakes and followed my instinct, I soon realised that in my subsequent role as Head of Fundraising and Marketing at the social action charity Toynbee Hall, that in being good at fundraising I could look to make a difference across a wide range of causes. Here was a job where developing innovation and income generation plans in partnership with organisations, I could see the charity sector grow and thrive. I was inspired by being able to 'make things happen', and it is this concept that has formed the basis of all my entrepreneurial activities ever since. In my opinion, the only real hallmark of being an entrepreneur is the ability to create something out of nothing, and especially when 'your back is against the wall'.

Just five years on from putting the full-time world of professional music behind me, I was in my element. I was working with a wide variety of people to create programmes across a range of areas including arts, education and social justice. The more diverse the causes the better, as long as I was curious about them – and each initiative fed new ideas into other projects.

I was then lucky enough to become Development Director of the London Symphony Orchestra based in the heart of the City of London in 2007 – which involved a whirlwind three years of fundraising and international sponsorship development. One of my first projects was the creation of a programme named 'LSO On Track' – a multi-faceted programme working across ten East London boroughs providing thousands of school children with music and arts education programmes and opportunities linked to London 2012 and the Cultural Olympiad programme. It was such a proud moment in July 2012, when I saw young people from across East London taking part alongside the London Symphony Orchestra in Danny Boyle's terrific opening ceremony in the Olympic Stadium in London's East End. Making this sort of grass-roots initiative happen on a world stage, was giving me an amazing energy for my day-to-day work.

At the end of 2008, during my time at the London Symphony Orchestra, Lehman Brothers bank collapsed and 20,000 people lost their jobs overnight. I knew at that moment that the world had changed and that the charity sector was therefore going to also have to develop, grow and respond if it was going to sustain itself and survive. As the UK economy started to wallow in recession, the idea for setting up *Cause4* was born. I felt that there was probably scope for a small organisation that could work more entrepreneurially in the charitable sector, to specialise in creating programmes of scale and to look at developing interesting partnerships that could navigate what was set to be an ongoing challenging financial climate for charities.

....and over several too many glasses of wine in early 2009 (with my two fellow Directors) this small idea became reality.

The entrepreneurial idea

In May 2009, *Cause4* began trading as a social enterprise.

Immediately we wanted to create a different sort of model, and a team that could work flexibly in partnership with charities and social enterprises for the longer-term. As such, we banned the 'c' word (consultancy), which often conjures up images in the charity sector of over paid advisors that are not held to account for the strategies that they create.

Cause4 supports charities, philanthropists and social enterprises as development and fundraising partners across the charity, arts, sports and education sectors. We seek to be a modernising influence and leader within the charity and social enterprise sector, offering relevant, contemporary solutions at a time when more creative, entrepreneurial approaches are much needed.

We work in three main areas - *strategy and fundraising, philanthropy and enterprise development* - and specialise in developing campaigns and programmes with strong potential to attract charitable support.

One of the keys to our early success was the creation of a new business model for *Cause4*. Our enterprising model keeps our fees low and allows the widest range of organisations to afford our services. It also means that we can provide the services of a whole team for a lower fee than it would cost a charity to employ one fundraiser. This means that the financial risk is shared by *Cause4* with the charities, philanthropists and social enterprises with which we work, making our model very different from most consultancy organisations operating in the charitable sector.

The model has proved to capture well the spirit of this Age of Austerity. Charitable Trustees and CEOs appreciate its transparency and cost-effectiveness, and in creating a model that clearly links expenditure to income, we also provide our staff with significant incentives for investing maximum effort and expertise into each charity over an agreed period of time.

ature *Cause4* the business and driving forward

We are now six years on, and the business is thriving. We have raised over £38m in charitable fundraising for clients, have a core team of 24 staff, have won multiple national and international awards for innovation and have a multi-faceted programme of clients from charities, philanthropists and social enterprises. We are also in a position where we are exploring a range of international opportunities to develop the business with hubs in Amsterdam and New York and to undertake major international philanthropy projects across the developing world.

It is rather difficult to understand how we've got to where we have - starting with a small idea that suddenly got much bigger. However, what has been important to recognise as we move out of start up phase to a more mature business, is that we have at least proved the concept, i.e. that there is a real appetite and need for the sort of innovation in programme development and fundraising for charities, social enterprises and philanthropists that we specialise in creating. The world has changed, and the charitable sector needs to adapt and modernize to survive.

We've put innovation at the heart of the *Cause4* and encourage all staff to take on their own programme development, business planning and ideas creation. One key innovation saw the launch of our Philanthropy Service in 2012. This new service targets top artists, entrepreneurs and sportspeople, as a professional, one-stop shop to grow charitable giving and through effective fundraising enables individuals to at least triple their investment. Current clients include a range of sports starts, artists and entrepreneurs. We also set up a new charity, The Philanthropy Foundation, to make it easier for a range of sports stars, artists and entrepreneurs to give, which is attracting a range of new clients. We believe that this work is a real 'game-changer' and will prevent the proliferation of new charitable foundations that have insufficient governance and structure.

Cause4 has also started developing corporate philanthropy models. These models encompass sponsorship, CSR and philanthropy, and hold incredible potential for staff engagement, as well as for tax efficient giving.

Our key challenges

With any fast-growing SME, our key challenge has been that the reputation and opportunities for the business have grown far faster than the infrastructure or staffing that we have been able to put in place. We are now seeking to embed as many processes as we can to ensure that we continue to deliver a quality service. We know that not taking care of our processes and clients as the business grows is a key risk for us.

However, the really key issue has been recruiting staff with the right entrepreneurial mindset to cope with the demands of the business and the fast-paced way in which we aim to work. Having brilliant people as part of the business that are able to deliver for clients is essential, and the speed of delivery of quality work takes most new recruits by surprise - however honest we are in the interview!

In particular, we have struggled to recruit senior people into the team to support growth. As such, it became increasingly obvious that we were going to need to 'grow our own' talent and therefore in 2010 we formalised plans to develop our own 12-month graduate 'Entrepreneurship' programme that would provide a solid basis for the future development of the business.

Our graduate programmes are now thriving with some 45 graduates and apprentices training with us in 2015 for future leadership roles in the charity sector.

The other key challenge has been a personal one for me – a successful, demanding business that would keep me busy is a dream come true – and in six years I haven't been bored once.

However, it is increasingly difficult to know how to keep fiery and energized with a 24/7 programme of delivery. The model we've created is intensive – the ability for us to develop the programmes for charities and fundraising is often the difference between success or failure and so the work is pressurized and the stakes are high….and after a solid run of 90 hour weeks for the first time in my career I feel on the verge of burnout – not an easy reality for a 'doer' to face.

There has been no hiding from this. I've had to look exhaustion in the face and keeping going at pace when the business has momentum is a constant test. One of the solutions has been to bring a great group of advisors and Board around the business – people that can advise impartially and honestly and who can both be supportive, and have the confidence to occasionally say 'no' or 'not now' to this ambitious founder.

Entrepreneurship most certainly isn't for the faint-hearted and recognizing your boundaries has to be the priority. Therefore, I've also needed to find a combination of support and activities that can help me cope with the demands of the business.

I now have a coach, swim regularly and make sure I make time for painting, music and other creative activities – and however hard it is for me to maintain this sort of discipline and to look after my own well-being, I have made these activities regular and non-negotiable aspects of my day-to-day portfolio.

Skills and networks

On starting *Cause4* I had just finished an MBA at Ashridge Business School, so I had some good generic knowledge of business. This was a great platform, but where I have really benefitted in developing the business is by becoming part of a number of accelerator networks.

In the turbulent journey of running a start up business, there is nothing so leveling as networking with other entrepreneurs, finding out the realities, sharing information and realizing that however challenging it feels for you as an individual, everyone is facing similar issues.

Cause4 has taken part in the Cranfield School of Management Business Growth and Development Programme and I've also been lucky enough recently to be part of the [Goldman Sachs 10,000 small businesses programme. This initiative, which provides](#) access to education and support services via programmes at top global universities including University College London and Said Business School Oxford, really demonstrates its power in its access to networks and the reflective time and challenge that comes from spending time with other entrepreneurs.

All of these programmes have given us great critical challenge and have allowed us to focus our strategy and to make sure that we were taking on the right work at the right time.

We have needed to focus on developing outstanding projects and programmes that could achieve maximum impact for the charities and social enterprises that we represent and to not get distracted by every opportunity that has come our way, however new and shiny! Learning to say no has been both important and painful in equal measure.

Investing in talent

Perhaps the area that I am most proud of is our graduate talent development programmes. In the business as a whole we are looking for people that are passionate about charitable causes and that have an entrepreneurial outlook and ambition. We are much more interested in aptitude and talent than experience. We also expect our staff to be passionate about professional development and to embrace our learning culture, both for them and the staff that they manage.

We knew that we needed to develop our own talent to grow the business in the spirit that we wished, so in 2010 we set up our 12-month, fast-track, graduate training programme - the *Cause4 Entrepreneurship* programme, which seeks to address the widely-acknowledged shortage of entrepreneurial development and fundraising personnel within the charitable sector.

We have trained 30 graduates so far and have funding to support another 50 graduates in the next three years supported by Arts Council England. Last year our graduate Associates contributed some £4m in charitable fundraising for clients.

The Associates also run our daily blog site at www.cause4.co.uk - aimed at being the sector's voice for critical commentary in the areas of fundraising, philanthropy and social enterprise. Undoubtedly, a useful arm for any start-up business is to have a group of 20-somethings in charge of its social media strategy.

We're now recognized globally as one of the leading authorities in non-profit blogs, and the blog site is also a fantastic vehicle to support our staff to develop their own voice and profile.

Cause4 has also set up an incubator hub for Creative Entrepreneurs in partnership with the Guildhall School of Music & Drama – building on our potential to create a training ground for a range of talented graduates. To support the development of new creative businesses run by actors and musicians in our offices in central London alongside our graduate programmes is proving to be an irresistible combination.

The programme includes access to mentoring, coaching, business planning, marketing and sales and funding. Graduates also benefit from use of *Cause4* office space for a 12-month period and are introduced to a range of entrepreneurial, community and partnership networks to support business development.

Learning from others

I'm completely passionate about giving young people opportunities that were not necessarily forthcoming for me; it is one of the great privileges of having set up *Cause4* to be able to create jobs and employment opportunities for graduates.

When I look back to the time in early 2009 when I began telling people that I was about to set up *Cause4* I had many people who told me that we would struggle or that I shouldn't give up a regular wage and a promising career in the charitable sector. It is not lost on me that most of these detractors were other women!

I think that female entrepreneurs in particular suffer from a lack of positive role models. This, coupled with the fact that women tend to be more cautious than cavalier about enterprise, means that there is a whole generation of young people (and especially females) that never take the plunge into enterprise. It is with this in mind that we have set up in partnership with Santander a new national network for fast-track female entrepreneurs to support others. Entrepreneurship is incredibly rewarding but it needs support and time – and the fastest learning for entrepreneurs is from others.

Within the busy world of *Cause4* we have also been careful to make sure that each member of staff has an external mentor, and I also find time to be a mentor for programmes such as the Aspire Foundation and Emerge Student Labs to support aspiring entrepreneurs.

Such schemes are 'win win' in allowing me to learn from others but also reminding me that it's a good thing to be bold and to keep going with a 'risk positive' mindset. After all - what's the worst that can happen in running a business – you fail, but even if catastrophe happens, you will have learned some important things on the way to the next venture.

Future vision

I can honestly say that setting up *Cause4* has been the best thing I've ever done – I've learned a huge amount, understood better my strengths and weaknesses, and experienced both success and failure in equal measure. In developing a new business model, we've got our supporters and advocates and a healthy share of detractors, as any disruptive new business is likely to have – so it will be interesting to see what the next stage brings.

My final thoughts are the importance of setting BHAGs – or Big Hairy Audacious Goals. Every good business needs them to keep firing, moving forward and to galvanize the staff and team.

In the next period we have three priorities of BHAGS for ensuring innovation and development in the fundraising sector including: training 250 new graduates into leadership careers, to raise £100m in new philanthropic investment and to set up one major entrepreneurial project each year that will be a game-changer for the sector, in 2015 we are looking at our digital offer to help our international aspirations. These are all exciting goals and we're hoping for great things ahead...

Michelle Wright

Michelle Wright (Chief Executive) trained at the Guildhall School of Music & Drama and played the violin professionally. A chartered marketer, manager and fundraiser, Michelle founded *Cause4* after leaving the London Symphony Orchestra, where her achievements in private sector fundraising led to her being judged the Best Upcoming Fundraiser at the National Fundraising Awards in 2008.

Since setting up *Cause4* Michelle has undertaken major strategic and business development projects, including campaign developments with a number of national charities and consultancy work for FTSE 100 brands developing their cultural sponsorship programmes. Michelle also specialises in philanthropy, having recently developed a number of major philanthropy projects for charities and corporates, and having set up new philanthropic foundations for sports stars, artists and entrepreneurs.

Michelle is a Fellow of the Guildhall School (FGS) and of the Royal Society of Arts (FRSA). She is particularly passionate about mentoring emerging entrepreneurs and is a mentor for Santander Breakthrough, as well as supporting the development of several new businesses in the field of creative entrepreneurship as part of a partnership with the Guildhall School of Music & Drama.

Michelle was the winner of the female entrepreneur category in the national Natwest Startup awards 2011 and is a top 10 winner in the Ernst and Young Future 100 awards 2011 for entrepreneurs under 35 that demonstrate innovation in progressing a responsible business venture. She is a gold, silver and bronze award winner in the 2012-2014 international Stevie Awards for innovation. In summer 2013 Michelle was invited by Lord Young of Graffham in 2013 to become an Accelerate 250 member for small businesses showing rapid growth.

In 2013 she was recommended by a panel of independent investors to be part of the Silicon Valley 100 list for businesses showing high potential. In 2014 Michelle was the first entrepreneur in the UK to receive the IWEC award for outstanding entrepreneurial achievement, and represents the UK as a National Champion for Entrepreneur of the Year in the European Business Awards. In 2015 she was invited to become part of the Maserati 100 list for entrepreneurs 'that give back'.

MY ENTREPRENEUR MAGAZINE

FOR AMAZING PEOPLE LIKE YOU

myentrepreneurmagazine.com

Creating an enterprising young Britain

Ben and Michael Dyer - The Ryman National Enterprise Challenge

Growing up for us seemed normal enough. Sure both of our dads battled with alcohol dependencies and going to fetch the family allowance from the post office was a morning out, but to us this was normal.

It wasn't until we went to high school that we started to notice the difference. Going around to a friend's house for tea you would notice that their dad was still at work past six o'clock. They had PlayStation and the latest games, they went abroad, had nice clothes and their dads drove nice cars. That's when the difference hit and we thought 'why haven't we got that'

This is not knocking any of our parents. We were living in post Thatcher Stoke-On-Trent which now had no industry. The Pot Banks famous in the area were shutting rapidly and the Pits had long since been flooded. We were in the same situation as many from our council estate high schools but it still didn't strike us as fair.

As cousins we would meet up most weekends while we were at high school, we went to football together, played together and then subsequently went to college together to study pretty much identical subjects. We would often talk about 'wanting more' and how when we were older we would have the nice cars and 'good jobs'.

After college in 2007 we decided to do something about it and being from a disadvantaged background has certainly helped form our sensational journey.

We set up in business after hearing about an advert from Staffordshire University asking for people 'who wanted to be their own boss'.

Not even sure what we wanted to do, we enrolled on the journey against the 'better' advice from most of our family and friends. Comment's such as 'Are you sure' and 'there's plenty of call centre jobs you could apply for' were common place.

But a job working in a local call centre wasn't what excited us. The belief inside that we could achieve more completely outweighed the £16,000 salary that the call centre would bring and instead we started our first business ...*The Altogether Company.*

The aim of the company was to deliver motivational workshops to young people to help raise their aspirations in the same way we had raised ours.

During the first couple of years we achieved a tremendous amount of success. We secured a two year contract with the Chamber of Commerce to deliver their Young Chamber programme and we became Princes Trust Young ambassadors. We were lucky enough to meet Prince Charles, Ed Miliband and Nick Clegg through our work and we also worked on the government's BAF Diploma as advisors.

In total we delivered our self-written programmes to around 30,000 young people, something which at the time we were extremely proud of.

All of these opportunities came about in our early twenties whilst still at University, the reason? Our fearless nature in telling anyone who would listen about our business.

This fearless nature was also the root cause of our biggest business challenge to date. As young men with friends in college and university, our social scene was pretty active. When invited therefore to take on a failing council estate pub, the meeting point when we used to travel to Stoke City games, an offer our head categorically said 'No' to but our fearless nature and entrepreneurial spirit got the better of us.

We found ourselves in the local bank asking for a business loan and sizable overdraft to fund the venture. They said yes due to the good trading figures of our education business and we took on the 'Red House' Pub and become amongst the youngest pub owners in the country.

On the face of it the transformation of the Red House after we took over was cosmic. We took the pub from a £2000 per week turnover to a pub turning over £7000 per week. Thursdays through to Sundays were packed thanks in no small part to us becoming the City's main 'Stoke City FC' pub and us making it the hub of our own social scene.

Underneath the surface however the problems were slowly increasing. The pubs increasing popularity with the younger generation had led to the police insisting we install door staff at the weekends. This coupled with the brewery tying us into a beer contract which increased prices the better we did meant that we were losing money at an alarming rate.

In fact, in twelve months we lost approximately £50,000. From two lads who had built up an education business from scratch and owned the busiest pub in the city we had racked up debts that our upbringings could not afford or service and we lost the pub and the education business when in 2011 we were forced to go bankrupt.

Going back to having nothing was arguably the biggest challenge we have faced. People were quick to say 'I told you so' and 'why don't you just get a job'. Instead, we decided to go back to university to finish our degrees and 'bounce back'.

During our year back in education we persuaded Staffordshire University to run a small enterprise programme with 4 local schools with a finals event being held at the University in Global Entrepreneurship week. The challenge went down a storm with pupils and teachers and we set up a meeting to discuss how we could potentially take this further.

It was at a meeting in the university coffee shop that we overheard a discussion between the employers stating how young people lacked the skills needed for the world of work. This just further enhanced our belief that it was time we provided a solution to this growing problem. We were still passionate about our enterprise work and wanted to prove to people that we had what it took to turn it into a sustainable business.

We sat down and brainstormed how we could become the market leaders in the enterprise market. We talked through how we should launch a national competition, how we needed to let every team who took part attend the National finals and finally how we needed a high profile name to front the competition. We also decided that we should call it the very grand sounding 'National Enterprise Challenge'.

We shared our ideas with family and friends and the response was typical of the area 'How are you going to do that' they asked. 'Your bankrupt with no start-up capital, why will top entrepreneurs work with you,' the negative voices in both of our heads told us they were right. How could we pull this off?

But despite the negative comments and thoughts our inner desire and passion kicked in, we literally had nothing to lose and everything to gain! We shared our idea with industry contacts and started contacting high profile names to see if they would front our programme. Fearless and with nothing to lose we spoke to a number of PR companies representing these high profile entrepreneurs and even we after a few knockbacks we were still hopeful of a September launch.

However, the summer came and went and we were left facing the prospect of getting full time work and not fulfilling our dream. At the very last minute came the break we were hoping for when one of our contacts Claire Young (Runner Up of The Apprentice) got in touch one evening to tell us she had been successful in persuading Lord Sugar to front the programme!

We were back in business! We registered as Youth Enterprise CIC and set about working on the challenge. It was the end of September so we didn't have long to get going. However, working with somebody of the profile of Lord Sugar meant getting contracts in place and by the time everything had been agreed it was Christmas.

We had no schools signed up, no website, no team, no office and no start-up capital. We needed 50 schools minimum to make it work and the most schools we had worked with previously in one school year was 41. We had six months to sell and deliver the programme and put on a finals event in London - somewhere we had visited only a handful of times between us.

Over Christmas we set about working on a team. Not quite the Avengers Assemble but it was a team none the less. We then set about trying to secure a premises. We put an advert on Facebook and managed to secure the back room of a local community centre for £20 per week.

In January 2013 from our back office at the community centre we set about calling all of the schools
In the country to inform them about the challenge.
In the first year we delivered our programme to 11,000 young people and 58 schools from across the country, gained the support of Staffordshire University and OCR and in July 2013 hosted our first ever finals in London where 700 people attended including Lord Sugar.
That summer we wanted to freshen up the challenge and we contacted another of our dream ambassadors, Theo Paphitis, to see if he would be interested in fronting the programme. He agreed and the deal also saw his company Ryman become the main sponsor.
In September 2013 the challenge renamed The Ryman National Enterprise Challenge was re-launched with challenges set by Ryman and Social Enterprise Gandys Flip Flops from London.
During the year we delivered to over 21,000 young people from across the UK. In July 2014 we bought 1000 young people to The Trentham Estate in Staffordshire for the second of our National Finals, less than one mile away from the council estate where we grew up.

We also became delivery partners for the Government's Start Up Loans scheme (the first recipients of a loan to become delivery partners) during our time delivering the programme we have supported over 150 businesses in the Midlands to the tune of over one million pounds. We also ran a live Dragons Den style competition for Start Up's in the Staffordshire area where six businesses pitched live for a share of £30,000 in grant funding in front of a 300 strong crowd.

This year the challenge has once again grown. Theo has continued on in his role as lead ambassador and Ryman have set the Key Stage 3 challenge. The Key stage 4 challenge has been set by The Alton Towers Resort with the Resort also hosting our finals in July this year, which is expected to be attended by over 1400 people.

The last few years has also not been without its challenges. We have had to let people go on the journey including close family members which was tough. We have had to learn how to deal with big corporate companies and their needs. But most importantly we have had to learn how to get the most out of a small team whilst getting them to share in our vision.

Over the last few years we have learned a lot, made plenty of mistakes but also achieved more than many thought possible. We have been able to use our disadvantaged start to our advantage by being fearless when communicating our vision for the business and ultimately selling our services.

Understanding the value of money and making sure that you spend every penny wisely has also been a great advantage for us. Never having anything as children has meant that we are always looking for a deal or looking to do things ourselves to save on costs. This definitely helped in the early months of re-starting the business back in 2012.

In the past we always thought about all the different ways that we could get the business to work and the day that we realised that there was no substitute for hard work was the day that the business took a turn for the better. When re-starting the business we would often work late into the night and at weekends just to save on money and make the business as good as it could be.

Our advice to anybody thinking of starting out would be to do something you enjoy doing otherwise it will ultimately be a struggle to get it off the ground. Tell everyone you can about your business, you never know who is listening or could be of help. Finally don't let anybody tell you that something can't be done, if you want it bad enough you can achieve it.

Another piece of advice that has stuck with us is to look into people and not up to them. Too often in the past we thought that people were better than us and that there was a reason behind why they were doing better than us. The reason wasn't because they were better than us, just that they were working harder. So find out who it is that is at the top of their game in your field and look into why that is the case, look at what they do and take note. If something isn't working, then make a change. Always remember to be you, but to be the best of you!

Ben and Michael Dyer

Ben and Michael Dyer are the Co-Founders of The Ryman National Enterprise Challenge aged 27 and 28 from Staffordshire, UK.

Helping young people make a change and get on in life

Fleur Sexton, Joint Managing Director, PET-Xi

Former teacher Fleur Sexton is the co-founder and joint managing director of PET-Xi, working with hundreds of schools across the UK to deliver intensive, immersive, motivational and inspirational interventions that have a positive impact on learner progress. This covers everything from
• helping D-grade GCSE students to achieve that all important C-grade which opens so many doors to further training and employment,
• ensuring newly arrived immigrant children get to grips with the culture and language of their new home and integrate fully into school life,
• steering NEETS (young people Not in Education, Employment or Training) towards a fresh start through employability qualifications and skills,
• boosting young learners towards best possible achievements in their SATs tests,
• providing catch up courses for years 7, 8 and 9, and
• providing home revision tools for individuals and families to make revision simple and stress-free.
There's no other training company with this wide an offering and with the same level of commitment
Here she outlines her business philosophy..............
I often hear people say "business isn't personal, it's just business" - I couldn't disagree more - business is very personal! It's about our dreams, our aspirations and about making the world a better place – not to mention that business provides the means by which we all look after our families and make our personal ambitions come true. It's what we do every day, it's very personal and you must never lose that 100% commitment and loyalty to both your business and your staff.
My business, PET-Xi, aims to help every single child to fulfil their potential, to help them grasp every opportunity and love what they are doing as they

take their place in society by providing training in everything from exams to language to life skills.

I truly believe that anyone can change their life by taking control of it. One of my earliest memories is of my grandfather Ron Neal who came from a very poor background in Coventry, but overcame all manner of challenges and built up his own automotive business in the 1950s. That showed me, at an early age, that you don't have to settle and stick with the hand life has dealt you.

The children we work with at PET-Xi have sometimes been placed in a difficult position because of family, or other circumstances beyond their control. Much of our work is centred on emphasising to students that they have the power to change things for the better. The courses, written and run by PET-Xi, show students how to make things right and how to get to where they want to be. Often students arrive at our sessions facing a bleak outlook, but leave with a determination to change their future. I actually set up an annual award in my grandfather's name for the young person who has shown the most initiative to change their life – The Ron Neal Enterprise Award.

With Ron having lit the flame, I think my passion for helping young people in difficult circumstances was sparked more than 20 years ago when, as part of my French degree at Nottingham University, I spent time teaching English in a culturally diverse area of Paris. Whilst there I gained my ESOL (English for Speakers of Other Languages) qualification and followed it up on my return to the UK with a PGCE at Westminster College, Oxford.

After that, my first job was at Exhall Grange Specialist School – a physical/sensory special school for blind children and those with other disabilities. This was an inspirational environment that celebrated and encouraged success and achievement. Watching these children overcome multiple barriers to learning and development encouraged me to develop new audio and kinaesthetic approaches to teaching. I clearly remember the day of the school's swimming gala, when I asked what a little boy, who had no limbs, just hands and feet, was going to do while the others were swimming. 'He'll swim like everyone else' – came the reply. I've never forgotten the power of that 'can do' attitude and have endeavoured to apply it to my thinking ever since.

Together with my husband Chris (my fellow managing director) who had taken an MSc in artificial intelligence, we launched our first product 'Teacher's PET' – an exam-based computer game to help learners with foreign language vocabulary. Our very first success was a French GCSE product for children to learn via a disc. That was extended to include German, Spanish, Italian and Panjabi.

Having set out to solve a specific problem, i.e. to help children with a sight impairment to retain vocabulary when learning a foreign language, the business began to gather momentum. The success of this 'simple yet highly effective teaching tool' (as described by Guardian Education) led to the formation of our business, PET, in 1995 and following a move into vocational training in 2004 the business was renamed as PET-Xi Training – the 'Xi' added to reflect the company's new focus around 'explosive inspiration' . Xi, 'explosive inspiration' is about creating an environment in which learners have that moment of Xi when they decide they are going to achieve something..

We had an idea and we wanted to make it happen. Other people will not take risks on bringing your ideas to life – it's down to you, plus there is so much excitement in making things happen and in being in control of your own destiny.

But while it may be exciting, it's not all plain sailing. We had no money to launch the business and funded it through our own salaries. The fabulous part of doing things this way is that it means after 20 years we still own 100% of our business, which is unusual. The downside is that it's a slower way of growing!

Another challenge came in 2004, when the government decided that it would no longer be compulsory for children to study a language in school. This meant that we had to be swift and nimble, moving fast to develop courses centred on enterprise. We did it.

Every company goes through some tough times – we're no different – but by investing in ourselves and being creative with the products we provide PET has emerged stronger.

And while growing our business we had some personal difficulties too. When my middle daughter was born she was very ill and I was in hospital with her for six weeks. She was not expected to survive but she did! She was a fighter who gave her all to win her fight and survive.

Watching her night after night struggling for breath - and also being in a place where I was so vulnerable and out of control of the outcomes myself - made me emerge from it all as a stronger person. I felt even more committed – aware that life is short and that there is no time to waste in pursuing your goals. I became more determined than ever and discovered even greater reserves of empathy and resilience. After this point I realised that everything was possible. No students were beyond redemption and motivation ... For everything there is a way.

This led to greater risk taking and a much bolder approach to engaging. We started taking on students who were considered to be beyond the point of motivating and engaging who in actual fact were just battling their own impossible battles in one way or another. For every one, we found a way to get them on track and we began to see some real miracles of engagement.

Incidentally - baby survived and some!! She is still one of my biggest inspirations.

I stay motivated by keeping highly involved with the business at all levels– I've now got three children and three dogs so I appreciate the backing of a top-class team which I trust beyond words. I only employ the best and expect the best from them in return.

All my staff have freedom of action and are never micro-managed. But I make it clear that it's freedom so that they can be the best and that I expect results and more! I would move mountains for my staff. They are family. I work at a very fast pace – which means they do too!

A swift change of business direction was required again in 2010 when the new coalition government set a greater focus on vocational learning training and GCSEs. Without the family feel and support within the business we wouldn't be able to write and provide these courses in such quick time since it involves PET-Xi people going the extra mile, working long hours and sparing no effort to make sure the children on our courses get every last drop of knowledge and inspiration while they are with us.

It's also vital to innovate. We were the first company in the UK to run intensive GCSE courses for young people on a results-based model and one of the first to run multi-media courses for languages in 1995. There is no other company which offers a combination of digital courses and training. All our training programmes are devised using our own methods and delivered in-house by our trainers who are dedicated to improving the lives of every person on our course – whether that be to help them pass an exam immediately, or in the longer term to improve their career prospects or their future educational opportunities.

We have also extended our work in teaching English as a Foreign Language with a ground-breaking course to help Slovakian Roma children assimilate into their new life in the UK and integrate and thrive in the classroom. Thinking outside the box, we came up with a course involving kickboxing which has taught them English and social skills while integrating them into school life at the same time. Studying a martial art was chosen specifically to help the children learn discipline and self-control, and also to act as an incentive. By allowing the Roma children to take part in something they enjoy, they saw an element of school that immediately appealed to them and this provided them with a reason to continue attending and working hard. It has helped these children, who were previously not 'school-ready' and consequently in danger of exclusion.

Work is very demanding, but at the end of the day I don't mind because it's my passion. It is important to stay passionate about the business you set up. Like every important relationship in my life, my relationship with the business is something I work hard to keep fresh, am always grateful for and never neglect or take for granted.

I also think it's vital to put something back into the community – we are a local company and keen to demonstrate our commitment to the region where we are based- Coventry and Warwickshire where our 50 head office staff are employed. This includes sponsoring the Young Chamber of our local Chamber of Commerce, establishing a charitable foundation which has raised thousands of pounds for local youngsters and buying locally every time – including most recently our company cars!

I also make sure that the business employs and mentors young people and gives opportunities to those who perhaps wouldn't be given a chance elsewhere – for example because of a bad work record or a criminal conviction.

PET-Xi is growing year on year by an amazing 20% and we are consolidating our growth by also growing the processes and organisational structure at the same time. This is where my business partner and husband and I work very well together. I have a vision and Chris has the strategy for actually building the road to that vision. In this way we combine strategic and operational working hand in hand. He describes it as I slash the new route through the jungle and he moves in and builds the road and infrastructure. It's a team work approach that works fabulously well.

Now 20 years on from where we first began, we are running a leading UK training company which delivers real results, impact and progression where it matters – to the learners. In 2013-14, PET-Xi completed intervention programmes for 300 schools nationwide, delivering 750 courses to more than 14,500 young people aged from 7 to 24. The business employs 55 full-time employees and 340 full-time, part-time and sessional trainers and is still growing. There's no other training company with this wide an offering and with the same commitment, dedication and drive.
Above all we care and will work to overcome any barriers to learning, whether they be cultural, physical or behavioural.

Fleur Sexton

Former teacher Fleur Sexton is the co-founder and joint managing director of PET-Xi, training providers working with hundreds of schools across the UK to deliver intensive, immersive, motivational and inspirational interventions that have a positive impact on learner progress.
Fleur's belief in education as a way to optimise life potential and her passion for helping young people in difficult circumstances make a change and get on in life was sparked more than 20 years ago when, as part of her

French degree at Nottingham University, she spent time teaching English in a culturally diverse area of Paris. Whilst there she gained her ESOL (English for Speakers of Other Languages) qualification and followed it up after her degree with a PGCE at Westminster College, Oxford.

Her first job was at Exhall Grange Specialist School – a physical/sensory special school for blind children and those with other disabilities. This was an inspirational environment that celebrated and encouraged success and achievement. Working with these children to overcome multiple barriers to learning and development encouraged Fleur to develop new audio and kinaesthetic approaches to teaching.

Now, 20 years on, Fleur and Chris are running a leading UK training provider – in 2013-14 PET-Xi completed intervention programmes for 300 schools nationwide, delivering 750 courses to more than 14,500 young people aged from 7 to 24. The business, with an annual turnover of £7 million, employs 55 full-time employees and 300 trainers and is still 100 per cent owned by Fleur and Chris.

Caring, dedicated and driven – Fleur's motto in life is 'to be the best you can and encourage fulfilment of potential by getting young people to celebrate every success'. She will work to overcome any barriers to learning, whether they be cultural, physical or behavioural.

An Insight into Entrepreneurship

John Stapleton, Co-Founder & Director Little Dish

Much is spoken about an entrepreneurs' ability – innate or otherwise – to overcome obstacles and challenges. Successful entrepreneurs are generally thought of as having the capacity to run through walls, uproot trees and get things done, especially in the face of adversity. However, in my experience, it really shouldn't be all that surprising that entrepreneurs possess these types of skills – along with tenacity, drive and, in many cases, stubbornness. Frankly, in the absence of these abilities, nothing much would ever get done. If entrepreneurs weren't, in the main, focused, driven and thick-skinned, their ventures would often never see the light of day and they would struggle to overcome the inevitable obstacles that lie in wait during the subsequent growth phases.

Without the resources and support systems of a corporate behind them, entrepreneurs have to do everything themselves. They must find ways to make things happen, while at the same time, often content with being told they haven't got much of a chance of succeeding!

From what I've seen in my 25-odd years of professional life, entrepreneurs are comfortable with uncertainty and risk. This is the world in which they operate. Therefore, personality traits such as application, commitment, determination and passion tend to feature highly in any entrepreneur's repertoire. To my mind though, the real difference between entrepreneurs and others is quite simple: entrepreneurs act on their ideas while others procrastinate and think too much about the challenges or get swayed by the naysayers.

Sometimes sycophantically, a debate rages as to whether entrepreneurs are born or made. Similar to the nature vs. nurture argument, there is unlikely to be any universal agreement any time soon. I believe, in the main, that they are made – but this "making" process begins from a very young age and not just once they enter professional life. I'd like to share how I became involved in the entrepreneurial world and spent the first few professional years figuring out how to relate to it.

Part One: In the Beginning

I met Andrew Palmer in mid-1987 as I completed my masters in Food Science in Reading University. Andrew had this wonderful or crazy idea, depending on your perspective. He wanted to introduce fresh soup to the mainstream consumer so they could enjoy it at home. Today, fresh soup is taken for granted, but back then, if you wanted to buy liquid soup you could only find it in a can. It was assumed that soup had to be sterilised and come with an 18 month shelf life. It was difficult to manage from the safety point of view. Soup was traditionally the product of left-overs from yesterday's lunch or dinner. When we first placed the words "fresh soup" on a carton and placed it in the chiller aisle, it created confusion – these two words didn't belong together.

Making and selling fresh soup through the retail chain was viewed as revolutionary. Andrew and I decided to join forces to bring this fresh soup revolution to fruition.

Being quite a left brainer and coming straight from a science-based education, I was analytical and logical in my approach. This can be an extremely useful asset in business, but when starting New Covent Garden Soup Co (NCGSC), I found myself in an unfamiliar, entrepreneurial environment. Scientists like to begin from principles, form a hypothesis, test it repeatedly and proceed once all the variables are not just known but proven. In a business environment – especially in a start-up – one doesn't have the time luxury that such an approach demands and one has to evaluate quickly, trial if possible, and then simply do. The partnership with Andrew – who was more of a right brainer – was very complimentary; we got on really well and this benefitted the business hugely.

The early years of NCGSC ware extremely dynamic, creative and exciting. In the main, we wanted it that way, but, in hindsight, it also developed a life of its own. Necessity is the mother of invention, so we really didn't have a choice with this. The demand generated in the marketplace meant we were constantly running to the next challenge. If we wanted to get this idea off the ground successfully, we had to move quickly, take calculated risks and implement, implement, implement.

This was due to us not only pioneering a brand-new category and developing a new concept but also the consuming nature of growth, giving us little time to introduce much structure to the organisation. Combine this with the fact that neither of us had much business experience – certainly not industrial or brand experience - two key elements which proved instrumental in the later success of NCGSC, meaning that in the majority we had to make it up as we went along.

The Early Years

My over-riding memory of the early years at NCGSC is how crazy is all of this? It was one big adventure. The downside was – if one had enough time to dwell on it – the tendency to be quite chaotic and without structure. At first I found that bit challenging. I was often confronted by the feeling that I was winging it – and, of course, to a certain extent I was! Remember, there was no "black book" on how to make fresh soup; as the pioneers of the category it was exciting, but at times, an unnerving prospect. My grounding in science clashed with the craziness of the early soup years, which were based on judgements with little relevant available information. At times, making decisions almost seemed like guess-work.

We realised early on that we needed to develop a completely new process to manufacture fresh soup – compared to the established, traditional process for making canned soup. The following three opposing objectives emerged quickly to be of equal importance:

i) ensuring the end product actually tasted of the ingredients used;
ii) making the product safe without sterilising it (i.e. the canned approach) and,
iii) ensuring the product had a commercial shelf life sufficient to survive the route to market through the retailers

In addition to dreaming up a new product and a new manufacturing process to go with it, we were also challenged with creating a new brand which would effectively convey the benefits of the product to our target consumer market. Essentially, a brand makes a promise to consumers – it explains both the functional and emotional benefits of a product to the customer. We were convinced that, if we could get the product to be as good as you could make yourself at home or even in a restaurant, the customer would come back for more. The trick was establishing how to get consumers to try it in the first place. Soup buyers exclusively shopped the "soup aisle". We needed to generate awareness for our new product concept in a different store location. This was a big ask – especially in a category which was dominated by retailer own-label – the chilled ready meal aisle.

I often felt like I was having a right-brain vs. left-brain argument inside my own head where the insight-driven, judgement, have-a-go approach to dealing with challenges and setbacks and taking advantage of opportunities would challenge the more established and analytical approach - and very often win. In those early years I couldn't quite make up my mind whether this was all too scary or whether it was extremely invigorating, inspiring and therefore fulfilling. On different days, even at different times of the same day, it seemed like it was both. My more dominant memory is the latter, so I guess this won out!

However, I reached a point of recognition, realising I needed to take action to make the situation more efficient. In more-or-less the following sequence, I took the following steps to deal with the challenge:

Carried on a Wave of Excitement

In effect, to start with, I didn't do anything particularly purposeful. I just allowed myself to be carried on a wave of excitement and enthusiasm – which was infectious. There really isn't much chance to resist the inherent force of a start-up in any event, so I stopped trying to figure out if I should. To be honest, I wouldn't have had it any other way.

Business School

I did however, yearn for at least a little bit of structure so I found time to go to business school during the evenings. This underpinned my authority and satisfied my technical and process-competence needs. I could now figure out the areas of the business, which I'd previously felt under qualified for and I could convince myself that I knew enough about them to make the decisions the business demanded.

Learning by Doing

Next, I learned that rather than needing to feel qualified to start a business and to break new ground, you are probably much better qualified than many others are, purely by making the decision to do it in the first place. A big realisation was getting to a stage where I allowed myself to recognise the essence of learning by doing. The value of experience suddenly dawned on me and what I now call my "MBA of life" took on a greater meaning. I recognised that official qualifications are excellent but that "figuring things out" by getting stuck in and so-called "street smarts" can often be much more relevant.

Keep It Simple, Stupid

One further lesson I learned from this experience is "don't try to over-complicate things" – as a left-brainer often tends to do. I still like to understand the detail in any given situation, but the real focus is on keeping things simple. Successful people have a tendency to seek clarity – and this is often the essence of simplicity. Just focus on doing the simple things well.

Jump Straight In

Also, as time went on, I realised everyone was winging it anyway – at least a little and almost always at the beginning. And this is fine – in fact, there is no better way to approach business. You have to jump in at the deep end and implement. This can sit uncomfortably with some. There is a tendency to feel it is only appropriate to manage and make decisions on a topic for which you are suitably qualified. You need to have a thick skin and not be fazed by all the no's you will get along the way, but passion and a belief in your idea and vison for your business will take you through. You don't necessarily understand this by going to university or by gathering qualifications. You only really ever begin to understand it when you get stuck in. Therefore winging it is a great asset and, in my experience, an essential approach which should be embraced.

Trust Yourself

The real break-through was to simply believe in myself and believe that I was actually quite capable or even good at certain things. Everyone brings something different to a business. It was important for me to understand and recognise the part I played and the benefits I brought to the team. Yes, I wanted to gather information, understand the detail and figure out how things worked. But, I could also see the big picture and was keen to get going, experiment, innovate and take risks. As a result, I could make balanced and effective business decisions. I also understood both categories of people in the business and on teams and had a good appreciation for what roles they played. I find this insight is a great strength in leadership situations and in facing challenges and I have used it a lot in my career ever since.

Leadership

Leadership style, in the context of the entrepreneurial spirit and starting and growing a business, is a very interesting phenomenon. I came to the understanding that a good leader relies heavily on highly-developed emotional intelligence and a keen sense of how to deal with adversity. These skills are borne out of understanding oneself and knowing what is important in managing people, developing organisational culture and building successful teams. This realisation was also key in my acceptance of my own abilities as an entrepreneur and as a business leader. It allowed me to play to those strengths over time, to trust the skills I had developed and to not feel I was winging it any more. The initial internal struggles led to significant benefits in the later years at NCGSC and when I set up my subsequent businesses. These were also invaluable lessons when it came to my food consultancy, advisory and mentoring roles, which I am now, happily, in a position to dedicate more time to.

Part Two: Taking Control

Figuring out the Process

It became immediately apparent at NCGSC that we needed to manufacture the product ourselves, unlike later at Little Dish. Apart from there being no out-sourcing option available at the time, we also wanted to protect our growing knowledge of what we believed to be the critical success factors of this venture. We felt that if we **designed, controlled and managed** manufacturing in-house, this would be a significant barrier to entry – and so it proved to be, especially during the early years.

The first step was to establish the right theoretical process to deliver our product objectives (see the three product objectives earlier). My background was clearly relevant to achieving this, but, at that stage, not very applied. Despite this, I developed an approach which we tested rigorously and the outcome was a novel process to manufacture fresh soup.

We successfully applied for patent protection, which filled us with confidence that we had something that would **work**, but also which we could exclusively apply and which would later become a significant competitive advantage in the marketplace.

Scaling-Up

The next step was to apply the theory in a pilot plant environment and then scale it up to factory level. We begged, borrowed and stole facilities, equipment and expertise in order to do this. Significantly, we secured, at this point, a listing with a leading high street retailer and this provided us with the leverage to approach venture capitalists in order to fund the building of a full-scale factory. The key was obviously raising a relatively large sum of money while not "giving away the farm" in return. Convincing the VC firm of the validity of the founders' vison and that the product would appeal to a significant proportion of the mass market, was the Holy Grail. We achieved this, not without an initial struggle, but with a satisfactory balance for all concerned.

With the cash secured, we bought a freehold site, refurbished the building and installed a lot of new shiny and expensive kit. It was vitally important to be able to rely on a process which guaranteed product consistency. Product quality in this case relied on the use of predominantly fresh ingredients and these, by their nature, already contributed some product variation. Therefore, the process needed to be very closely controlled and not contribute any further product variation. The controls imposed on the process secured this, but required significant investment and we proceeded to launch the product nationally.

Establishing a National Brand

And so onto our next challenge: creating and developing a national brand, with very little resources remaining following the investment of most of our VC cash in the manufacturing facility.

When talking about brand building at speaking engagements these days, I emphasise that a business needs to invest ahead of the curve. We were initially doing the opposite! Unsurprisingly, this led to difficulties. The way we circumvented this, at least for the first few years, was to concentrate on product innovation and PR. In fact, one went hand-in-glove with the other. We introduced a wide range of products, most of which performed very well, and ran PR campaigns around their stories. In some rare instances we actually launched some products which we didn't necessarily believe would sell well to the mass market, but would generate column inches.

One such example was Borscht. This is a beetroot-based soup of Ukrainian origin and is popular in many eastern European countries. It is a very distinctive soup with a particular flavour and a vivid colour. Prior to launch we were never convinced as to its marketplace appeal. In the end, the product sold, at best, to mediocre levels. However, the media coverage we received.

We also introduced a Soup of the Season and later a Soup of the Month, each product carrying the same product barcode, but with a different product inside the carton each season/month, which was another industry first at the time. This approach was, in fact, the only option open to us, as it was relatively inexpensive.

After all, we didn't have the funds for the more typical brand-building efforts such as traditional advertising. Remember, this was long before the advent of social media marketing opportunities, therefore we had to be both innovative and frugal with our marketing efforts. We were perhaps lucky that we had the breathing space over the first two years or so in which to adopt this approach.

After this, we saw competition increase – in particular from the retailer own-label sector, but by this point we had established a significant lead in the market and we began to generate the revenues which in turn, funded more necessary and mainstream marketing initiatives.

Developing Consumer Awareness

Challenges have come to my three businesses in many shapes and sizes and I believe it is one of the virtues of an entrepreneur to not be fazed by them. At NCGSC, we were told from the beginning that it was a crazy idea, that no-one would pay three times the price of a can of soup for a so-called fresh version and even that we risked killing someone if we didn't completely sterilise the product. At Little Dish we got push-back like: "mothers will never trust a non-established brand" and "adult food will do".

The main challenge in establishing a consumer brand is developing good customer awareness. Coincidentally, at both NCGSC and Little Dish, the first major commercial breakthrough for both brands was a product listing in Waitrose. This was a significant milestone as it signified the beginning of trading in the high street retailer chains – essential if one has national brand aspirations. An initial step like this changes everything for all stakeholders. This was followed by a successful trial and listing in Sainsbury's (in the case of NCGSC) and in Tesco (with Little Dish), which proved the appeal of the brand to the mainstream market – again, quite significant.

Other breakthrough moments at Little Dish, possibly less commercially significant in their own right, but potentially more impactful in the longer term were the receipt of awards such as *Best New SME Brand* (Marketing Society Awards), *Quality Food Awards* (Junior Q Awards) and *Loved By Parents Award* (Best Baby/ Toddler Food Award). The *Loved By Parents Award* was probably the most significant and rewarding to us at the time, as it demonstrated consumer recognition and provided us with validity in the eyes of parents; our target market.

During the early stages at Little Dish, growth was slower than we liked. One of the main reasons behind this was an apparent guilt complex associated with ready meals.

A genuine sentiment and concern from mothers – our key customer base – was that by not cooking or preparing food from scratch, they were bad mothers. We had to work hard, therefore, to reassure consumers that providing their children with Little Dish products when you just didn't have time to cook from scratch, was a really good alternative.

Our message focused on the belief that while cooking at home is always best, Little Dish is a healthy, convenient and tasty option. This reassured mothers that relying on Little Dish every so often did not have to be a guilt-ridden choice – in fact, far from it! Once we were able to articulate this and get our customers recommending our products to each other, it became a little easier for us to build momentum.

Part Three: Lessons Learned – and putting these into practice

Lessons are still around every corner and I hope I never stop learning from them! In the context of lessons learned at NCGSC which, in the main, have been re-emphasised at Little Dish, the following are probably the top five:

1. **Don't always give too much credence to conventional wisdom**

If we had done so at NCGSC we would never have commenced the project. As an entrepreneur, one needs to have faith on your vision and stick to what you believe will work. This doesn't mean not taking good advice on board, but this should be in the context of perfecting your value proposition; understanding your target customer and amending your route to market in light of new information. At Little Dish, I had the benefit of NCGSC behind me and therefore felt justified in not worrying about the number of knockbacks we got in the early days. My belief is that the more no's you receive, chances are a yes is around the corner.

2. **When adversity strikes (and it will), don't ditch your personality traits and early life experiences – they got you this far**

Someone once said "show me someone who has overcome adversity and I'll show you someone who has done something worthwhile". Essentially, if you don't get out of your comfort zone you won't do anything worthwhile. In doing something worthwhile, you will attract some form of adversity – often repeatedly. This is just a fact of life and when it happens, one shouldn't take it personally.

In dealing with adversity, don't always believe you need to have faced a problem in business successfully before you can feel confident in dealing with business problems. In my experience, strength of character is vitally important to an entrepreneur. The qualities of tenacity and passion required to follow your vision come from character and this is formed just as much (if not even more), outside business as within. In the early days of NCGSC I originally believed I had to wipe the slate clean when entering professional life. I quickly realised, especially in the chaotic adventure that was early-days NCGSC, which I knew just as much as the next person about how to deal with problems, setbacks and challenges. I didn't get this from business, as I was incredibly inexperienced at the time, but rather from my childhood, my upbringing and by learning from events unfolding around me.

3. Not everyone can grow dramatically with a fast-moving business.

An entrepreneur tends to surround themselves with like-minded people. Those who are self-starters and who like autonomy. Individuals like these move quickly; they feel comfortable with change and uncertainty and generally think similarly to the entrepreneur.

As the boss, it is easy to think everyone is like this – especially if demand is strong and you may be struggling to keep up with it. However, many people in an organisation (and at one stage we had 120 employees at NCGSC, the majority in manufacturing) don't want constant change and feel threatened by uncertainly and risk. This realisation escaped me initially and at one stage I promoted a very good team leader to shift-manager. Unfortunately, the added responsibility didn't sit well with him and he regressed into a shadow of his former self. This was not his fault, but mine, for not being aware of the strengths, limitations and comfort zones of the staff around me. Since this realisation, I have been able to make better judgements about the suitability of staff to roles and this has benefited the business.

4. Monitor performance on a daily basis and communicate it strongly

I cannot over-emphasise this enough. Firstly, in an FMCG business with a short shelf-life product which is delivered to high street retailers on a seven days a week basis, the business moves far too quickly to rely on monthly management accounts for a steer on how the business is performing. One needs weekly and, in some cases, daily KPIs to keep on track and to be able to react to problems or properly take advantage of opportunities.

Secondly, once everyone understands what part they play in the performance of the business they can see, independently, the impact of the efforts they are contributing. This unlocks a synergy which is difficult to achieve in any other way. It's almost a case of: "monitor and measure something and it improves of its own accord", simply because you are looking at it constantly.

5. **Get all stakeholders aligned behind the main business objectives as soon as possible**

Doing this before a major decision needs to be made or a problem solved will be more beneficial in the long-run. It is key that shareholders, the board and management are all on the same wavelength regarding the major strategic issues. If not, this will lead to strife and wasted time and possibly missed opportunities later on. The most obvious potential point of conflict can be when to exit the business. If this is not clearly agreed at the outset – and circumstances can and do always change – then individual agendas can take over to the detriment of the business. This is especially the case when institutional investors are involved as they are governed by the time frame of the fund to which you belong.

Part Four: Where I am Today ….

I have recently stepped back to a non-executive director role at Little Dish, which has given me the opportunity to focus more on providing business advice, guidance, coaching and mentoring to both early-stage and developed growth-phase businesses.

Since returning from the US in 2003 I have lived in Munich. Setting up, growing and developing a business based in London, such as Little Dish required a lot of travelling and many days away from home. I wanted to achieve a better balance in my personal life, so following a lengthy but successful succession plan at Little Dish, I have been able to achieve this.

I have thoroughly enjoyed becoming NED in my own business, unusual though it may be, and I now serve as NED on a number of other boards, in addition to providing advice to other growth-phase businesses.

Since starting this phase of my career, it has struck me that through the process of setting up and growing my three businesses, I have probably come across 80% or more of the challenges, road-blocks and difficulties in starting and growing a business in this space.

By continuing to provide value-added input to businesses who can benefit from the experience I have gained over the last 25 years I continue to learn, which I find extremely fulfilling.

It is also interesting to, from time to time, recognise myself in others as I was back in the early days of NCGSC. Those who are either starting out or grappling with the growing pains of a successful business.

Entrepreneurs need to learn from their own experiences, just as I did, so I'm not proposing to circumvent this. However, I hate reinventing the wheel. So instead, why not leverage the last 25 years' experience and help others essentially following the same path, by putting their ideas into action?!

John Stapleton

John Stapleton is a results-focused entrepreneur, business leader, CEO & Non-Executive Director with over 25 years' experience in creating and building consumer brands in the FMCG sector in both the UK and the USA. A founder of three successful start-ups, John is an expert at developing new and innovative consumer-focused products & categories and has wide-ranging experience in operational management and strategic leadership roles.

John co-founded the New Covent Garden Soup Co Ltd in 1989, which pioneered and established the fresh soup category in the UK. In 1998 he moved to San Francisco, where he co-founded Glencoe Inc., bringing the fresh soup concept to the United States.

On returning to live in Europe in 2003, John established a consumer food consultancy and has worked with a number of varied clients across the FMCG sector in the UK, US, Germany, Belgium and the Czech Republic. He has worked with a wide range of companies including large corporations (e.g. Unilever-Bestfoods North America) as well as numerous start-up and growth-phase businesses.

In 2005, John co-founded Little Dish which supplies fresh, natural foods for children over 1 year. Little Dish, which created and established the toddler chilled food category, can be found in all national UK high street retailers and is the dominant brand in chilled toddler food (69% market share).

John is a graduate of UCD (Industrial Microbiology); Reading University (Food Science); The University of Westminster (Business Administration and Finance) and holds a marketing qualification from the Chartered Institute of Marketing (UK). John lives with his wife in Munich, Germany and speaks fluent German.

Am I an entrepreneur?

Raeleen Hooper - Snap Franchising

Am I an entrepreneur? Not in the sense of having an idea and starting my own business like the many inspirational and entrepreneurial women in Australia, and indeed worldwide. Many of these successful women and their businesses started from a simple, passionate idea of care and concern to make others' lives better. Now with technology, the great enabler, we have never before seen so many women use all their skills, initiative and nous to carve out their career and be proud of their achievements.

Two outstanding women entrepreneurs that I think really epitomise the essence of an entrepreneurial spirit is Lesley Gillespie, Co-founder, Executive Director and Joint CEO of Baker's Delight and Dr Catherine Hamlin, Co-founder of The Addis Ababa Fistula Hospital.

Lesley Gillespie with her husband, were honoured as a "champion of entrepreneurship" at the 2014 EY Entrepreneur of the Year Southern Region awards. Lesley, with her philanthropic work, has seen Bakers Delight raise more than $7.7 million for the Breast Cancer Network Australia through the sale of its pink iced buns.

Dr Catherine Hamlin, an Australian obstetrician and gynaecologist along, with her husband Dr Reg Hamlin, co-founded and opened the world's first medical centre in Ethiopia. The Addis Ababa Fistula Hospital is dedicated exclusively to providing free obstetric fistula repair surgery to more than 34,000 women suffering from childbirth injuries. Although Dr Reg Hamlin has passed, Dr Catherine Hamlin, at over 90 years of age, still continues to drive the success of this amazing organisation.

Both of these women are obviously extremely talented, great leaders, passionate and dedicated to their work. What sets them apart is their devotion to help others. I have observed these attributes through my life as not just the foundations of entrepreneurial business owners, but also with many women I have had the pleasure to work for, work with, as well as mentor and develop.

When I first entered into the world of sales within a highly male-dominated, global organisation I was excited that my first Sales Manager was a woman. This is where I met Julie who managed me in a team with males and two other females. Julie in her late forties was sophisticated, smart and a great mentor.

Julie definitely insisted on more discipline, training and commitment from the three girls in the team than the men. She constantly pushed us to be independent and to reach our personal and company goals. The impact of Julie's drive meant that all three of us went onto other successful careers by implementing what we had learnt from her - confidence, positive attitude, self and financial achievement, an unwavering work ethic through discipline, as well as the ability to adapt to pressure situations.

Julie never asked us to do anything she wouldn't do herself and it was ingrained in us that hard work would make up for any shortcomings until skills were developed. It was only as I was moving onto another organisation that I discovered Julie had been financially supporting her husband, an inventor. Julie provided support to her husband with the business plan, sales and marketing and the finances for success.

I have also come to recognise that the entrepreneurial bug is not restricted to any age, time frame or any particular level of education. Emma in her late twenties, single and pregnant started her entrepreneurial journey managing her own café. Emma possessed boundless energy, flowing ideas and a desire to be independent. Working in the café, Emma developed the concept of creating pre-made pizzas to distribute through independent grocery outlets. Soon enough the concept was picked up by supermarkets however Emma unfortunately couldn't gear up to meet the supermarkets' volume.

I was fortunate to work with Emma as a member of the sales team I managed. Very early on Emma was exceeding targets and out-performing the rest of the team. It was very clear that the entrepreneurial spirit of 'having a go' and not taking no for an answer laid down the foundations for a highly successful career in corporate sales. However the freedom and sense of personal achievement through owning her own business was deeply ingrained in Emma. So, whilst raising her children and tending to the family, Emma started her own communications company and continues to do so successfully today.

Sue, a teacher by trade, with two teenage children and a supportive, accountant husband didn't start out consciously on her entrepreneurial journey. Sue was 20kgs overweight and very unfit. Not liking how she looked and felt, Sue decided to change her life. Through discipline, hard work, commitment and great support, Sue lost the weight and got fit. It was these attributes that set Sue on her new business venture.

Sue invested in a fitness and health centre and became her own boss. Hard work? An understatement. Sue worked a minimum of 12 hours per day, six days per week (not including the time the business was on her mind). Starting from scratch, Sue spent all of her time building local business relationships, motivating people to get fit and lose weight and, most importantly, recruiting and inspiring a great team to help her with the challenge of growing the business.

As you would expect, Sue achieved success and was very proud of her profitable fitness business and new lifestyle - a long way from teaching. Sue never wavered from the foundations of her success and, every day, the people Sue worked with witnessed her total dedication and passion through hard work, discipline and commitment to her team and clients. Sue went on to repeat her successful formula and opened a second fitness centre. Then disaster struck. Sue was diagnosed with breast cancer.

Already working 12 hour days, six days a week, Sue had to figure out how she would continue to run her business while undergoing the treatment and getting the rest needed to help her through this difficult time. Many would have shut up shop to deal with the treatment but Sue, through the great support from her family, friends and employees, managed to oversee her business at the same time as fighting this devastating disease.

Six years on, Sue is still happily married and helping her children launch their own careers. Her fitness centres continue to change people's lives by inspiring them to be healthy and happy.

I had the pleasure of working with Sue and when I asked her what she would put her success down to, Sue said it was simple. Be passionate about what you are doing and make sure you have a strong support network around you.

I have also worked extensively in franchising where I have been amazed at the women who have taken the risk and invested in their own business through the franchising system. This is where I have really seen the trials, tribulations and excitement of success with being an entrepreneur.

In the early 2000's, there were a couple of ladies who had been at home raising their families and managing the household. Their children had moved on and they decided to have their own business to enjoy their own sense of achievement. Even though it was a franchise system, they still needed to possess finance skills, sales and marketing skills, great relationship skills and the ability to manage people and time; arguably the most difficult element of being a business owner.

These women faced many challenges, particularly in the beginning. The initial struggle of juggling family at the same time of starting a new business was probably the biggest hurdle as owning your own business is not a nine-to-five job. If you are not working in the business you will be busy working on your business and even when you think you are taking a break, it will be in the back of your mind. Often these women business owners tell me they have guilt. Either being away from their family working in their business or being with their family and not working on their business. The term 'jack of all trades and master of none' is often referred to by women business owners and having a strategy to deal with these feelings is critical, particularly in the early days as major adjustments take place.

The women who were able to acknowledge this early challenge of lifestyle change have a strong business plan in place and, most importantly, have the support of their family and friends to push through this stage of business ownership. This is also the time when doubt comes into play…..'what have I done?' Simply by acknowledging this as a normal reaction and talking about how you are feeling with your support network will help keep confidence levels up.

Then there is the tough stuff…….. as the saying goes, 'when the going gets tough, the tough get going'. I haven't met anyone yet who is great at all the skills that are required as a business owner when they first start out. This is where the tough times start. You have to identify your strengths and your areas for improvement. Great business owners and leaders make sure they have the best skilled people around them to help them achieve their goals. Whether that is people employed in the business or the advisers and support network, this is the key for long term success.

Too many times I have seen new business owners think they can do it all, however everything from managing finances and suppliers through to sales and marketing and building relationships takes different skills. You need to identify what you are really great at and what you like to do. Then be brutally honest with yourself and understand what you don't do so well. The next step is to recruit the best person, adviser or supplier you can afford and empower them to get the results you need.

In fact one more paragraph on this, honesty is the best policy……with yourself! Don't fool yourself and think you can do a task if you haven't had the training for it, if you are uncomfortable with it or lack confidence. That is not to say that as you grow as a business owner you won't develop these skills but you will have enough pressure on you in the beginning that it is best to work to your strengths and that will make it easier to get over some of the early roadblocks.

The two critical factors I have witnessed for initial success is top line sales and managing cash flow. Cash is king. So many business owners get busy making sure their operations are slick that they don't focus on sales. Mastering sales skills and sales planning will be imperative for successful growth of any business large or small.

Make no mistake, marketing is essential for your brand awareness but if you suffer from not being able to network, build relationships and talk to people about the value of your products and services, you will need to recruit the best people you can to do this for you. It doesn't matter if you are a bricks and mortar business or online; customer service, sales and after sales care will be the foundation for long term success.

I can't stress this enough. Sales, if it hasn't been one of your skill sets, will be a major challenge. Know intrinsically what your sales need to be, the cost of making the sale and how you will get the sale. It is all about the planning.........fail to plan, plan to fail. This doesn't need to be complicated There are state based governments and local organisations that can provide help and support to guide you through the planning stages and don't forget to reach out to your network.

That's why franchising is often very helpful for people who want to start in their own business but may need some of the expertise of planning and the safety net of support. Franchising also has a proven brand that can save you hundreds and thousands in investing in your own brand. However, with franchising you need to use their system so your entrepreneurial needs will have to work within the franchising framework.

Being your own boss and making your own decisions, without a doubt, is one of the very rewarding aspects of being an entrepreneurial business owner. With this comes managing people. Remember you are passionate about what you do, you have big plans and you hope to build a successful, long term business that provides you with the freedom to meet your personal goals. However, unless you have buy-in from the people you recruit, empower them to grow to meet their own personal goals and provide them with their just reward, you will spend an inordinate amount of time building and re-building a team of people to help you grow your business.

Recruitment and development of people takes time and effort. Thriving businesses have the best people who are passionate about the brand and love coming to work every day. If work is a chore then expect your people to act like it is. Without a doubt the most successful entrepreneurial people and businesses I have had the pleasure to work with are the ones who are heavily invested in their people and their development. Even to the point of helping their employees launch their own business.

Having said all of that, the consistent attributes I have seen in successful, entrepreneurial women are the absolute belief in their own abilities, passionate and confident in their offering and an unwavering desire to succeed and help others. Be brave, don't be afraid of failure and, most importantly, enjoy the journey.

Raeleen Hooper

Raeleen Hooper was appointed General Manager of Sales and Marketing at Snap Franchising in November 2011 then appointed to General Manager of Franchise Services in 2013. A key member of Snap's Executive Team, Raeleen has over 20 years sales, marketing and management experience including nine years at Snap.

Raeleen is responsible for the Sales and Marketing division and presides over the development of industry-leading sales and marketing systems, support and training. Raeleen is also an integral member of the senior management team responsible for the strategic direction of the organisation.

Raeleen has completed a marketing course at the Australian Institute of Management, sales courses with the Huthwaite Institute as well as a Certificate IV Workplace and Assessor enabling her to deliver many sales introduction and performance improvement training courses and workshops. In 2014 Raeleen completed a Diploma of Franchising and a Diploma of Management.

Raeleen has a keen interest in emerging internet marketing tools and also enjoys snowboarding as well as spectating and helping coach netball having played at a representative level for many years.

Happiness Is The New Black (And White)

Ben Hutchinson – Ginger Sport

On the face of it, my background and upbringing in North East England was far from likely to make me the subject of a book about entrepreneurs. Having said that, I don't define myself as an entrepreneur or view myself as anyone special. I'm just an ordinary bloke, with a lot of ideas, who runs a business. As clichéd as it sounds, looking back, I can see that the events of my life, leading up to where I find myself now, very much shaped who I am and gave me the inspiration and determination to be where I am today.

The second youngest of four boys, I was born in the early 1980s in Newcastle upon Tyne, a typical working-class city of the north east. I was from a working-class suburb, born into a skilled working-class family. My dad John was a second-generation fruit and veg wholesaler. It was expected that I would probably move into the family business like my father, and his father before him. He'd be up at 2am to get ready for work. My mam June always worked, and she worked hard. She ran the local caff, arranged flowers for the church, and raised four boys. She earned respect. She always told me, if you're going to go into something, don't do it half-heartedly. She had an entrepreneurial spirit and a strong work ethic, and she still runs her own successful cosmetics business. There's a special place in heaven for mothers with four boys I'm sure.

From the outside, I was a typical lad of the north east. I was brought up with football—a religion where I am from—in the same way that I was surrounded by cold and rainy weather, but that was part of what made football football. Football was my passion. Football was my life. If I was not playing football, I was coaching it, watching it, and studying it. I was obsessed with anything to do with the "beautiful game", and even more so if it was to do with Newcastle United Football Club. I wasn't particularly interested in the academic side of school, and I couldn't see much relevance. Football was my focus, not school.

My dad knew a lot of people through his work. When I was about 16 a restaurant customer of my dad's arranged for me to meet Derek Forrest, Head Coach of the Football in the Community program and an Academy Coach at the Newcastle United Football Academy. I was a pretty shy kid, and a bit overwhelmed. Derek became a massive influence in my life. He was always there, and he's still an outstanding mentor to me today. I spent my late teens shadowing him as a coach and gaining coaching qualifications. I remember one of the happiest days of my young life was when he told me I would be given a Newcastle United FC tracksuit. At age 18 I became one of the youngest ever in Europe to attain the UEFA B coaching license. This is where I focused my efforts, and to me this was a much bigger achievement than doing well at school.

I knew football was my passion, but now I had a potential career path to focus on. I realised I wasn't going to be a professional football player, not because of lack of talent, but because I developed the killer instinct too late. To be a football player the psychology is important as well as the skill. Although I did eventually develop that win-at-all-costs mentality on the field, it was too late for a playing career, and I'd have to say that sometimes I didn't care too much for that side of my personality.

As a kid I always seemed to have an eye for an opportunity. Due to their cult-like popularity, it was nigh on impossible to get a season ticket to watch Newcastle United play, and the waiting lists to get one were long. For several years, from the age of about 15, I became an agent for the Newcastle United FC's Super 7 lottery. In exchange for a coveted season ticket, I would collect the weekly £1 entry fee from about 300 houses in the district. I became so busy with it that I started recruiting people to work for me, including my brothers and my brothers' mates. I had enough season tickets for all of them. At least three of my customers won the £10,000 weekly prize, and I got to stand in the middle of the St James' Park stadium at the presentation of the novelty cheque with 50,000 of my closest friends, not to mention being invited to the corporate box with the winners. Not bad going for a teenager. Not only were there some great perks, but it taught me a lot about money management. I had to keep spreadsheets on who had paid, who hadn't, be responsible for handling other people's money, and balance the books.

By my late teens and in my final years of high school, I somehow managed to complete a couple of A levels, but not having much focus on the academic side of things, I hadn't realised I would need at least three A levels to gain entry to university. At any one time I was working anywhere up to four or five jobs, and averaging about five or six hours sleep on a good night. I was always looking for sources of income, and I seemed to have a bit of a mind for business. It was like a bit of a game, and I liked to compete with myself. I suppose you could say that competitive football instinct was coming out. Not one for sitting still, I loved the physical side of manual labour (and still do). From 6am to 8am I worked on and off for my dad doing the fruit and veg run. From 9am until 4pm, I worked at St James' Park—the hallowed ground of Newcastle United FC—either as a tour guide taking kids on ground tours and regaling them with my extensive knowledge about every aspect of the club, or coaching juniors in the community. From 6pm-10pm I was a pizza delivery boy. If I wasn't delivering pizzas I would help my mam in the caff. From midnight until 1am, I would take phone orders from restaurants for fruit and veg for my dad. Friday and Saturday nights were the busiest for the restaurants, and that didn't leave a young lad much time for a social life. Sometimes I would be staggering home from a night out, but I'd always be home in time to take those midnight phone orders. I can't be sure that the restaurants didn't get 51 bananas instead of 15 carrots, but I was disciplined, if not slightly sozzled.

Around the time of the UK housing boom in the early 2000s, one of my older brothers was talking about how, if he'd bought such and such a house down the road, it would have made this much money by now. I was about 19, working several jobs, and my ears pricked up. That sounded like a business opportunity to me. I saved up a £2,000 deposit for a £30,000 flat, and within 18 months it had doubled in price, so I sold it.

It was around this time that I met my wife Jennifer. A Yorkshire lass, she had moved to Newcastle for her work in the finance industry. I met her at a bar, and like Cinderella I had to leave before midnight to literally discuss pumpkins with dad's restaurant customers, but I must have made some kind of impression because I got a second date, and we're still together! Jen certainly made an impression on me. She is an incredible and strong woman. In her own calm and unassuming manner she provides a balance to my sometimes wildly enthusiastic ideas. Without her I couldn't have achieved what I have. I have so much respect for Jen as a person. I couldn't have hoped for a better person to spend my life with. So with money in my pocket from the sale of my flat, and the encouragement of Jen, I entered university as a mature-age student. At age 21 I paid for my university education upfront and completed a degree in sports development. I sailed through my studies quite easily, but for some reason I still couldn't see the relevance of academic studies, and I never really focussed on it with any great interest or enthusiasm.

One afternoon, in 2005, I was coaching some kids at the Newcastle United FC training ground. To my amazement, Newcastle United football legends Paul 'Gazza' Gascoigne and Peter Beardsley came over and joined in. Before I knew it we were having a kick about. Gazza was on my team, and I was scoring goals and winning with these two legends of the game. I was star struck. I was so excited I wanted to tell my dad about it straightaway. Unfortunately my mam and dad's marriage also fell spectacularly apart that very night.

Although I probably didn't realise it at the time, the breakdown of my parents' relationship was a turning point in my life. Emotionally I had to grow up. I had been a bit naïve about people and the world around me. After a period of grieving, and the inevitable fallout and recriminations that followed, I became emotionally stronger and resilient, more independent, and more worldly wise. I realised I couldn't rely on my parents, much less anyone else, to take care of me indefinitely. I had to be responsible for my own emotional and financial wellbeing. Looking back, I realise that it was probably the best thing that ever happened to me in terms of my learning and emotional growth.

At the time it was better to be out of the house and focusing on work, away from all of the emotional upheaval. Over the coming months and years I threw myself into my work at Newcastle United FC and then moved into self-employment as a coach for various organisations and councils. I started coaching at the Football Development Centre at the local North Tyneside College, where kids who weren't doing their A levels completed more vocationally based subjects. While I was at Newcastle United FC I coached every week as a part of a program teaching trade skills to older men from disadvantaged backgrounds. When the contract came up for renewal, I won it as a self-employed coach. When the government cut funding to the program, I still turned up every week and did it for free. In conjunction with North Tyneside Council I started a football program for kids with disabilities. They became established as a club called "The Dazzlers", they got uniforms, and they played friendlies with kids from other mainstream clubs. The idea took off and other similar clubs opened up in the district, until these kids were playing in their own league. Seeing what some of these kids had to go through opened my eyes, and really shaped my ability to deal with adversity and get it into perspective. I believed then, and I believe now, that sport is for every person and every ability.

I became involved in the Northumberland Council's "Positive Futures" program for older kids who had wound up in juvenile detention and generally came from socially disadvantaged backgrounds, including drugs, alcohol, and abuse. While I was there initially to support non-football related activities, it quickly became evident that what these kids were interested in was football. So once a week I coached a session for 16-20 year olds, males and females, with four staff supervising for every kid playing. Whilst many of these kids had next to no respect for adults, I could gain respect for my abilities as a footballer. Sport is the great leveller, and for an hour or so every week these kids felt like someone's equal on the football field, and for that hour they felt accepted. Football was the catalyst for some of these kids to make improvements in their life, and it became an opportunity for older ones to mentor some of the younger ones.

I quickly learnt to be grateful for what I had, as there were many people who would be grateful to have the opportunities I had had. I also learnt that not only did I love football, but I had always loved working with kids. I had found my passion and now a purpose. I was doing what I loved and felt I was making a difference. By this stage I had become pretty much full time with "Positive Futures". At the bottom of my heart, I knew I couldn't work in this environment forever though. I also developed a taste for travel in the mid-2000s visiting Egypt, France, Spain many times, and Australia.

Over the years I had become overweight and undisciplined with my health and lifestyle, and my mam was a great cook. It seemed that my lack of knowledge and discipline to fix these problems was a symptom of my emotional state. I felt like I needed to send myself on a journey of self-discovery, and consequently I became obsessed with running, in addition to my football obsession, and a growing list of other sports. Derek and I always ran together at the same time each day. We discussed anything and everything while we ran. Combined with my innate personality, and my mam's advice, I never did anything by halves. The aftermath of my mam and dad splitting up made me more determined and disciplined. I got to a point where I had to be the best at running. It was like a competitive mind game that I played against me. Running early in the morning I had time to clear my mind and think. I had ideas and inspirations. It was a time for meditation and reflection. The environment didn't bother me. Moreover, I wouldn't let it bother me. I would run in sleet, rain, snow, the cold, and in the dark. It got to a point where I plotted out, and ran, a five-hour marathon on the beach. Jen even came and visited me for an hour to witness the spectacle. By now, nothing about me surprised her. I was like some kind of Geordie-style Rocky Balboa crossed with Forrest Gump and Bear Grylls. I had to be better than I was the day before. I had to be the best version of me. What I learnt from my obsession with running was that adversity didn't bother me. If it came, I tackled it head on. I almost welcomed it, as I found immense satisfaction in finding solutions to my problems, whatever they were.

I had discovered on this emotional road trip that being uncomfortable, and getting out of your comfort zone, makes you learn and learn quickly. If you force yourself to be uncomfortable, to go into the unknown, you can conquer what you fear. My philosophy had become one of just plunging in. So in 2009, my desire to learn and grow, coupled with a taste for travel, saw Jen and me pack up our lives, leave our friends and loved ones, and travel halfway across the world to live in Australia. We already had the platinum card of Australian immigration in the form of permanent residency visas, but we weren't doing anything about it. Early in 2009 we took a holiday and reconnaissance trip to a few Australian cities to decide which one would be right for us. When we got to Brisbane we knew it would be the place for us to start our new adventure.

Jen's mum had tragically passed away a few years earlier from MS. She was only 50. She would have done anything to have those opportunities, and so in the spirit of gratitude and living in the moment, and with youth on our side, we took the opportunity that was sitting in our laps. In mid-2009, we left for Australia on the adventure of a lifetime. Packing up the house we had bought together and selling most of our possessions, including our car, was no small feat. We also had our beloved dog Millie to bring with us. Everything was fine until we got to the airport, and I saw my mam and two of my brothers standing there waving me goodbye. It suddenly seemed so final. We had one-way tickets, no possessions, a dog, and I had no job. We had less than $1,000 to our names. We were saying goodbye to everything and everyone we knew. We only had each other. I spent the next three hours bawling my eyes out on the plane.

Arriving in Brisbane it seemed hot and humid to us, even though it was winter – most definitely out of our comfort zone. I was 27 and had spent 10 years of my life coaching football to children in North East England. Football was my blood, but soccer (as they insisted on calling it in Australia), was not the most popular sporting pastime in Queensland by any stretch of the imagination. We had left one life, not knowing what the next one would look like. We loved life in England, but the unpredictability of starting a life in Australia, and the possibilities and potential for new experiences and opportunities, was exciting to us.

We spent our first three days living in a bed and breakfast in a leafy northern suburb close to the centre of Brisbane. On day two we found a house to live in, about 10 minutes south of the city. It had no furniture, and we had one suitcase each. With a background in finance, Jen found a job easily. After less than two weeks, I had two jobs. At night I was working at Lifeline as a residential carer for at-risk kids in care. Again I discovered that sport is a level playing field, and these kids could be themselves having a kick around with the ball. I stayed there for about a month. By day I was coaching kids' soccer with a local franchise. Pretty soon the kids and parents loved my sessions, and I was doing what I loved. I had great ideas for business growth and innovation, but I couldn't move the owner out of his comfort zone and convince him to take the risks I was proposing. The fear of what could go wrong was too strong. Another franchise approached me about buying into their company, but then they wouldn't talk to me because I was working for one of their competitors. In the end, I gave my notice and wished him all the best. I soon learnt that when people say no to you, it can present an exceptional opportunity. In this case I am so grateful that he said no to me, or I may not have been motivated to start my own business. This was definitely a case of when one door closes, another door opens.

In October 2009 I started Ginger Sport with a bag of balls, an orange t-shirt, and a handful of kids. At my first session I was standing alone on a school oval with no kids, in my bright orange shirt. Although the feelings usually pass quickly for me, I still felt that fear and self-doubt creeping in. I didn't know if it would work, and I didn't know if it was even worth my effort. After investing everything I had into it, with no guarantees, I realised I had to make it work. I had to market it, run it, manage it, and live and breathe it. Because this was my passion, I knew I had the drive and determination to make it work, but still the figures wouldn't stack up. It dawned on me that if I employed a coach I could take on more work, so I did. The big lightbulb moment for me was when one of the mum's suggested I come and talk to her at her work - a childcare centre. She signed up to do a weekly session at her centre, and she suggested I talk to her friend down the road at another centre who also signed up. It never occurred to me to coach at childcare centres. Agreeing to talk to this lady taught me to never close yourself off to potential opportunities or ideas, even if you don't think they'll work. Consider any opportunity before dismissing it. Within just one year 2,000 kids were playing soccer with Ginger Sport. We now coach at around 400 childcare centres. I learnt from my mistakes and inexperience and forged ahead.

Some of the early lessons I learnt were about spreading yourself too thin. Stick to your strengths, and outsource the things you are not good at, or don't have time for. For example, I realised that copious amounts of writing are involved in running a website, newsletters, training staff, and everything in between. Writing is not my strength, so I discovered that one of the parent's was a talented writer and editor, and so Ginger Sport's professional relationship with Fiona Thompson from Readford Group was established and continues to this day. Another parent complained about me being abrupt and rude on the phone. I wasn't being rude at all, but it dawned on me that it was my accent, and it was a case of lost in translation while I was rushing between coaching sessions. I realised I needed to hire an admin person who could deal with the growing number of parent inquiries. I couldn't continue to coach every child myself, so I hired one coach, then another, and another. Today we have 50 coaches and 7,000 kids playing soccer every week in parks and childcare centres across South East Queensland. It really struck home when Jen was due to give birth to our twins, and coaches were turning up at our house at all hours because we didn't have office premises. We got some premises quick smart, let me tell you!

I also learnt that along with relinquishing control, you have to do less white knuckling, let go of the steering wheel, and give people a chance to learn by doing things on their own. You need to let people have a chance to fail.

If they fail, they'll learn more. As a mentor to my own managers, I have to let them know that it is ok for them to let the staff under their supervision fail from time to time, so they too can learn from their mistakes. As an employer the pieces of paper saying you studied hard are nice, but they don't impress me overly. What impresses me more is if you have hands-on experience, and you are willing to give things a go and learn by doing. That shows you have qualities that matter to me. It relates to my philosophy of just giving things a go. Don't hesitate. As they say in the classics, what doesn't kill you makes you stronger.

I've learnt that every situation is a chance to grow and learn. My personal experience taught me that. From adversity you can find positives. You can find solutions to your dilemmas. If someone says no, another door will open. Starting a business is scary, but what's worse is not starting at all. I've heard the locals say, "have a go ya' mug", usually when barracking for sporting teams. It has become my personal and business philosophy. Find what you love and what makes you feel good. What are you passionate about? To me greatness is defined by people who pursue their passions, because that is what makes them happy. What makes you get out of bed in the morning? Then plunge in and take the first step. The pool is always the coldest when you dive in, then you get used to it. Prepare your mind to know that yes there will be drawbacks. It won't be problem free. But if you expect there will be challenges along the way, you can then focus on finding solutions to overcome them when they come. And they will come, and sometimes there will be spectacular failures, but you will be ready to face them head on. You can learn as you go, but you need to put the key in the ignition and start the car, or you'll just sit in your driveway going nowhere. You have nothing to lose and everything to gain.

If missions and visions are important, then ethics and values are critical. Think about what is important to you, and write it down. These will be your rules to live and work by. I always recommend flexibility in approach, but when it comes to your core values as a person, these are the things you won't compromise on. Integrity, gratitude, and enthusiasm are big ones for me. I have many more, but these are key. If something you are about to do—or something someone else wants you to do—will compromise your core beliefs, that's a major red flag.

Your values should be reflected in your business, but your business shouldn't change you or your core beliefs. For me it's not about wealth or a power trip. It's really important to be clear on your values, because recruiting staff with the right attitude, and who share the same values, can be a game changer. To me, the right attitude is more important than whether you have the actual skills for a specific job. When you find the people that are a good fit with your values, invest in them. If you stick to your values, you attract people with the same core beliefs and motivations. If employees have the same values, then they are more likely to support and implement your vision for the business.

In business, and in life, I try not to be judgemental. I have my views and ways of doing things, and they work for me. On the other hand, I am never beyond listening to new ideas. If you judge, and dismiss an idea out of hand, then you close your mind to the possibility of doing things in new and innovative ways. You are saying that my way is best, and I'm not interested in learning what you have to say or contribute. That is foolish as you close yourself off to the potential of fabulous new ideas and opportunities. In business, new ideas and opportunities are what makes your business grow and thrive. It's called change. Embrace it. Open you ears and mind, and listen.

When you do listen to people, you tend to find out what it is they actually want. You have to be flexible on the journey, rather than just focus rigidly on an end point. There doesn't have to be a clearly defined route in getting there. Have an idea of where you are going, but if you end up on a detour you are still on the road trip. You need to go with the demand. You will just as likely miss an opportunity to provide people with what they want if you stick rigidly to a fixed path. When you find out what people want, don't focus on making money, but focus on offering them value. Don't make money your goal. If you make offering value the goal, then the money will follow, because people will recognise the value in what you offer.

I've had jobs that others wouldn't do and might see as menial. I saw them as opportunities to achieve my goals, and without them I wouldn't have learnt some of the important lessons that help me run a successful business. One of those lessons is how to get along with people. Getting along with people is a great skill, and in all facets of your life you will come across many different kinds of folk. I started off as a shy kid, but my experiences have given me a lot of confidence and inner strength. One of my strengths is my ability to engage and build a rapport with most people I meet. I don't judge because I don't assume.

I take people on face value and deal with them respectfully. I don't think of myself as better than anyone. The only person I want to be better than is me. I want to be better than I was yesterday, health wise, business wise, and values wise. I want to do more, and I want to learn more. I want to be more.

Here are some of my final tips and observations for people getting started in business.

- People who achieve and appreciate their success, usually go through the mud at some point in their lives.
- Look after your mind and body. Exercise often, eat well, and set yourself up for success in all areas of your life and work.
- Take advantage of freebies. Take any opportunity to market your business for free, and put your name out there. I still do this.
- Celebrate small achievements, and recognise they are leading to bigger things.
- Keep reinvesting in your business, rather than taking money out of it.
- Focus on delivering value, not making money.
- Remember it's a game. It's not what defines you.
- Be real, and be good to people.

- Stay true to yourself.
- Choose your own path. Don't let other people choose it for you.
- Stick to your core values.
- Don't begrudge other people their own success.
- Be prepared to reshape direction and be flexible.
- Don't say no to opportunities.
- Staff should feel your passion and presence, but you don't have to be physically present all the time.
- Notice the energy, and shift it if you need to.
- Go against the grain, and shake things up if need be.
- Don't be swayed into behaviours just to conform with the pack.
- Tune into the environment, and tune into what people want.

The take home message I would give to anyone who wants to do something with their life, whether it be starting a business, a course, a hobby, or a relationship is to strap on your boots and act on it. Just start, and deal with the consequences as you go. Do I think I'm successful? Well that's for history to determine.

But if success means finding happiness, following your passion, finding your purpose, doing what you love, facing challenges head on, and continuing to learn, then on my terms it's been a successful game so far.

Ben Hutchinson

Having travelled halfway across the world to begin a new life in Australia, Englishman Ben Hutchinson conceived and created Ginger Sport in 2009 with nothing but a passion for football, a bag of balls, and a handful of local kids. Inspired by Ben's passion for football and fun, Ginger Sport combines fun and healthy activity, for children aged from 2-10 years, for thousands of children across South East Queensland. In just six short years, Ben has created a thriving first business based on nothing but his love of people and his love for the "beautiful game".

Creating beautiful environmentally friendly yoga mats

Jensen Wheeler Wolfe – The Little Yoga Mat

When I turned 50 I had much to celebrate: a vivacious five-year-old daughter, a great marriage and my 20-year run with cancer had ended. This seemed an ideal time to start a 2nd career.

Yoga was a staple in my life. I'd dabbled in it for years but now I got serious and became a Vinyasa yoga teacher. I taught classes all around Manhattan, led workshops in Costa Rica and studied with many teachers. Yoga transformed my life.

What I like best about yoga is its simplicity. A flat surface, open mind, and basic understanding of alignment so that you won't hurt yourself is all you need. The feel-good rewards are immediate.

In 2007 I was asked to teach a classroom of twenty 2-3 year olds at my daughter's preschool. That's allot of kids! The space was small and carpeted and I wasn't quite sure how to make it work. I created an inner circle of kids with an outer circle of parents and the kids did some yoga but mostly ran around. I needed to find a better way to organize the chaos and create boundaries so I could effectively teach the class.

My solution was to bring mats for all the children. I went home, cut up a stack of adult mats and made mini mats. One adult mat became four toddler mats. The kids loved having a mat their size; it was just like Mom and Dad's. The teacher liked that the mats created a safe zone for each child during yoga class.

Parents called and wanted to purchase more mats, so I searched online and couldn't find any yoga mats for the under age four set. This, I decided was my opportunity to start a business. I'd identified a need in a niche market and what I trusted most was how the idea organically unfolded. The next two years, when I wasn't fact checking for Glamour magazine, were spent putting all the pieces together to create a company—something I'd never done before.

In 2011 I launched The Little Yoga Mat; mini hip eco-friendly yoga mats for toddlers and babies. My goal was to create beautiful environmentally friendly yoga mats that appeal to mom and tots alike with fresh designs and lush colors. The designs are based on authentic yoga poses (sun salutation for the SUN mat and lotus pose for the LOTUS flower mat). We sold out of our first batch quickly with placement in toy stores; yoga studios and high-end department stores like Anthropologie and Barneys.
We're now entering our third year in business with plans to expand the product line by adding a larger size mat with a new design for 5-10 year olds. Boasting a bit, we've won numerous awards, had great press, were a featured company in Alibaba's IPO and sell in over 200 stores nationwide + Denmark, Australia and Africa. Kids yoga is booming and we plan to grow along with it.

Taking an idea from concept to creation is not for the faint of heart. It's detailed diligent work and requires vision, tenacity and a huge leap of faith. I have many positive entrepreneurial traits; I'm creative, driven, passionate and organized, but I don't like taking financial risks. It's a challenge but I continue to take the risk anyway.

Since I started my company I've been happy to be a role model for other budding momprenuers by demonstrating that it is possible to start a new career as a middle-age working mom. I advise moms to take small steps every day and try not to overwhelm themselves with the big picture. In five years you will know if you want to continue down this path or not. Don't over think it. It's more important to start and see what evolves.

When I see a child doing yoga on my mat or receive glowing compliments from parents or toy store owners that understand what I've created: a quality, durable, safe chemically free-product that's esthetically pleasing and makes sense, it's all worth it.

Yoga is something you and your kids can do your entire life. It's terrific for stress relief, strength, balance, coordination, confidence, circulation, and focus. Yoga is not competitive and compliments any sport. I like being a part of this message.

I'll now share three hurdles that I've overcome on my journey as a small business owner. My hope is that by sharing these experiences you will avoid some of the bumps.

1. GOAL SETTING

Many people, magazines, webinars, blogs, friends will tell you how to run your business and where your company should be in X amount of time. "You know what you need to do…" listen with distance. They may have a good idea, they may be wasting your time, but in the end you need to follow the path that makes sense to you. It may be a challenging path, but it will give you peace of mind because it's yours.
Do set goals for yourself, but make them your goals. Revisit the goals every few months and renew or edit. They should guide not guilt you.

2. MANUFACTURING ABROAD

Also not for the faint hearted. If there was a guidebook we'd all be following it! I had to manufacture my eco-mats in Taiwan and China because I could not find any U.S. options. Communicating with a factory overseas takes patience and an understanding of their culture. They don't have the same holiday schedule and their business practices are probably different that what you are used to. My advice, check and recheck your order. Ask many questions and prepare to pay inspectors that you trust to check your order before it ships from the factory to the U.S. as well. No one will care about your product like you do so put lots of checks in place to guarantee that the factory will manufacture something very close to what you ordered. Find peace with less than perfect, but as close to perfect as possible.

3. CASH FLOW

I had $60,000 saved to start my business and naively thought that we'd sell the 2,000 mats in our warehouse and have $ for the next order. What I didn't account for is the expenses that add up like cardboard boxes for shipping, credit card fees, ink cartridges, promotional materials, and liability insurance. We definitely needed more than $60,000 to stay in business and that's the reality of a start up. We weren't doing anything wrong; it takes money to stay in business and more money to grow. Have a plan for cash so you can stay afloat. I hear the cash flow situation gets better after 5 years. I'll let you know.

Jensen Wheeler Wolfe

Jensen Wheeler Wolfe lives with her husband and 9-year old daughter in Hell's Kitchen, New York

From idea to reality

Alex Hunn - freemarketFX

Having started a few businesses now, it's clear to me that passion and perseverance are two common themes and necessary qualities for any founder or group of co-founders. Without either, I don't believe it is possible to achieve success – and it is important to stress that success can be measured in a number of different ways, not just financially.

All of my businesses have been involved in the Financial Services sector. For some the technology and regulatory infrastructure was already in place (similar to a franchise opportunity), which obviously had a big impact on how quickly the business could start generating revenue. As it was an entirely new concept, for freemarketFX in particular, the business required building from the ground up. Before deciding on any of my ventures, I spoke with others who had already been through the pains of growing a business in the areas I was looking at – these discussions were invaluable. It laid out the bare truths of the challenges ahead and set a realistic expectation of the mountains we had to climb.

The idea

In some respects, my decision in founding freemarketFX was an easy one, based off my background and experience. During my career, I have worked for banks such as Credit Suisse First Boston and Deutsche Bank AG. My last employer in the Financial Services sector before starting my own companies was MF Global, at the time the world's largest brokerage house.

My experience is specifically focused on exchange-based products and this was the inspiration for freemarketFX – a currency exchange that targets companies that, as a requirement of their business, make or receive payments in a different currency. Foreign exchange is regarded as a complex product, which suits the current market incumbents perfectly – it's profitable to operate in a space that only a few understand. It is, however, a market with few happy customers, especially around the service they receive regarding cost, transparency and efficiency. Through both business and personal experience, I too was dissatisfied with the current status quo. I realised trading market technology and methodology could be adapted for a new foreign exchange model. Free from legacy technology platforms and systems, we were able to build a new sort of financial services provider (a 'fintech' company) – freemarketFX.

Our goal is simple: to make an inefficient, expensive and opaque process transparent, efficient and cheap.

Proving yourself

But all startups face the same challenge – namely one of proving themselves. You've got to prove your idea, vision, technology, service or product, route to market, customer appetite and engagement, your team's ability to execute, your ability to attract investment (if needed) etc. The list is endless. The reality being that all this disappears when you have an operational product. Why? It's simple, you go from thinking and talking to actually doing – and that is a massive mind shift as to how your business is perceived, both internally and externally. Once operational, your learning curve is steep and problems that you never anticipated become a reality. That is a great place to be because now you have to address real, rather than theoretical, issues.

Starting any business is a huge challenge – but when that also includes regulatory bodies and global bank relationships, the challenges are multiplied. These two particular challenges required significant investment – not in terms of cash – but in time commitment. And when you're starting a business, one thing that is not on your side is 'time'.

Unusually for a start up – one thing that really helped us in the early days was patience. There is a saying in the start up world – fail fast. Basically, try things quickly and learn if they don't work. We didn't, however, believe that was an appropriate strategy for a B2B solution operating in a regulated environment, so we focused on an incremental building block approach.

Focus – One step at a time

There is a great quote by Francis of Assisi – 'start by doing what's necessary; then do what's possible; and suddenly you're doing the impossible'. I think this is very true. When you think about what is ahead of you, it can be daunting. But it is all about taking one step at a time. A very astute and successful entrepreneur once said to me: 'It's amazing what one man can achieve' and I think there is a huge amount of truth in that – application and hard work go a long way.

So, how did we do it? By taking small and logical steps as part of a clearly defined strategy.

1. We got regulated.
2. We secured a global bank relationship.
3. We launched a beta service.
4. We secured commercial funding.
5. We publically launched.

Have no doubt, there were many components to each and every one of these steps. Some took longer than anticipated, cost more than we had forecast, or just proved harder than expected. However, knowing the end goal kept us focused and allowed us to successfully execute on our plan. Having patient and understanding Shareholders who had a clear roadmap of both our vision and challenges from the outset was also a massive advantage.

So what have I learnt along the way? This list is not intended to be exhaustive, but here a few things that I think can impact a young business.

1.　　People – businesses are all about people

It's an old cliché but it's so true. Businesses are all about people. Get good people doing the right things and progress can be phenomenal. Get the wrong people doing the wrong things then you get tension, an unproductive working environment and problems. A divisive atmosphere at a start-up is a disaster because each person is so important in a small team.

Throughout my career there is no doubt that people have had the biggest influence on any business. I have been hugely fortunate to work with some highly talented and gifted individuals. More importantly, surrounding yourself with people who share your vision, have the same ambition and are aligned in remuneration with you is critical. This, rightly so, often means providing equity incentives. Getting the team moving in the same direction with the same risks is not an easy thing to do, but essential.

In general, people that engage with start-ups also tend to have an entrepreneurial can-do attitude. Therefore, structuring a remuneration package that aligns you both is often easier than anticipated. If this proves to be hard, then very often it is a sign that you have the wrong person. And it should be fun, although I appreciate that can be hard when you are stretched to breaking point!

2.　　Get operational

Earlier I spoke about 'proving' the business. Nothing is truer than when real customers start using your service on a regular basis. Issues that you never expected suddenly become a reality or more importantly, strengths that you anticipated might not resonate in the way you would have liked. So with each new customer, we would ask him or her for feedback on their experience and, if they're happy to, to provide a testimonial about our service. Customers have nothing to lose by telling the truth, so if you have a happy customer with a willingness to speak out, you will find this makes sales and marketing much easier. In our experience, we found that businesses were only too delighted to comment on our service and be associated with the brand when they realise the benefit it provides.

The concept of social selling is a good one – and one I very much believe in (and is a very cost effective client acquisition). Customers often know and talk to one another. A good experience can result in a recommendation and therefore, a quick sale or solid endorsement. There is nothing more rewarding than being referred and to hear customers talking positively about your service. It is the reason you founded the business – so you are realising your vision! In addition, happy customers frequently go the extra mile to help you out or provide positive critique on workflow and process development. When you're building a service, designing around customer feedback is a good way of ensuring you're moving in the right direction.

3.   Where to concentrate your resource

One of the challenges we had was a slightly ironic one, in that the market was almost too big. So when we were talking to both customers and investors, we appeared to cover a multitude of sectors as diverse as: corporate finance, clothing/apparel, music software and cosmetics – although in the early days, we didn't have any detailed understanding of a specific sector. Whilst we knew there was significant opportunity, targeting numerous sectors at once showed us we needed to prioritise.

As a result, the first thing we did was to undertake a deep profiling of the market, devising specific client acquisition strategies for each route to market channel. There's no right or wrong way to do this. You will understand what works best for your company and how to achieve this. It is, however, critical to understand how you get in front of, and ultimately convert, your target customers.

4.   Communication

It sounds obvious, but it never ceases to amaze me how few people truly communicate. Starting any business is a stressful and lonely time. I found that by constantly talking to those around me, explaining our problems and asking for input alleviated this. Moreover, it makes for a collaborative environment, which is significantly more productive. Giving people the confidence to freely communicate their thoughts, perceptions and concerns in the very early stages of a business can only result in a positive outcome.

5.   Keep things simple

Keep things clear and simple – I cannot emphasis this enough. Your first set of shareholder documents, description of your proposition, your route to market, your use of funds – it doesn't matter what it is but keep it simple.

Customers want to get your proposition immediately and understand quickly how it will help and enable their business. Investors don't need a highly complex and difficult shareholder structure or financial model to review, negotiate and then sign up to. Keeping things simple means life is significantly easier for everyone involved in your business.

6.   Process and structure

In my limited experience, most entrepreneurs are not particularly process-orientated individuals, which is not surprising. After all, it is the reason that you decided to start your own company – to get away from large, process driven organisations to create and deliver something unique and special (at least in your eyes!).

But process and structure are critical. Whether it's process of workflows for client on-boarding or delivering a well structured fundraise for potential investors. Getting this in place early will ultimately be hugely beneficial as your business grows.

7.   Where to base yourself?

London is the financial services capital of the world and an excellent place to start a financial technology business. Our access to global bank partners, global customers and investment capital has provided us with a platform that would have been harder to achieve in other jurisdictions. In addition, the investment capital has been greatly helped by the UK Government's Enterprise Incentive Scheme ("EIS"), which allows investors tax relief on early stage investments. It was a very easy decision for us in terms of headquarters, but for others I suspect it might not be so clear-cut.

What advice would I give to someone wanting to start a company?

The short answer – loads and I have touched on the first one already in this chapter. But rather than leaving you with one particular point to think about, here are a few, based off my own experience, which I believe are vitally important:

-       People. Surround yourself with good people. They are the sole reason your company will be a success – you cannot do it alone.

- Things go wrong – it's a fact. Accept it and carry on – it happens to us all.
- It takes longer than you think. It always does and good investors know that.
- There is no substitute for perseverance. If you want it, you need to hunt it down.
- Make a decision. Making no decision is worse than making a bad decision (which can be rectified).
- Accept criticism, and get used to it, as there will be a load coming your way in the early stages of building your business. More importantly, if it is justified, learn from it and use it to your advantage.
- Work backwards. Where do you want to be, and what are the drivers that allow you to get there?
- Don't take cash for the sake of it (which is hard when you are looking to scale your business). Think carefully about whether the interests of those investing in your company and your interests are truly aligned. With technology, bright people, energy and a small amount of cash – it's amazing what can be achieved.
- Be realistic. Achieving 5 per cent market penetration of your target customer sector in Year one is not going to happen!

And finally – what do you want out of life?

I have three simple objectives in life: To learn, develop as an individual and to add value. They don't all need to happen at once, but as long as I am achieving one of them all the time – then I am happy.

I wish you all the best. You only have one life – live it.

Alex Hunn

Alex Hunn is the founder of freemarketFX. He has over 20 years of investment banking and financial services experience, specialising in multi-currency, multi product macro portfolio management sales and structuring for exchange-traded derivatives. During his career, Alex was a Senior Sales Executive for MF Global, which was the world's largest exchange traded derivatives brokerage house. Prior to joining MF Global, he was a former Director of Deutsche Bank AG London and a Vice President of Credit Suisse First Boston, working within their capital markets and fixed income divisions providing global coverage to central bank, real money, hedge fund and institutional clients.

Creating solutions for problems

Robert Gavin – NDD Group

Before I had a family and my own business, I was a great fan of Science Fiction films and books, especially the ones that dealt with time travel and alternate realities. I was always interested how the slightest decision could affect your life and send it off on a totally different tangent. In many ways I feel that this has been reminiscent of my life to date; I had always been entrepreneurial as a child, interested in business and creating solutions for problems.

I suppose the first true example of me being an entrepreneur was in high school when I was about 11 or 12 years old. The school principal had ideas and ambitions of having a school newspaper and I saw this as an opportunity of not only being in charge of the newspaper but also running it like a business, which meant obviously to make a profit. Back then growing up in a small village there wasn't much news to be reported so to add content, the newspaper was mainly comic strips, jokes, quizzes and gossip. I remember our first edition, we printed about 300 copies, and with a bit of use of social media or as they called it in the early 90s "word of mouth", we had queues all the way around the building and we sold out in the space of two lunch times.

By most people's perspectives it was a great success, the problem being, and is most often the case in business is what is seen as success for one person may be seen as an utter failure from another perspective. Case and point the principal was very pleased to see such a popular first edition, and I'm sure it would have looked good on his resume to compare his newspaper readership to other schools in the area. However, in that day and age, the comparative printing costs were very high and it didn't take us more than the third edition to realise that our printing costs alone were more expensive than the sales prices of the newspaper.

Not only that, but the price for us to break even would have made it more than most students would be willing to pay for it, ergo successful newspaper, unsuccessful business. This was a really great learning experience for me as an 11 year old because I realised two irrefutable facts for any business to be successful. Firstly, it needs to have a products or service that people want. And, secondly, it needs to make a profit to do so. It goes without saying that I achieved the former but failed abysmally at the latter. So this experience really nurtured and educated me for my second business which I undertook when I was 14. Again fellow students where my marketplace, but this time the product was fashionable t-shirts which my friend's brother had designed. This time I knew straight away what we needed to sell to make a profit, my friend and I gave t-shirts to all the best looking and most popular jocks in the school on the provision that they wore them. I suppose you could liken this to present day sponsorship deals, all we asked them to do was to tell anyone who asked where they got them from. Again this old fashioned method of social media meant we were in the amiable position of people coming to us for orders.

We managed to sell out in the first week alone which meant we were able to get some more which we then sold out again two weeks later. In total we managed to sell 200 t-shirts which was not bad considering there were only 250 male students in the school. Third adolescent experience of being an entrepreneur was working at a shoe shop, which my aunt worked for. The owner then went on to be awarded a knighthood from Queen Elizabeth for his service to business whereby he would buy defective shoes from the biggest shoe companies in the world and would then sell them to people of lower income or export them to Africa or India. Whilst only working minimum wage on an hourly basis, there was no real incentive for me to increase revenue for the business or to increase sales but being the perfectionist I am I always strove to find ways to add value and to make improvement.

In my teenage years, up until the age of 18, my entrepreneurial desires were pushed to the side due to the typical teenager's insatiable need to be popular, socialise more with my friends and to study hard to get into the best university I could. In short the typical pressures of being a teenager. It was also a time when, and certainly this was the case for myself, where your inner voice or desires of what you want to do in life are drowned out by the desires of the other people in your life friends, family, the media, teachers, etc. That is how at age 18, I found myself heading to university to earn a degree in Chemistry. Growing up in an environment of humble means, and having worked whilst studying for the last three years. I was adamant that university was going to be something I was going to pay for by myself without any financial assistance from family. It was a tough decision to make, made tougher by the fact that most of my friends did not only get all of their tuition paid but most of their social needs paid for as well. To help me achieve this skill, I took a part time job at the local supermarket stocking shelves. Whilst there were many times during that period of my life when I really disliked the job and the pressure it put on me, (not to mention the heavy work-load from university, and the embarrassment of having to help friends find the milk and yoghurt), it did help me achieve my goals in university. In fact so much so that in my first year of university I was not only able to pay for my tuition fees from my part time work but I was also able to make a profit.

If anyone has ever studied science in university or worked in a science field, they will most likely agree with my opinion of science, in the way that it operates in the black and white, yes and no, fact or fiction. This black and white nature appeals to many of my best friends today who work in these fields, but for someone like myself who is very creative and likes to operate in the different shades of grey I felt it stifling and restrictive. Therefore when I was offered the opportunity to do some volunteering and teach at the local primary school I jumped at the chance.

I enjoyed the experience so much and found it so liberating and creative that I decided within two weeks of doing this volunteering at the local school that my goal of doing a PHD in Chemistry and working in the pharmaceutical business wasn't something that I really wanted to continue. Shortly after I spoke to my tutor at university and I changed courses and enrolled to do a teacher training course instead. The next year while I was training to be a teacher was probably one of the hardest years of my life. Not only was I studying 60 hours a week for my course, but I also had three part time jobs as well. This probably took my work load up to 80-90 hours a week. In fact, there were at least three to four days each week that I left home at 6am and didn't get home till 10 or 11pm. Throughout my life, I've always enjoyed being busy and the worst feeling for me at any one time is the feeling of boredom. So whilst my working hours seemed excessive to the people around me and was cause for concern for my friends and family I thrived and grew from the challenge it created. Through a lot of hard work and perseverance I also managed to secure a teaching position at one of the most prestigious schools in the area. Around about this time in my life which was 2002, was the period of great economic success in the UK. Property prices and the economy were at an all-time high, many of my friends had moved down to London for the high salaries that it promised them, and I was certainly by far the happiest of my friends at their job but also, unfortunately, the poorest. Many people prior to me entering the teaching profession had warned me of the low salaries, but it wasn't until I actually became a teacher that I realised that living in a very middle class expensive city in the UK whilst earning a low salary, creates a lot of financial stress. Crunch time came for me really when I realised that with my salary and the property market that I couldn't even afford to buy a studio apartment where I lived. That realisation came like a short and hard punch to the gut, after all I rationalised, I work 80-90 hours a week, have two degrees but still cannot afford to buy my own place.

This prompted my decision, in addition to the wanderlust I had since I turned 18, to apply for teaching jobs overseas, and that's why I found myself over the next few years living and working in the Middle East and Asia. One of the places I lived in over the next few years was Shanghai, China. And for someone who has entrepreneurial tendencies like myself there was no better place for those entrepreneurial ideas to be nourished. Whilst I am always committed to what I have at hand, teaching at a private school overseas allowed significantly more free time than it would teaching in England. And what with Ebay becoming more popular I saw an opportunity to replicate what a lot of companies were doing in China at that time, buying products cheaply and selling them directly to customers via Ebay at a marked up price. With the right contacts and volume, I was able to buy beautiful silk ties for $1 each and was able to sell them on for up to $30. Pashminas, purses, scarves, all low cost and low weight items with significant mark ups, in the few months it meant I was earning more through ebay than I was with my salary as a teacher. This was a tremendous learning experience for me because I realised the importance of having good relationships with both your suppliers and your costumers. Whilst the price of the silk ties were incredibly cheap, there were suppliers that I could get for less than 25 cents a tie, however these were of much poorer quality and when you use a service like Ebay, feedback and customer loyalty is very important and not something to be taken lightly. In fact I carry out my business today with the same rule, keeping costumers happy is one of the most important aspects of growing and maintaining your business, because without the satisfaction and loyalty of your costumers, then it's impossible to grow and run a successful business. It is interesting to note, for all my life up until that point, I had always been an entrepreneur in addition to having a day job. Looking back there were probably several reasons for this, firstly none of my friends or family had ever had their own business, so every time I broached the subject of leaving my day job to focus on a business was met with concern and fear on how I would managed without a steady income, and the comforts of a regular pay check.

Looking back now I realise that I asked the wrong people for advice and counsel, what I should have done is asked someone who had their own successful business, surely they would have given me a more optimistic and positive response. Looking back all they were doing was trying to protect me, from a risk that they would not have been willing to make. And that was why it took me a further two years before I was able to have the confidence to leave my day job and to start my own business without any safety net of a regular pay check.

Most people start their businesses when the global economy is strong, however, I ended up starting my business when the global economy couldn't be any weaker, in the early stages of the economic crisis. And in many ways it was this crisis which gave me the idea in the first place. I had always been an ardent fan of property and real estate, perhaps in many ways this harped back to the many afternoons I would spend playing monopoly during my childhood. In Europe, property prices were falling dramatically and many real estate developers had lots of property that they were unable to sell either because the buyers couldn't get finance, or because their prices were too high and people were no longer willing to pay them. In many ways my first business was reminiscent of Groupon but for real estate and property. I would negotiate to purchase large amounts of houses or apartments from developers, oftentimes at much as 50-100 units in one go, and due to the volume of the units would negotiate significant discount off current market value. I would then sell these on to a waiting list of buyer and real estate investors. In many cases the discounts could have been up to 45%, for investors this was a great deal for them because they could buy property as such great prices locking in instant equity from day one. Developers and banks were happy because they were able to liquidate some of their properties that they weren't able to using traditional methods. My company got a commission from every unit sold, which when you look at the volume of unit property sold, was very profitable indeed. In my first week of starting my business, working from a laptop in my spare bedroom, I made a profit of 55,000 USD.

Two months in, I was selling 40-50 properties a month, with no staff, just on my own and still working from my spare bedroom. The level of success I experienced so quickly took me by surprise and made me realise and really turned my understanding of business on its head, whereby most businesses lose profit in the first year and maybe would start to make a profit in year two or three. I also learnt the power of leverage, by achieving more with less, I worked hard to teach myself everything there was to know about paper clip advertising, and used the skills I'd learnt to increase the database of property buyers. Consistently every week I would have over 1000 new property buyers signing up to my property service to buy discounted and distressed property deals. Replicating this model, I then went on to achieve similar success in other property markets around the world, this included Spanish and Portuguese luxury villas, hotels in France, and finally took me to the USA.

Like Europe, the USA had been hit hard by the credit crunch, one of the cities probably hit one of the hardest was Detroit. Due to a falling population and therefore falling tax base, as well as high unemployment, Detroit was having significant problems and therefore many areas of its property market had fallen significantly in value. In many cases 60-90%, over a one to two year period. One of the traits of entrepreneurs I believe is finding opportunities where most people find problems and in Detroit, I felt that this was an opportunity to take advantage of. Although I had spent most of my adult life living and travelling around the world, I had never been to the USA, so I was a little bit apprehensive when on my own I flew to Detroit to get boots on the ground on the areas in which I was going to negotiate foreclosure deals directly from the bank. Detroit's riverside and General Motors building is a beauty to behold, but several miles behind that, some of the neighbourhoods were quite intimidating initially. I remember walking down and seeing some of the property we were going to acquire from the banks and seeing bullet holes in some of the doors and one in every five houses being burnt out and gutted. However, there were streets that were luckily far more pleasant whereby the owners had fallen into financial troubles and were due to be foreclosed by the bank. The first deal we did from the bank was for about 50 single family homes, whereby my company purchased, renovated them and sold them own to private investors around the world. This provided safe, high quality and comfortable accommodation for lower income families.

Oftentimes in business, it's very easy to get carried away with the bottom line, revenue and profit. And whilst these are important, equally important is to make sure that your company provides a service that helps people. This was clearly demonstrated to me when after our first month of operations in the Detroit property market, one of the tenants that we had just rehoused reached out to me personally to tell me how her and her children had spent several years living in squalor and run down houses, terrorised by street gangs and the house that she was now renting was the first house she had felt safe in. In business success or failure oftentimes comes down to timing, my company had operated in Detroit at just the right time, but due to our success many other companies had tried to copy our model and compete with us. So what had started at us blazing a path, soon ended up with us being one of many companies all competing for the same deals. Fortunately, another market even more exciting than Detroit was coming to the front, and that market was North Dakota.

North Dakota, throughout the twentieth century had experienced several short term oil boom bust cycles, but it was only with the advent of new technology called hydraulic fracturing or fracking for short that oil companies were able to really tap into the billions of barrels of oil trapped inside the shale formations underground in North Dakota. This led to a huge influx of workers literally tens of thousands all migrating from other states to North Dakota for well paid jobs in the oil and service industries. Many of these jobs allowed people without a university degree to earn six figures or more, however, due to the fact that North Dakota is one of the least populated states in the USA there was simply no housing to support these tens of thousands of oil workers.

It was common for the Walmarts in Williston, North Dakota to be littered with tents and sleeping bags most nights, and in the winter people would huddle around fires. People who were pulling in a thousand of dollars a day were sleeping on the streets like the homeless. When I saw this first hand I realised that not only was there an opportunity to do business to provide high quality housing for these workers, but also provide somewhere warm safe and secure for them at the same time.

Those first few months of having boots on the ground in North Dakota were a steep learning curve for myself and my company. Not only were we having to deal with creating a new market, but also having to deal with a challenging and often fragmented planning, zoning and permitting processes, as well as dealing with a severe lack of utilities. For example, development real estate in most part of the world, and there would be an availability of sewage, water and electricity.

However, this was far from the case in most places in North Dakota, oftentimes we had to build our own waste water treatment plants, bring in electricity and water line from sometimes three miles away. Weather was also a challenge, developing real estate in the UK or places like Florida, provided a 12 month building season, however this is certainly not the case in North Dakota.

Being just south of the Canadian border, in the great plain area of the Mid West, meant that temperatures from November to April could fall as low as -40 degrees Celsius, which meant that instead of a 12 month building season sometimes it could be as short as 6 or 7 months. In order to overcome this obstacle we prefabricated our housing units, built in factories in states in the south and would bring them up on trucks.

The third significant challenge was workforce shortages, in order to tackle this we brought workers from out of state and provided free housing and food in order to incentivise them to work for us. Our first lodge named Great American Lodge, opened over a year ago and is currently providing high quality furnished studios for over 400 oil workers, as well as three meals a day.

In total, we expect by the end of 2015 to have 2,500 housing units in western North Dakota, and already provide housing for some of the largest oil companies who operate in the area. When I look back on my life and think of about my five year old self playing Monopoly, and at the risk of sounding overly sentimental, it's almost like subconsciously my head and my heart were guiding me to make decisions for what has been and continues to be my passion in life, being a real estate entrepreneur and every tangent in my life at different stages have brought me back full circle.

I thought it would be appropriate to finish this chapter by highlighting some of the qualities which I believe have taken me to where I am today in business.

Risk Taker: Open up any dictionary and look up the word entrepreneur and you will find the word risk or risk taking somewhere in the definition. Entrepreneurs are no more intelligent than the average person, but generally they are more open to taking risks. When I talk about risk, I don't talk about irrational risks, like driving without a seatbelt or risks associated with chance such as playing roulette. I am talking about calculated risk, where an opportunity has been assessed from multiple angles and both the chance of success and the potential gain are significantly more than the chance of failure or potential loss.

I believe to be a successful entrepreneur and both an understanding and willingness to take those risks is vital. Whenever I am at a party and I meet someone new for the first time and they ask me what I do for a living, after I tell them they invariably tell me about their business idea. In fact I think that at most points in most people's lives they have an idea to start a business, and what stops most people from taking their ideas forward is a lack or desire to take a risk.

Integrity: It's easy to get jaded in business when it always seems to be about the bottom line. Whilst the bottom line and profit is important, what I believe is more important is the way that you conduct business. Rome wasn't built in a day and for anyone looking to make a quick profit and willing to sell their morals and ethics in exchange for money there will always be opportunities and unsuspecting victims for them to make a profit. However, I was raised to treat people the way you are expect to be treated back, and this is the same way that I conduct business.

If I or my company makes a promise to someone we always fulfil our promise, if we sign a contract we abide by that contract. If we have used a product or service then we pay for that product or service on time.

These simple ways of acting with integrity may seem basic but it's surprising how few companies operate in this way and by acting and conducting business with integrity you easily stand out from the crowd. Whilst I'm not religious, it has been proven to me time and time again that there is an element of karma or serendipity in this world and if you put out good vibes into the universe inevitably they will come back to you ten- fold.

Prioritising: How often have we heard the term from someone's lips, I have no time. I try never to use that term myself because I realise that it's not that I don't have time to do something, it's just that I don't think it's a good use of my time. Like any entrepreneur my business takes up a huge amount of my time, which means prioritising is key.

You can't do and have everything in life so it's very important for people to choose what they consider to be the most important for me that is my business, friends and family. TV is a big no no, and I generally watch less than one hour a week, as often as possible I try to combine more than one activity together to be more efficient with my time.

Most of my conference calls are not done at a desk but rather while I am out walking and getting my exercise for example, usually I try to keep the intensity of exercise to a management level as it tends to put people off on the call when they can hear you pants profusely on the other side!

Robert Gavin

Robert Gavin is a serial entrepreneur and a leading and trusted figure in the global real estate and investment industry, and is the Group CEO of NDD Group and associated companies.

Robert has been featured in prestigious media such as Money Week, The Economist, The Telegraph, Al Jazeera and The Financial Times, to name but a few.

Born into humble circumstances, Robert is testament to what can be achieved through hard work, creativity and dedication. Robert is often mentioned in the media with his insights into the world of real estate and investments and his opinion is respected by many journalists worldwide. Having worked and lived in the Middle East, China and South East Asia, Robert brings a global perspective to his companies, which gives a unique advantage to their loyal client base around the world.

NDD Group are an award winning developer who are undertaking commercial developments in and around oil fields in the USA, to provide high quality hotels for oil and construction workers from companies such as

ExxonMobil, Chevron, Halliburton, Hess, Schlumberger and BP, as well as those in the service sector for both short and long-term rental basis.

NDD Group's latest project, Williston Heights, will comprise of 570 luxury apartments in Williston, the city with the highest rents in the USA, which will set a new benchmark for quality, sustainability and lifestyle for the discerning investor and tenant.

NDD Group is the fastest growing and most respected provider of full service, accommodation in the Bakken oil fields area whose revenue for 2014 is on target to exceed $120 million.

Striving For Success – From Physiotherapist To Sock Entrepreneur

Luke Goodwin - GripSox

What if it fails? What if there really isn't a need for my product in the marketplace? Is it going to be too much work? These were just some of the questions I pondered when preparing to take on a new business project.
For me, it made perfect sense! My clients were already complaining about slipping when performing their exercises at my physiotherapy and pilates exercise studio. How could this problem be resolved? If my clients had this problem, then surely others undertaking this form of exercise around the country and overseas must be experiencing similar issues.

The only problem was that this was a whole new type of business venture for me. My Physiotherapy degree had not taught me anything about how to run a business, so it was only through jumping in the deep end as a novice physiotherapist and starting my own physiotherapy and pilates businesses that I had a few minor clues about what was involved in running a small business.

But again, this new business venture was to be quite different. It involved actually making a physical product. The only thing I knew about socks was that I wore them most days. I had no idea about what was involved in sourcing a manufacturer, the production process itself, marketing a product or other essentials such as importing/exporting, foreign trade and intellectual property. The list goes on…
Despite all of this, I was up for a new challenge. I'm not one to die wondering. I immediately began to undertake my own research and started to read anything and everything about those newly required business skills that appeared somewhat foreign to me.
I decided to write a business plan. This was not something I had done when starting my initial physiotherapy business. On that occasion the

opportunity presented itself quite suddenly so I made more of a "gut-feel" decision. Luckily for me it turned out to be the right decision and set me on my way as a small business owner as well as a physiotherapist.

When I say "business plan", I don't mean a one thousand page business SWOT analysis. I like to keep things fairly simple so it was more of a Q and A session that I conducted with myself. I know some people are hugely focussed on writing long extensive business plans before planting the first seed, but I am not one of these people. I like to make a few educated decisions (guesses) and then get on with the task at hand. Sometimes I think that people get so caught up in the "nitty gritty" of things that procrastination is the ultimate winner.

So, after several weeks of my own self-designed R&D methods, I was slowly beginning to think to myself, "Hey! This little side project of mine may actually take off!"

The all-important sock manufacturer had been established. Tick! Now to finalise the design of how I wanted my non-slip socks to look. As I was just starting out with this new product, I didn't want to offer my customers too many options. Instead, I decided to take the lead of the great Henry Ford who, when asked what type of motor vehicle his customers could have, he replied "you can have it in any colour you like, as long as it is black." If it was good enough for one of the greatest entrepreneurs of all time, then it was good enough for me. Having said that, I did at least give my customers the option of two different sizes from which they could choose.

Before I could complete the design of my non-slip socks and commence the much anticipated production of samples, there were a few more important things to organise. This included thinking up the all-important name of my new product, and along with that, taking all the necessary precautions to secure important intellectual property (IP) rights.

Not only did I have to think up a "catchy" name, but like a good game of rock, paper, scissors, I also had to determine who triumphs out of

Trademark, Business Name and Domain Name. Better still, was the name I was going to choose available in all three of these formats.

So, what was going to be a great name for a pair of socks that had grip on the bottom? Whilst I was tempted to call in the focus groups, marketing and advertising gurus, or anyone else prepared to throw in their two cents worth, I decided to go it alone. I mean really, there must be some logical name for my new product.

And so, without too much further analysis the name "GripSox" was born. I quickly set out to have my new product name registered as a Trademark, Business Name and Domain Name. Whilst the latter two formats were quite instantaneous, the registering of a Trademark is a little more time consuming as it can take several months for all the checks and balances to take place and for you to receive the tick of approval.

Not only had I registered the name "GripSox" to be trademarked, but I also registered my new logo as well as our catchy slogan, "Don't slip up on falls prevention!"

It was now time to crank up the engine on my new business venture and start making my new GripSox® product. It didn't take long before the first prototype pair of GripSox® was in my hands. I immediately tried them on to see if they lived up to my expectations and, did in fact, prevent slipping whilst walking and exercising. They did! It was now time to place an initial production run of 6,000 pairs of GripSox®. "Fingers crossed they sell", I said to myself.

As I mentioned earlier, there were a lot of business and entrepreneurial skills that I lacked before commencing my new business project. However, as time went by, I was becoming more and more confident that I could learn these new skills and apply them accordingly.

It is said that a big part of being an entrepreneur is to always see the "bigger picture". With that in mind, and whilst I was awaiting my first shipment of GripSox®, I started to brainstorm all the different types of markets that I could tackle in order to increase my product sales. Whilst I initially designed my product for my pilates clients, I was already thinking of the bigger problem that is people slipping over in the hospital, aged care and domestic settings. As a physiotherapist, I had seen first-hand the physical, emotional and financial burdens that falls had in the community, so it was now my mission to see if my new business project could have a positive impact in these specific markets.

The day finally arrived. After a great deal of hard work and careful planning, my first shipment of GripSox® had been delivered to my door and on 1 July 2005, GripSox® were on the market…cue the applause!
Whilst my own pilates clients were all over them like a rash, I was still awaiting that elusive first sale to a customer outside the four-walled confines of my own pilates studio.

Fortunately it didn't take too long. Seventeen days to be exact! It was beginning to look as though an earlier mail out to some local pilates studios was starting to pay dividends. One by one more studios were placing their GripSox® orders. Whilst they weren't massive orders, the ball was rolling nonetheless. To say I was a little chuffed would be an understatement.
The next few months saw regular orders coming in and our list of retailers was steadily growing, both here in Melbourne, as well as interstate.
And then it happened! Our first enquiry from an overseas pilates studio wishing to purchase some of my GripSox® to sell to their clients. Could this really be happening? Was GripSox® going global this early in the piece? I'm sure this wasn't how it was written in my business plan. But then again, who am I to halt progress?

Before long, we had retailers all around Australia as well as in three other countries. Already I had begun to plan my world trip to go and visit these retailers who had taken a punt on me. Unfortunately to this date, that still hasn't occurred. As anyone who runs their own small business would know, it's very easy to get caught up in the day to day running of your business, and a lot harder to step back and enjoy watching it grow. There's always that next sale just around the corner that you don't want to miss.

Whilst most of our early sales were to pilates studios and physiotherapy clinics, the other markets that I had envisaged would greatly benefit from GripSox® soon started knocking. Hospitals and aged care centres from around the country and overseas were interested in using GripSox® as part of their falls prevention strategy. Falls in these organisations are a huge problem that can prove to be very costly financially as well as having a negative impact on their reputation for patient care and safety. Add to this the physical repercussions suffered by the individual.

As a result of several very successful hospital clinical trials using my product, it soon became apparent to these organisations that the small cost involved in purchasing some GripSox® for falls prevention far outweighed the alternative consequences.
And with that we had reached our first "tipping point" for this new business venture.
The next few years continued to be a lot of hard work for both myself and my yet to be mentioned business partner (AKA my wife!).

Whilst not all start-up businesses intend on becoming a family affair, indirectly, a lot of them turn out that way. They say that marriage is a two way street, and from what I've experienced in establishing several businesses to-date, you definitely need the support of a loyal and understanding partner, especially in the early days of the business. A partner who understands why you might be up until midnight checking emails, or who is happy to drop everything in order to get an urgent delivery sent out to a very important customer. Fortunately, 99% of the business discussions that my wife and I have had in relation to my (our) business start-up venture have been very positive, despite the occasional hiccup along the way. Not to mention the arrival of two children during the early phase of our business development which further required a whole new lot of juggling skills.

Whilst most of my story so far sounds all rosy and cheery, there certainly have been hurdles along the way. Some of these include early teething problems with my manufacturers; customers quickly becoming competitors with rival (yet very similar) products; the occasional lost order in the mail; swings in foreign currency; controlling stock from three separate locations; registering certain trademarks (both locally and overseas); and last but not least, finding time to take a break from the day-to-day grind of running your own business.

However, despite all of these minor obstacles along the way, I can honestly say that not once have I thought of throwing my hands up in the air and saying, "I give up! It's all too hard!"

This, I believe, comes back to me possessing what I see as being **twelve important traits of a successful entrepreneur.** In no particular order, they are:

- Passion
- Motivation
- Confidence
- Drive to succeed
- Ambition
- Dedication
- Avoids procrastination
- Risk-taking
- Intuitive
- Hard working
- Determination
- Positive thinking

Whilst it may not be necessary to have all of these traits, the more of them you have when the going gets tough, the more likely you are to come out the other end successfully.

It is hard to believe that in just over three months it will be the ten year anniversary of my GripSox® product being launched on to the market. I don't know where the time has gone, but I do know that it has been an enjoyable adventure filled with many learning experiences along the way.

From an initial start-up idea, to a product that has now been sold by over 200 retailers in thirteen different countries and used by more than 150 hospitals and aged care centres for falls prevention, I can gladly say that the long hours of hard work have been rewarded.

The past twelve months have seen a GripSox® distributor appointed for the North America region as well as relocation into a much needed bigger distribution warehouse.

The funny thing is that the job only seems to be half done.
With significant sales growth in recent years and a positive outlook for the coming years, it's time to set some new goals, and who knows, I may even have to write a new business plan!

Luke Goodwin

Luke Goodwin is a Physiotherapist, Entrepreneur, Business Owner and Start-Up Consultant.

Luke, who is based in Melbourne, Australia, has in a short period of time established himself as a very successful small business owner and, through the launch of his GripSox® (non slip grip socks) product, now has an international presence.

Luke was only 24 when he set up his first business- a Physiotherapy practice. He expanded his business a couple of years later by setting up a brand new Pilates exercise studio. This has now been further expanded in the past few years into a Health & Wellness Centre in Brighton, Melbourne.

In 2005 Luke launched on to the market his very own GripSox® product. Since then, Luke's GripSox® product has been sold by over 200 retailers in Australia, UK, Europe, North America, New Zealand, Asia and the Middle East.

They have also been used very successfully by over 120 hospitals and aged care centres in order to reduce the number of patient falls. Read some of the clinical trial results...

It has been Luke's entrepreneurial traits like passion, determination, vision and perserverance that have seen him become a successful businessman in the healthcare industry.

GRIPSOX®{non-slip safety socks}

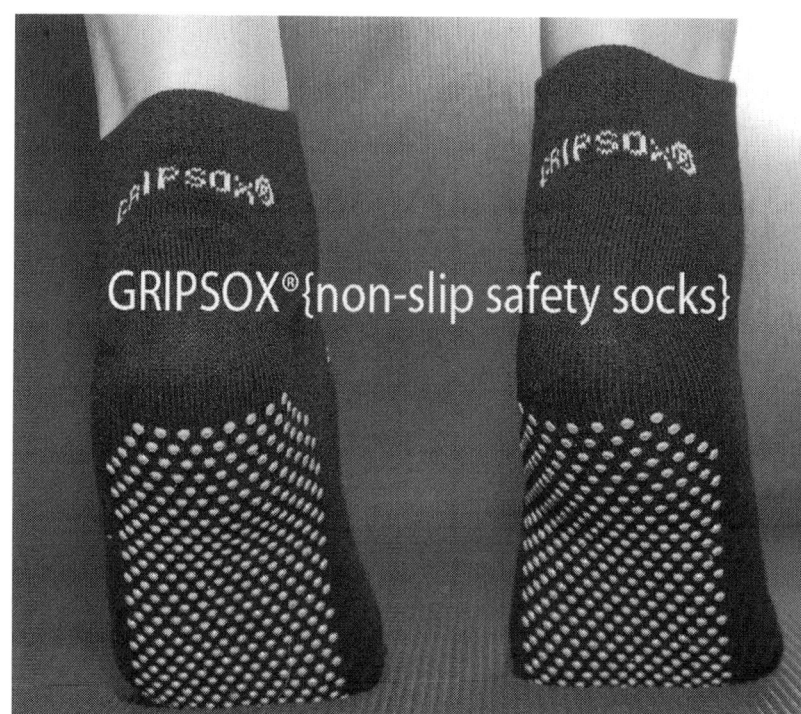

Designed by Australian Physiotherapist Luke Goodwin

MAKING A DIFFERENCE WORLDWIDE

Healthcare, Hospital & Aged Care, Pilates, Yoga, Exercise

Don't slip up on falls prevention!®
Ph. +61 3 9591 0500   www.gripsox.com

Creating a business full of energy and positivity

Erika Clegg – Spring

From the age of twelve, Erika Clegg knew she wanted two things: one, to work in advertising, and two, to own an agency. She might not have known what innovation truly meant then, but all her natural instincts pointed towards the fact that this would very much be part of the equation too.

Of course those were the days of the big agency brands, forged in the flames of the hedonistic 1980's. Erika's passion for the industry grew, in no small part, from her father's clear love of his dealings with agencies in his role as marketing director of Princes-Buitoni. What other career could combine the thrill of the dramatic arts, the creativity of the visual arts, the sheer confidence of career politicians and the social life of a bon viveur?

So, as a teenager, Erika became an avid reader of Campaign, Design Week and all the other industry publications that arrived home in her father's briefcase. She watched VHS agency showreels until they wore out. Throughout her teens, she prided herself on knowing the agency rankings, wins and losses every week. She took on work experience in advertising and design agencies in London and the North West as often as school would allow. This was her plan: get a junior copywriter job – she had a fancy for Young and Rubican – and work her way up to the board by the age of 30.

But when Erika left university in the summer of 1994, Britain was deep in recession. Her final work experience position demonstrated the stark impact of this on the industry: the award-winning copywriter's office in which she was stationed was empty, as were the five offices either side. Her focused plan to become a successful copywriter suddenly, rudely, seemed impossible.

She took her first job selling digital print to ad agencies. Although a far cry from her long held, cherished copywriting dream, she recognized that this job would allow her to learn the crucial nuts and bolts side of agency life. It's funny how things work out - learning the ability to trudge, sell, bounce back from rejection, deliver on promises, negotiate, delve, chat, learn new things and trudge once more, combined with her original creative instinct, has become the very backbone of Erika's subsequent success.

Eighteen months later came Erika's next career move, to AMD - a small full-service agency specializing in work with property developers. The benefits of a fast paced environment and of being closely mentored by the agency's extraordinarily ambitious, demanding and focused female owner were immense, though – as with all truly worthwhile training – it was hard. Starting as a graduate trainee, within a year Erika was as a matter of course working fourteen-hour days, leading the marketing strategy, creative direction, writing and project management of client accounts. She put her head down and fast tracked to become an account director within three years, working on the Nomura sell off of ex-military housing under the Annington brand, and much of the Saint George/ Berkeley Homes regeneration of London's riverside estate from Kingston to Docklands.

She developed a real passion for community engagement. In managing the marketing for different sites for Annington, she had pioneered a hands on, very localized approach, visiting every site in person and making sure to meet the real community influencers. These sites were often in places where housing was hard to come by – some coastal resorts, for example, where second home owners had driven up prices – and so the Annington properties, always sold at around a third less than market value, represented great opportunities for local people to get on the housing ladder. Erika had uncovered the real needs of those communities, found out where people congregated, got details of local employers and even the names and contact details of potential purchasers. It came down to knowing where the factory noticeboard was and on what night the WI met.

This blossoming understanding of community need had a real, formative resonance for Erika. Her grandparents lived in the coastal market town of Southwold, in Suffolk, and over the years, as she and her parents had moved up and down the country, Southwold had come to feel like the place that was really home for her, and indeed she had bought her home here even though she worked in London.

The town has many natural advantages that make it a prime holiday spot: unusually high rates of sunshine, a long sandy beach, comparative proximity to London. Add to this a great local brewery, beautiful beach huts and a pretty townscape, and you have one of the most charming small town communities in Britain. But house prices bear a close relationship to London too, and the opportunities for locals to pursue skilled careers are conversely low. As Erika developed her own career in London, she was increasingly aware of this, and often wondered if there was anything she could do to help her beloved hometown.

When AMD was acquired by Bell Pottinger, as part of an aggressive growth policy to become the largest communications group in Britain, the pace stepped up further as the agency moved from its charming small mews office in Kensington to a four-storey office block just off the King's Road, Chelsea.

As rewarding as this work was, Erika became frustrated by the dearth of creative opportunity and she moved on to become client services director at global top 5 agency Attik's London office. Her time at Attik was fuelled by the creativity of one of London's most talented studios. Clients including household-name fashion designers and DJs flocked, as did banks and building societies, keen for some of the 'cool' to rub off onto them. It was in many ways the opposite of her first jobs, where client had been king and – whilst not always right – was never told 'no'. Attik was the best in the business and had the ego to match. Clients did what they were told. The agency was big, bold, sometimes brash, and brave. And then it came to an end.

Where were you on the 11th September 2001? Erika was standing in the studio in Attik with her colleagues, each in stunned silence as they watched the screens, pop videos wiped off them by a horrifying scene of planes, smoke and falling, dying people. Those heady days of transatlantic trade stuttered from that point, taking years to find their confidence again. Within a few months, many of those colleagues had left, Erika amongst them – one of many ripples from an event that has become a place marker in history.

Erika moved on to another agency – headhunted by her original mentor at AMD – accepting a job that was about systems and process, neither Erika's passion nor her strong point, but an opportunity when one was needed. This job saw her start a new learning curve helping to oversee the merger of two businesses and mutual relocation to a new office.

But at home, something was happening which was to take her eye off her career – doubtless aided by this shift into the back office, for which she still thanks fate. Her boyfriend, the architectural photographer Simon Hazelgrove, was in the process of fighting for custody of his three year old daughter, and after ten months of expensive and frustrating legal wrangles, the court decided that he should indeed take on her care formally. With her customary taste for a challenge, Erika - an only child with little experience of young children - offered to quit her job and look after Georgie. She decided to set up a consultancy that she could run flexibly from Simon's or her own house to cover her mortgage on her home and living expenses. And so, at 28, that's what she did.

For the next three years, Erika was Georgie's main carer, juggling this around work with a handful of clients for whom she pulled in freelance designers, photographers, exhibition riggers and others as needed. It was a happy time in many ways, allowing her to reconnect with a really hands-on style of account management as well as to integrate herself in to her new family. Her own renewed love of the industry coincided with a difficult time for photographers like Simon, with the rise of digital driving down day rates and reducing the available work for a growing pool of photographers.

Simon's experience of owning and managing a large photographic studio stood him in good stead to become involved in setting up a business, and Erika's long standing ambition to launch her own agency had now reached a crescendo.

So, soon after their marriage in March 2005, they agreed to do just that.

Erika's desire to support Southwold's sustainability as a community had not dimmed, and so – in a sharp twist of accepted thinking – she decided that the agency would be based, not in London, but in the seaside town. It made perfect sense in so many ways. Southwold is packed with creative people, and at the weekends London's media flocks to this pretty bit of coast. Home to Adnams, her plans for her agency's brand values aligned perfectly with those of the high quality, community focused brewer. People love Southwold, just as she and Simon hoped people would love their agency, but of course it was crazy in so many other ways. For many, the seaside symbolizes relaxation, retirement, leisure – none of those would be the case for this ambitious pair and their business. Southwold is two hours by train from London, longer by road. Nobody had tried to set up a business like this in the town before, with the exception of a few consultants dividing their time between city and coast, and a small specialist education-marketing consultancy.

This was where Erika's natural optimism and determination came into play.

She would make her agency become a national player from this seaside town. The emerging digital revolution that had taken the gloss off Simon's photography would underpin this. The days of cycle and motorbike couriers were gone. The clean air of the Suffolk Coast could bring inspiration even to the most jaded mind. Instinct told her that this could work. She and Simon agreed that Erika would go to Southwold, to live and work in her little house there for three months to give it a try. So in the autumn of

2005, she headed to Suffolk armed just with an old laptop, some case studies and 500 business cards emblazoned with the name 'Spring'.

The Spring name was a conscious decision from the pair to create a business that would be full of energy and positivity. The implications of growth and nourishment are intentional, and the secondary meaning of Spring – something which creates bounce – an equally applicable brand characteristic. In addition, the name is short and simple, wouldn't have to be spelt out, and has some emotional meaning to anyone who hears it.

That autumn was pleasant in Suffolk, with little of the chill breeze that can sometimes whip around the coast. Erika set to work getting to know the regional community, to see if the agency was likely to be able to grow organically starting with local work. In the third week of Spring's gestation period, she found herself sitting next to the inspirational expert on lateral thinking, Edward de Bono, at an event, and wasted no time in seeking his advice. This policy of asking and listening has been a key feature of both Spring and Erika's growth; still now, the agency has Spring Hero lunches in which big names from the industry and outside it join the team for lunch and to share their experiences. She joined the Chamber of Commerce, got to know the local press, took the regional papers and scanned them daily for possibilities. She wrote to business owners, brand managers, venture capitalists and property developers across Norfolk and Suffolk, making as many meetings as possible.

It was a hard slog, but enormous fun. No money was coming in, and travelling around East Anglia takes a lot of petrol, so every foray out had to count. Erika made lots of contacts and the Spring name started to become familiar within both the Southwold and the wider regional business communities. But work was not yet coming in. Simon and Erika had agreed that the three months would only be counted as a success if it generated work – and by Christmas Eve, 2005, it hadn't. Ready to pack up and start scanning the job pages of the Guardian, Erika accepted that she'd tried, given it her best shot, but had ultimately failed.

Then the phone range, and in that phone call – taken at the kitchen table of her tiny Southwold home – Spring was finally born.

The call was from the operations director of East Anglia's largest social housing business. They'd heard about Spring on the grapevine and felt the agency might be able to help them. They had to sell 1,500 great value, shared ownership houses loitering on their books and were committed to build many thousands more over the next few years. It was a crisis, in no small way. The challenge was made for Erika and for Spring. All this required was a really good property marketing campaign combined with solid community insight – two things they had by the bucketload, albeit from their past lives. By early January 2006, Simon and Georgie had moved up to Southwold too, Spring had hired a designer and a small office and life in Suffolk as business owners and as a family began in earnest.

The next three years were like riding a galloping horse without a saddle much of the time. Spring grew fast, employing up to seventeen staff by 2009. In its second year, the agency brought in a net profit of 32% - a fantastic achievement in an industry where 20% is considered ambitious. It hit the Design Week top 100 in year two. Clients poured in, intrigued at finding such an ambitious, energetic business in Southwold.

From the start, Erika took Spring's community responsibility seriously. She set the agency's Five Point Ethical Code, of which one of the five is community. The other four ethical codes by which the agency steers its course are respect, sustainability, integrity and nurturing people. This clear moral compass is an important brand asset, but also, Erika believes, a secure platform for the agency's growth. Aware that the agency's services were unlikely to be of value to many people in the town, she ensured that the townspeople would at least benefit from them. Spring's staff became a feature of Southwold, shopping on the High Street and flocking to the beach at lunchtime and Erika offered pro bono work for community events and celebrations, supporting charitable endeavours and even setting up, marketing and providing box office for a town Concert Series.

Staff came from the local area, but also from further away, often bringing family with them. Over the years, new Springers' partners have also set up businesses in the region, finally able to realise their own lifetime ambition in the way that Spring brought Erika's to life. Whether the agency is making use of skills already here that would otherwise leave or lie fallow, or drawing new people up to the region, the impact on the town is entirely to the good.

Spring began to draw in an interesting mix of clients, as Erika focused on growing the business entirely through project income and building up a good portfolio of work. From the start, she set out to provide a full, ongoing service to Spring's clients, recognizing that the best work comes about once relationships are established. But its financial growth was underpinned by that original large, stable client. When a business finds itself in a position like that, warning bells ring. Every overhead Spring had was pretty much supported by the fee income from the Shared Ownership property marketing. It meant that the agency's work for other clients tended to be, if not exactly pro bono, certainly for love. Spring produced some beautiful work but undervalued themselves financially, leaving the agency open to risk.

It was clear to Erika that the risk needed to be minimized by recruiting more sizeable clients, but world events had more power than even the most ambitious sales development programme could hold off. The property market crashed – and, without private sector property development, there's no shared housing, since it comes as part of a planning agreement. So the spend that was keeping Spring's overheads covered abruptly dropped by 90% in one single, memorable meeting.

To add to the impact, at the same time Erika was pregnant, and her occasional absence left Spring exposed to two members of staff whose objectives differed to Erika's own founding principles. The repercussions of these difficult times and of their eventual departure were deeply felt, and Erika learned the hard but valuable lesson of how important shared vision is for a personality-driven business like Spring, as well as the need to identify and deal with people who are causing that vision to suffer.

The 2009 credit crunch turned into the 2010, 2011, 2012 and 2013 recession. These were lean years for businesses of all natures and sizes – and to survive, every business had to adapt, rethink their strategy and simply become a whole lot better at what they did. Such a turbulent start to the recession for Spring meant unreliable cashflow and a team with equally variable morale. It was clear to Erika that these were priorities, if Spring was to survive. If this wasn't enough, competition from agencies across the UK was hotting up. Every agency head including Erika knew that clients needed watertight strategies and bold, well-crafted creativity to consider signing off a budget; and that those budgets were getting smaller.

And so Erika and Simon made the bold decision to invest. Invest in training, invest in non-executive directors, and invest in morale. Erika found the chief executive of Britain's most-awarded, chart topping brand consultancy as a mentor. Two high profile, enormously experienced Non Executive Directors joined the business in 2009 and 2012. Spring's management team expanded, taking in staff beyond the directors. A stakeholder scheme was established, allowing staff to share in the information about and benefits of profit, as those profits started to grow. Agency staff were given an open chequebook for industry books, magazines and website subscriptions. Other new perks that Erika instigated included twice-yearly funded cultural trips for all staff, Friday gym sessions and negotiated discounts in Southwold shops and restaurants – which all benefited the community too.

The team – smaller through natural movement rather than redundancies – started to gel again, to regain trust in each other. Of those who had been at the agency in the really hard time, it's true to say that their love for Spring had never dimmed, and Erika ensured that their love was rewarded in a wide range of interesting ways.

Sales throughout the tough recession years were of course paramount, and Erika focused hard on getting out, meeting clients and potential clients, and raising the profile of the business with the people it could help. Plenty of donated time, events, speeches and marketing were became her focus as the recession dragged on. Amazingly, it worked, and although growth slowed, Spring did continue to grow year on year, even without the big client. Profitability was impacted, but every month Erika ensured that the agency paid its bills on time, pulled in work with a great scope for creative inspiration and grew its reputation. Simon's skills were perfectly applied to client services and supplier management, with his attention to detail and uncompromising dedication to the success of projects making Spring a very safe bet for its clients.

Over the course of this time, Spring took on a number of significant projects, each in their own way a landmark for the agency's professional confidence, growth and innovation.

Spring became Champagne Bollinger's digital marketing agency, growing them from a place of no social media and digital to having the confidence to take on their own content strategy in-house, over the course of three years. Working with Bollinger saw the Erika and the team heralding James Bond movies, becoming a leading authority on the days' racing at Royal Ascot, rubbing shoulders with the England rugby team and running hugely popular literary competitions for fans of Hay.

Adnams approached Spring to launch their American pale ale, Ghost Ship, asking the team to deliver a social media competition. With customary innovation, Erika's answer to the brief went way beyond expectations – with Apple style landlord launch breakfasts, a VIP party, blogger recruitment and a mind blowing experience where the brewery itself transformed into a galleon, exploded and came back to life as the eponymous Ghost Ship, all through the power of 3D projection. Only then, with the results of this filmed, edited and up on YouTube, did the briefed social media competition commence. The level of preparation Spring undertook guaranteed the success of the competition, with take up at such a level that the video sharing autoreply crashed and Adnams sold half a million pints of Ghost Ship in just two weeks.

Politics, too, got the Spring touch as the agency launched the Conservative Party's conference retail zone – they were the first party to realize the commercial value attached to 13,000 delegates trapped in one place for three days – and, the next year, designed the party's official Margaret Thatcher commemorative materials, earning extensive media coverage across the world. As Erika grew up with Margaret Thatcher in 10 Downing Street, the Queen on the throne, a strong headmistress and many other amazing female role models – it's little wonder that she's always had an intrinsic belief in her right to a career and a family, as well as a deeply ingrained sense of her responsibility to those around her. To undertake this work in commemoration of one of those women felt in many ways like coming full circle.

EDF Energy, who plan to build a third nuclear power station at Sizewell on the Suffolk coast, recruited Spring to manage their community planning consultation following a protracted pitch. They recognized that Spring would be an invaluable partner in delivering a robust and genuine consultation programme, a skill Erika had brought to Spring from her AMD days, and this kind of work has become a sizeable part of the agency's output.

As the company continued to face up to the economic realities of recession, Erika became a board director of the region's Local Enterprise Partnership as well as the industry's Design Business Association. She balanced this by working on the strategy and creative delivery of key accounts, as well as providing quality overview for all agency projects, and regularly speaking at events and conferences on matters related to business or CSR. This allowed her to create impact through her skills and the business's activities, helping to build the reputation and scope of the region as well as her own industry.

As the recession finally abated, and always with an eye on progress, in 2013 Spring repositioned itself boldly as The Agency for Change. It had become clear that their best work was always for the boldest clients, and so Erika made a conscious decision to set out to find those types of client in a positive way. Another strategic brand decision was to create a suite of photographs for the brand, depicting the Springers in the dawn light. Fashion-led in style, the images made a positive feature of the agency's East Coast location and made Springers the stars. This clear, uncompromising presentation of Spring's assets became a platform for renewed growth in 2014 and 2015.

At the start of 2014, Spring launched a brand new website for regional tourism body Visit Suffolk. The client had taken the bold step of moving away from Britain's standard provider of tourism body websites – the reason this was bold is because the business in question had gained something of a stranglehold on the database, making it almost impossible to extricate a regional destination website from them. Erika instructed that Spring would put itself on the line to support their client, offering to match the scale of the database by the time the website launched. From commission to launch, with Christmas in the mix, there were just ten weeks to make this happen. Without Erika's willingness to share her client's risk, the project might well have fallen at the first hurdle. Two Springers dedicated at least three working weeks to phone calls, meetings, emails and otherwise building the database of Suffolk tourism, having agreed a nominal reward per sign up. When the site launched on the 2nd January 2014, the database was at full strength – and what's more, every single one of those was an engaged subscriber. Acknowledged by industry leaders to have broken the mold, the site received unsolicited praise from digital media and design press as well as tourism, and won awards for its design, content and marketing across both industries.

It was perhaps no great surprise, then, when the Moroccan Tourism director in London called Erika, asking her to tender recommendations for the country's tourism marketing in Britain and America until 2018. To fulfill this request the agency had to recruit a new French speaking account handler, and Erika and Simon thought long and hard before doing so. Tendering is a risk; large new clients are a risk – especially overseas. But go for it Spring did, submitting a 27,000 word proposal within a matter of weeks. Shortly afterward, the agency was awarded the account, and now works alongside Moroccan tourism bodies and businesses both in the UK and Rabat, with three Springers full time engaged on the project.

From this, too, came Spring's commission to promote Norfolk and Suffolk as an unmissable Cultural tourism destination, a project which has seen Erika make trips overseas to share insight and experiences with other cultural destinations, thus raising both the agency's and the project's profile.

Many of Spring's clients are manufacturers, some of consumer products, like luxury chocolate maker Booja-Booja, some of specialist equipment, like football kit manufacturer Mark Harrod and garden office market leader Smart. The ethics of a successful British manufacturer – quality materials, attention to detail and a streak of innovation – echo those of Spring, and are also a good part of the reason why manufacturing is returning to Britain again.

One of the things Erika often says she loves most about her chosen career is the way it allows her to get behind real change and economic growth, with a limitless capacity to be creative, exciting and pioneering. That one day she can be in the studio working on concepts to launch a new beer, and the next speaking about skills and opportunity at a political conference, is a source of great pleasure to her.

And yes, like many women in her position she is acutely conscious of family, and juggling the best choices for the two children. Her son Will, now 5, attends school in Southwold and has au pairs, but Erika makes no pretence of being anything other than a loving Mum and he is a regular feature of the office, just as Springers are often to be found at Erika's home, pushing a cat, dog or chicken aside to sit down. Work and home just rub along together, as they must.

Walk into the Spring offices today and you'll find more than 20 people, all friends with one another and their clients. You'll find sun streaming in through the windows most days, and laughter ringing around the desks every day. You'll also find people studiously embedded in developing briefs, researching opportunities for clients, loading content to websites, developing design across brands, creating comprehensive content plans.

Over the past four years, Spring's focus on its people has earned it the accolade of Most Innovative Independent Employer in the east of England, alongside Benefit Cosmetics. Amongst its peers, the agency was earning a good reputation too, being listed at position 8 in The Drum's most respected list in 2013, and rising by two places to number 6 in 2014. Other awards have included Corporate Engagement gongs for the Southwold Concert Series, regional business awards and strong recognition of the agency's design and marketing work.

Spring is now bursting out of the old Victorian print works that has been home since 2006, and by the time this book goes to press will, with luck, have taken up residence of a large Georgian Manor House on the town's High Street.

Erika's vision for the agency's future remains ambitious. If pressed she'll say that Spring is getting ever closer to the agency she knows it can be, but there's a long way to go. Those tough recession years held the agency back in some ways, though the Spring that emerged was far more what it has to be to meet that vision.

Her early career means she knows exactly the size of agency she wants: no more than 30 people, to maintain that family feel and shared knowledge of client projects. She also knows that Spring must constantly maintain balance between a good client experience and a great client result, holding what she refers to as a maternal care for clients' successes.

Creativity in thinking, design, writing, technology, production – in fact, the whole approach – are fundamentally important. And if she ever stops being almost childishly excited by the emergence of brilliant ideas, she'll stop work.

That twelve year old girl, with her passion for the industry, would be pleased – though undoubtedly she'd be pushing for more and better, too!

Erika Clegg

Erika is co-founder and executive creative director of British communications design agency Spring, which she launched with Simon Hazelgrove in 2006. She is also a board director of the Design Business Association, a trustee of the Norwich Theatre Royal and the Southwold Music Trust and a British business ambassador for UKTI. She lives with her young family and animals just outside Southwold, Suffolk.

Spring is a communications design agency which specialises in brand consultancy, destination marketing, digital marketing and multi-channel communications programmes. Clients include the Moroccan National Tourism Office, the National Trust, the Norfolk and Suffolk cultural tourism programme and EDF Energy. As the sixth most peer-respected boutique agency in the UK, Spring rewards its team with benefits including stakeholdings, fitness classes and cultural grants.

An English entrepreneur in France

Catherine Broughton - holidaychateaufrance.com

I never imagined I'd be an entrepreneur of any sort. And now that I am one, I cannot imagine being anything else.

I trained as a teacher and taught French and Spanish for twelve years. My father was a doctor and my mother a professor of Latin. My background, therefore, was academic and when we first moved to France, three little children on tow, I assumed I'd get a teaching post of some sort.

We were utterly broke. We had lost everything almost overnight in England, the bank repossessed our house, our youngest was barely a year old, my husband's business in property development had crumbled in the blink of an eye during the property slump, and we were crawling.

We were among many hundreds – thousands – of families who lost out financially at that time, but there was no way we wanted to allow circumstance to reduce us to a council house or even a rented property.

So we moved to France. Like so many other British families before and since we – so naively! – thought that life would somehow be "different" once we got to France. Well, it is different – it is in French !

I thought I'd be able to get a teaching post and my husband would go in to the property business as he had in the UK, ie buying up cheap properties, restoring them and selling them at a profit. But no. Although English was (and perhaps still is) badly taught in French schools, they didn't want me. My qualifications were not valid, they said. My husband had bought, with the help of local banks and my language skills, four derelict little houses going for a song. But the French do not have the same hunger for owning property as the British have; there are rules and regulations for anything and everything, and it was nigh-on impossible to forge forwards. It seemed to us that the French system was designed to make life as hard as possible and I was desperately homesick.

And so I set up business selling houses to the British. I asked the local notaire (like a lawyer) if it was all right to just set up business and he assured me that it was. He was wrong and I ended up in Court over it ... but that is a different story altogether. Because my clients, almost uniquely British, loved a bargain and bought very cheap semi-derelict properties, my husband's business was the renovation and restoration of them. His business operated off mine.

One of the first things that struck me was how clueless I had been. As a teacher I had been on the academic staff of a secondary school, I was a post-graduate and tri-lingual, I had already travelled around the world ... yet I was so clueless. I think this is often the way, particularly in a job like teaching – you live in that one world and never see beyond the job.

I was instantly amazingly successful. I gathered dossiers about properties for sale, relying largely on the local notaires and the jungle-drums, and sold them to the British. It worked like magic and within a matter of months money was rolling in.

 A bit of a sweeping statement, but I sometimes think that only people who run their own businesses really know what work is. If you are employed by somebody else, you go in to work, do whatever it is you have to do, then go home again. You get paid for it. It may be easy stuff or difficult stuff, but essentially you get paid for a specific job and it is up to you to do it properly.

People who run their own businesses have to create a situation, in our case out of thin air, out of which they can earn some money. Nobody said to us "do this and I will pay you for it". We had to make it possible to pay ourselves I, in the first instance, had to persuade my client (having got the client at all) to buy a house in France. Not just any house in France, but a house on my books. In order to get to this situation I first had to place advertisements in magazines and newspapers in the UK. This was long before the internet. I then had to answer the phone, the fax and the post several hundred times, enclosing details of five or six properties each time, in order to get one solitary client into my car. I worked out that for every 200 sets of details I posted, I got one client. Out of the clients who got as far as looking at properties with me, about one in every seven would buy.

Having got the client to agree to buy something – invariably an old fermette in need of repairs – I then had to get them to sign papers called a Compromis de Vente, which is a kind of promise to buy. At that stage I also had to persuade them to part with a cheque for 10% of the value of the property. This was sometimes done in the office of a notaire, but was also regularly done in my own little office at home with the washing machine chugging away in the background , the smell of burnt toast and the sound of children playing. The cheque was always made out to the notaire. From that moment responsibility should have fallen off my shoulders and onto his, though it never really did, and it was his job to do a search while I kept the clients informed.

Of course, the clients always referred back to me, from sensible questions like the perimeter fences to silly questions about the height of the skirting boards. If something went wrong it was always my fault – even the weather seemed to be my domain – and people never wanted to pay for anything.

It was, however, a neat little business. My clients looked to me for sorting out utilities and insurances for their properties, and I was able to make a small charge which helped to swell my commission a little and – Lord knows – we needed every penny.

The situation was, nonetheless, fraught with difficulties. I had never dealt with this sort of thing before, and now I found myself translating contracts, advising people about building permits, talking with banks, interpreting at the notaire's office and generally stepping a long way out of my comfort zone. The job involved endless driving, first to view properties and then to show people around. I was so short of money that I had to ask my clients to help with the petrol on several occasions – something that turned out to be illegal in France, though Lord knows why. And that was another thing – I wobbled constantly on a thin line between doing something illegal and keeping on the right side of the law. Everything went via a solicitor, so you'd have thought it would be fine, I paid tax and VAT ... yet nonetheless kept getting letters from this authority or that, telling me it was interdit to do whatever I had done. Frequently this was something so simple – like the petrol money example – and often it was something ridiculous like not translating my own forms.

I was ruthless. I had to be. Whether you are selling a property or a packet of Smarties – you have to sell it. That is the whole point. Being kind did not come in to it – though I hope I was never unkind. I could often see people making totally unsuitable choices, not least because very few of them spoke French, but at an early stage learnt to keep my opinions to myself and just get on with the job.

Rule no.1: I think that is one of the first things I'd say if asked about being an entrepreneur: you have to be tough. You are selling your product, whatever it is, and that is your aim. Lose sight of that and you will not succeed.

Sometimes people comment that it was lucky that I spoke French. Well, the ability to speak French has nothing to do with luck actually! I learnt it. But apart from that no - it was not necessarily an advantage simply because it meant that everything fell on to my shoulders. If the phone rang, if somebody came to the door, if the children needed help with homework or teachers needed to see me, I had to deal with it myself. From talking to the bank to the tax man and the accountant; from waiters to vendors to petrol station attendants – I had to do it myself. My husband could not speak a word, the children (although they learned very quickly) were too young. I was alone with it and it was a long uphill grind.

But it was precisely that long uphill grind that taught me so much. I was fantastically energetic and willing to learn. Each hurdle was a lesson learned, a step up the steep ladder. Sometimes the hurdles seemed insurmountable – the French bureaucratic system truly did its best to break me – but I clambered over to the other side, as it were, and learnt from it.

Rule no.2: And that is the second thing I'd say to anybody who asked about being an entrepreneur: learn from your mistakes. Learn from all the things that go wrong, all the things that are difficult. The mistakes you make are a crucial part of the solid platform you are building.

It took its toll on me, however. It sounds nice, doesn't it, driving people around, looking at properties ? But competition from local French estate agents was vicious – positively nasty in fact – and the whole thing gradually ate away at my nerves. I earned good money and had come to thoroughly enjoy having money on the account. But I needed to look for something else, something more gentle, or I felt I'd just crack up.

Rule three: recognize the difference between giving up and changing direction. So many people say "I don't want to give up yet" as though they are facing failure. Changing direction is not the same thing. You need to know which way you are heading, and if it does not seem to be working out, you need to be practical.

And so one day we drove past a big old house called the Chateau de Rochebonne. It was on the main road and stood gloomily staring out through half-dead trees, closed, semi-derelict, grey and depressing.

"I wonder which idiot is going to buy that?" asked my husband.

We did. It was us.

We will convert this lot in to holiday lets, we decided. Once they are built, all we have to do is take the bookings. Simple enough.

We had left England six years earlier, broke, depressed and up to our eyes in debt. By the time we bought this property, six years later, we had cleared all our debts, which were considerable and were able to pay cash for the house. Admittedly it was very cheap at the equivalent of £75 000 for a small chateau with 6 acres of land. With three small children – they were now aged 6, eleven and twelve – we moved in to our derelict chateau a few days before Christmas.

Rule no.4: An entrepreneur cannot be afraid. Do not be afraid. If you are going to say "but we haven't got enough money" or "it is too cold" or "I can't do that and work and care for the children" – you will not succeed. The key to your success is knowing that not only you can do it, but that you will.

My husband had the right skills, and that was a huge advantage. You need, of course, to have the skill sets to go with the enterprise. Had we been setting up a cooking and singing school we would not have succeeded because neither of us can either cook or sing. Mark you, you can raise the capital to pay somebody who does have the right skills, but nobody will do it in the devoted and determined way that you will. No matter how much you pay somebody, the bottom line is that you do it best. Your own heart and love and strength is the very thing that pivots the project forward, and that is something only you can provide.

We did take on a labourer. It is a big mistake to not delegate where you can. The trick is deciding which bit of the work (and the work was massive) to give him to do, and which bit to get on with ourselves. Our middle child, William, became our best man in many ways, though he was only eleven years old. And even Pips, our daughter, was brilliant at loading and unloading wheelbarrows. Funny that. Children usually complain about helping their parents, but ours loved it.

Within two years we had restored the chateau and converted the barns in to eight cottages. We did this on a shoe-string budget, and with the help of banks who were at that time very keen to lend. Everything was a juggling act. We juggled taking from Peter to pay Paul. We begged and borrowed as and where necessary. We both became brilliant at making do and at using an item designed for one thing as something totally different. Necessity is the mother of invention. Lateral thinking, imagination, energy, stepping out of the box – these are crucial attributes.

And speed. For us speed was a hugely important element in our success. Because of shortage of funds, it was essential that we got the chateau and the cottages all let to holiday makers as quickly as possible. The deposits they paid financed the next part of the project. In just five months we raised the roofs on the barns, laid ground floors, installed staircases and upper floors, all plumbing, all wiring, all rendering and plastering and painting. And the furnishing ! Our youngest, Jake, rushed back and forth with me to local shops (the nearest "local" one being a good half hour's drive) loading up with beds and mattresses, chairs and side tables, sofas and shelves, pots and pans and crockery and duvets ... on and on and on, and always frantically looking round for the cheapest option. A great deal of what we bought was second hand.

Rule no.5: when something goes wrong (and plenty went wrong for us), ask yourself what advantage you can get out of it. How can you turn this dreadful setback in to something you gain from ?

A huge storm hit France at that time and took away the roofs we had just finished and destroyed all the lovely trees that protected the property from the main road. Windows were smashed in and stocks ruined. It was a bitter setback for us.

It was very difficult indeed to find an advantage in the situation – yet there was. A team of village men turned up, looking for work. Just clearing the smashed roof tiles and windows that lay strewn all over the ground represented several weeks' work, and we explained to these men that we could not pay them till the insurance had paid us. They agreed to work on that basis and in fact turned out to be a brilliant team who went a long way towards helping us get the properties all finished and ready for holiday-makers in good time.

Years have swept by. I spend my time writing (I have published several books) and sketching. Our properties are full every year, and many of the holiday-makers are people that come back year after year. I take the bookings, all of which are on-line, and my husband oversees maintenance work (which is constant). We come and go as we please. We have a caretaker and a gardener, and a team of excellent cleaning staff. During the winter months we travel – at the time of writing we have just returned from a six-week tour of India and Sri Lanka. We own a property in England and another in Belize; we stay in one or the other as the moods takes us. Many people would give their right arm to be in our boots, but very few of them have the remotest idea about what we overcame, the risks we took and the work we ploughed through.

Catherine Broughton

Catherine Broughton was born in South Africa to English parents. Her father's job as a doctor of tropical disease took the family all over Africa for many years, till Catherine attended the University of London when she was 18. She trained as a teacher, and then went in to business. She has lived in Spain, Belize, New Caledonia and Switzerland during her adult years.
She and her husband bought their first property in France in 1989 and have lived there off and on since. Catherine Broughton's first book "A Call from France" was published in 2011 and the others followed rapidly. She has three adult children and three grandchildren, is a keen supporter of a variety of charities and enjoys water-colour sketching and interior design.

Creating something of your own and seeing it come to life

Heidy Rehman - Rose & Willard

I spent almost 14 years climbing the corporate ladder at one of the largest investment banks in the world. I was a stockbroker or, more specifically, an equity research analyst. Analysts cover sectors within regions.

Initially based in London, the main hub for the UK and Europe, I'd started with housebuilding and construction before moving on to hotels and leisure. For the last four and a half years I'd been based in Dubai covering Middle East & North African chemicals, materials and construction. I spent my days analysing and assessing the financials, strategy and valuation of companies, questioning CEOs and debating with investors.

It was intellectually challenging, financially rewarding and rarely were two days the same. It was a good living, with status, and there was more of the ladder to climb. People often ask me why I chose change. I was at a point where a choice was becoming inevitable. Every analyst chases and covets the illustrious top ranking of the two main City surveys – Institutional Investor and Extel – as voted by investors globally. I was top ranked in both surveys and across two sectors.

Professionally, I'd arrived but knew I needed to make a decision. Should I fight to retain my titles, change sectors again, opt for an upward but more managerial, administrative route or should I try something new? This crossroads coincided with me seriously evaluating my place as a woman within the vastly male-dominated arena of investment banking.

I had always felt that women had to do that much more to prove themselves. After so many years this was starting to take its toll and I believe had set the wheels in motion for a new direction.

As I contemplated what to do next, I began to think more seriously about the perception of women in the professional working world. What I undoubtedly knew was that this would play a part in whatever path I chose. How we present ourselves can influence a person's entire opinion of us. For women, who are judged much more readily on their appearance, this is all the more important, especially when it is mostly the positive opinion of men in positions of power that we seek.

What I began to realise was that women lacked choice when it came to personal presentation or, more specifically, there were insufficient wardrobe options for professional women. I'd struggled with this myself. While I did well enough I didn't have a luxury budget and high street wasn't a genuine option; it was aimed predominantly at a younger market and, to me, also represented an ethical compromise.

Being a professional woman I was aware that I needed to pay close attention to what I wore but not so much as to be considered frivolous or superficial. I needed to be readily identified as distinct from the secretaries but not to appear too concerned with my appearance. There was no easy or ready answer. Speaking to a few of my female peers I found they also struggled with the same issue.

My conclusion, as an analyst, was that there was a gap in the market. But who to fill it? Gradually I started to think; why not me? I'd had the benefit of some very good advice in my life; someone had once said to me 'don't be afraid of change' and this had spurred my move to Dubai, away from almost all that was familiar, but one that had worked out very well. And, in all seriousness, other people had done it so why couldn't I? And so I did.

The first thing I did was to do what I was used to – gathering information about what I needed to know. I read books, pored over industry articles and CEO interviews, making notes of what needed to be done. There had to be a formula, or so I thought – incorporate a company, register a trademark, hire people, buy some fabric, contract with factories to manufacture some products and market them.

What I hadn't anticipated was the reality of tying it all together and with people in between. It dawned on me very quickly that analysing companies is one thing, starting and running them is a whole other ball game. The first part was easy – an online application to Companies House. Endeavour Clothing Ltd was born.

What I hadn't anticipated was the lawyers telling me that NASA had the rights to all things Endeavour. I needed a new name, one that not only captured the essence of the brand but also one that no one else had considered. It took some time but Rose & Willard (which means feminine and bold) finally surfaced and was perfect.

The problem now was that I was still in Dubai and had another two months before my visa expired, the tenants had vacated our London home and I could return.

Aware that I was no fashion designer, I knew I needed one. And where else to find one than London's Central Saint Martin's. Adverts went out, applications came flooding in and the interviews started. What I needed was someone who could creatively translate my commercial vision into reality. The challenge I faced was that most candidates simply saw me as a funding tool for their own aesthetic vision. And I didn't just need a designer, I needed a pattern cutter. Researching and reading about these roles had seemed simple enough but what I didn't understand was how I could test them at interview. I also realised that I needed
to acquire and understand a whole new industry vocabulary.

For the first time in a long time, I was lacking experience. After finally relocating permanently to London I believed I could properly focus and slot the various pieces into their respective places. I was fortunate to find a good studio with plenty of natural light and started ordering in equipment. While I busied myself with arranging this and organising the administration and budgets, I delegated to my first two staff the task of reviewing candidates as potential new team members. With hindsight I should have taken a much more proactive role in this as not all our hires proved to be the right ones although it was only as delays and errors occurred in our production line that this mistake transpired. What I needed was qualified, dedicated and capable staff, all hungry for the opportunity.

After a few months it became evident that such skills and talents weren't broadly reflected across the team. Aware from previous experience that even one weak member can undermine an entire team I decided to take decisive action. I was all too aware of managers who had stuck with bad hiring decisions in order to avoid the admission of having made that wrong selection in the first place.

What was new to me was actually being the person to tell another that they no longer had a job. Perfunctory was the only way to approach it. I had the rest of the team's jobs to consider. This all coincided with a delay to our launch. Understanding the practical implementation and realistic timetable of a critical path was unfamiliar territory for me. The pattern cutting took far too long. The ordering of our fabric choices was also hindered by our lack of scale versus the required minimum ordering thresholds imposed by a number of mills. And then there were the factories; aside from finding those we thought could deliver the appropriate quality, our order quantities again were often too low.

It was a new reality for me; coming from a place where requesting a meeting with the CEO of a multinational organisation had posed no problem to liaising with much smaller factories and mills for whom we were of little or no significance. What I needed to do was make myself, and my company, important. My familiarity with the clear demarcated lines of corporate culture inspired me to impose a high level of professionalism throughout my team and the way it worked. We would have structure, responsibility and accountability. No timetable, no cost and no task could be open-ended.

Interestingly this didn't transform me into some kind of dictator. Rather, the team responded positively. They actually valued the limits of the parameters within which they were now expected to operate. My belief that creative people respected and needed fluidity in their work has now been somewhat redrawn. Many react equally positively to a more formal framework.

Progressively the team was coming together. And for any new team member I decided to break with the traditional hiring approach. Working in the City I had seen first hand how the privilege of class and the networking opportunities that offers can propel a person's career. To my surprise I saw this reflected in the fashion industry where interestingly there is also a snobbery attached to luxury versus high street experience.

In order to secure an initial footing on the professional ladder any graduate's CV needs to include internships and at the correct establishments. The challenge for most aspiring, fashion-related graduates is that internships were, and to a large degree still are, unpaid. Indeed some do not even receive travel costs. Unless parental or some other funding can be sourced for costs of living during an internship the only option is to seek alternative paid work. Without internship experience industry doors are usually closed and so the less fortunate are faced with the dilemma of having to reluctantly opt out of fashion.

My working class background was certainly not one of privilege. Having my own company made me realise that I could either reinforce the status quo and take advantage of unpaid interns or change course. Despite the cost I opted for the latter. Not only that I chose to reject the traditional method of hiring. My previous experience of recruitment consultants and their general lack of understanding of transferable skills made me adamant that I wouldn't look for square pegs for square holes. What I wanted was to offer opportunities to people who could demonstrate sufficient ability and a strong appetite for the job regardless of their experience.

This led me to hire people who no recruitment consultant would likely ever have suggested; and these have been the best hiring decisions I have made. It has taken time but much of the foundations have now fallen into place.

I take an active role in every aspect and process of the business. Our critical paths run to order, we have an established set of suppliers and manufacturers with options on others and operate strictly within our ethical boundaries.

What I also needed to master was the marketing side of the business equation. Having once been the customer I have always felt a genuine understanding of the market I am aiming to serve. The challenge, however, has been in establishing and cultivating any relationship.

The British womenswear market is worth over £20bn per annum but is highly fragmented with even the largest players having less than 10% market share. Not surprisingly, and as evidenced by any magazine, the customer is swamped with advertising. The challenge I faced was how to stand out from this very busy crowd, a crowd which included brands with budgets multiple times larger than mine.

What I learned as an analyst was that it was futile to try to be better when my competition was already exceptional. What I learned was that I had to be not only the best that I could be but also different. Otherwise we get lost in the crowd; and the womenswear market is a very large, and often very slick, crowd. While I was sceptical at first I hired a PR firm. My first foray proved an incompatible pairing mostly I believe because their approach wasn't differentiated.

In my second search for the right PR firm I deliberately looked for something different. That is what I believe I have now found. A PR firm with an alternative approach and one which is open to any good idea has proven to open doors for us that we may never have knocked upon. So ultimately, while I have relied on my own resources, there are those of my team and the partners we have chosen that have set us on a path which I hope will be long and fruitful.

In terms of the advice I would offer to those considering the world of entrepreneurship there are of course words of caution:
- Set a timetable and then double it; most tasks take longer than expected. Entrepreneurs are usually natural optimists. They also need to be pragmatists.
- Calculate a budget and then double it. See above – time really is money.
- The boss, in any company, can never be anyone's friend. In a small company where informalities are more commonplace and where there is little or no formal hierarchy this can prove more personally demanding. For example, if the success of the business demands that a non-performing member of the team is replaced it can strain personal relations between the boss and the remaining team members.
- Free time will become a thing of the past; you will eat, live and breathe your business. Even when you're not at work, the business will likely be at the forefront of every thought.
- You have to be able to multi-task. No part of the business really operates in isolation and every part is always moving. To lose sight of one part can destabilise their entire chain. It is not the case that the entrepreneur needs to be able to undertake every task, rather they need to know whether each member of their team is delivering effectively and meeting deadlines. BUT, nothing is as rewarding as creating something of your own and seeing it come to life. I recall a chat with a friend once about my trepidation at trekking alone around China. Her response had been 'well, if you think like that you'll never do anything'.

Heidy Rehman

Heidy Rehman is the Founder and Managing Director of Rose & Willard, a British womenswear brand based in London. Heidy was born in Newcastle. She moved to London and studied Mathematics at Queen Mary & Westfield College, University of London, gaining a BSc (Hons) 2:1. She is a Fellow of the Association of Chartered & Certified Accountants. After stints at the Office for National Statistics and the Medical Defence Union she spent almost 14 years working as an equity research analyst for Citi. During her career as a stockbroker, Heidy covered a wide range of sectors in the UK, Pan Europe and MENA (Middle East & North Africa). She was ranked top analyst in two sectors for the last two years of her stockbroking career.

A PR agency success story

Charli Morgan - The Cult PR

Six years ago, I was getting thrown out of Robbie Williams's dressing room; spraying champers into Amy Winehouse's beehive to celebrate her ill-fated Blake Fielder-Civil engagement; replacing my carefully-researched George Clooney interview questions with a shame-free pitch to be his debut Mrs C and generally being a canape-chasing, nefarious ne'er-do-well on my showbiz Goss column at the Daily Star, which I secured at the age of 24.

I'd hungrily pursued Journalism since sproghood, when I'd churn out endless fanzines with Pritt Stick, battered typewriters and my dad's work printer. If you'd told me then, that I'd quit my beloved profession and would now be running a multi-award-winning, London PR agency, I'd have guffawed myself cross-eyed.

But that's exactly what happened and my experience on the other side of the PR fence has given us the unique insight to take on eyeball-bulgingly exciting clients and grow so quickly that I have whiplash.

I wrote for a veritable Pick 'n' Mix of titles, from 'respectable' publications like The Times, Telegraph and Daily Express to the weirder end of the newsagent's spectrum, like (the now-defunct) Bizarre Magazine, where I'd cover weddings between dwarves and giants or people who lived their lives as Manga characters. I also wrote 24/7 feeds at global news agency WENN and interviewed stars in my other guise as OK! Magazine TV's launch presenter.

I met fellow journalist, Matt Glass at the Daily Star. Like me, he had dealt with Blighty's myriad of PR agencies from the desks of a range of publications and was amazed by how lazy, unimaginative and unhelpful a majority of them were.

We saw the best and worst of PR from this enviable position and learnt what did and didn't work.

When the recession's shadow grew darker over the newspaper and magazine industry, our teams shrunk and we found ourselves writing more pages and rapidly taking on additional duties - features, news, events, interviews, splashes.

The most successful PRs understood the radical shift in our roles and helped us, by knowing our titles inside-out and providing content for specific sections, targeted to our readers and with the speed required to meet our tight deadlines. Obviously, this was mutually beneficial, providing their clients with publicity; making our jobs easier and earning our gratitude and increasing dependence on them, sometimes resulting in us running weaker stories, to promote their more challenging clients as a thank you.

The best agencies also understood that journalists have little time and are constantly invited to events and bombarded with tedious releases, so laziness is not an option. It was essential to put together snappy, original, exciting or newsworthy events, stunts and releases to get their attention.

The increased workload and dwindling staff numbers also meant that journalists couldn't get out as much to cover events, so the news often had to be brought to them or events worked around their schedules. And (alas) PRs could no longer rely on buying them long, boozy lunches as bribery for coverage, because writers simply didn't have the time and urgently needed a mountain of strong content to fill their growing page responsibilities.

Sadly, creative and proactive PRs were rare gems and the majority simply flooded everybody with the same, dreary releases, with no individually-tailored pitches or consideration about their story's suitability for the journalist or title. They compounded this, by following their ill-judged pitches with nagging calls and emails, inquiring whether the sports editor would be writing about the new, turkey-flavoured blancmange they were launching.

The recession also marked the beginning of the dark days of journalism, leading to redundancies, strikes and overworked teams. This was combined with the unfortunate impact of digital journalism's growth, which meant that more and more magazines and newspapers were shutting down.

A mixture of frustration at the PR industry's increasing laziness and the dawning realisation that Journalism's halcyon days were over, led Matt and I to an epiphany. We had the contacts, the intimate understanding of a newsroom and enviable experience on the other side of the media fence to set up the sort of PR agency that journalists like us desperately needed - this would guarantee success for our clients and in turn, our business.

I briefly worked at another PR agency, to understand what programmes and databases were used by the industry and to learn the procedures they followed, to employ at the agency we were secretly preparing, which we christened The Cult PR.

We were apprehensive about starting a new business during the recession, but it actually benefitted us, because companies were forced to save money by leaving the big, expensive agencies and coming to less costly, boutique agencies like ours, which had smaller overheads and more to prove.

Proving ourselves, amassing positive case studies and word-of-mouth endorsement to develop a strong roster was our initial challenge. Our first client was a fairly mundane docu-film, about the decline of the bee population. At that time, there was little interest in this issue and our newspaper backgrounds made us horribly aware of how tricky this would be to excite media interest.

The client had a non-existent budget for launch activity, so we convinced a fancy dress shop to loan us a bee costume; I hand-sewed a strip of material across the costume, emblazoned with the film's title - which I unpicked before returning - and we persuaded an actor friend to play the bee in a short film we made about a bee's last day on earth, ticking dreams off his bucket list.

Using our celebrity contacts from our time as journalists, we managed to convince Liam Gallagher to film a piece with our bee for free, which was an enormous coup. This was just days after Oasis split up, because Liam had cancelled their V Festival slot, claiming to have a sore throat - the pair have still not made up to this day.

Being a little squiffy, Liam threw his arm around our bee's shoulders and passionately pleaded to the camera: "Save the f*cking bees. You need honey for your Rolls Royce (voice) and without it, we're f*cked."

This footage - and subsequently, our 'bucket list bee' video - went viral and the image of Liam and our bee (complete with the film's title branded across his costume) filled the pages of the papers the following day. The story exploded, with NME naming it their favourite story of the year and The Guardian launching a satirical counter-campaign, for the bee to save Liam Gallagher.

This paved the way for us to place more serious features and news stories, exploring the issue of bees dying out and promoting the film and its findings in-depth, alongside interviews with the movie's creators.

This put us on the map and showed future clients that with some imagination, the right contacts and experience, you don't need a massive PR budget to create a major campaign. It also helped us prove that clients' advertising budgets were better spent on considered PR campaigns resulting in reams of editorial, which consumers actually engage with, rather than one piece of advertorial, which is flicked past.

However, while we had the PR skills and our roster quickly grew alongside our clients' publicity, neither of us had any previous experience or real knowledge of business, which was our biggest challenge. We have learned our business lessons the hard - and often, very costly - way, through harsh experience over the past six years.

For example, our first employee was a friend, who looked after in-house events for a big magazine. She joined our agency to head up our events arm and in less than three months, she had stolen £20,000 from us.

We had been far too trusting and naive and gave her too much freedom and power in a company we'd painstakingly worked so hard to build. We had allowed this to happen, by giving her unfettered and unquestioned access to our business accounts; allowing her to sign off contracts in The Cult's name; believing her excuses for the outgoings, due to our inexperience in that area, and naively failing to check up on her - even paying ourselves less to ensure she had a full wage when our funds mysteriously dropped.

We spent the following year in legal battles with her. She was finally found guilty - in both criminal and civil lawsuits - of fraud by false representation and sentenced to community service and a suspended prison sentence. We didn't realise how easy it could be to defraud a business and get it written off, until she declared herself bankrupt, meaning she only had to pay back a small amount.

We did, however, keep our hard-earned reputation intact and made it more difficult for her to defraud future businesses, by running prominent stories in the PR trade titles about the ongoing cases and her eventual, guilty verdict.

The £20,000 theft within such a short period in the business's early days, plus the legal costs and time spent fighting her in court put a significant strain on our agency and briefly set us back.

But we learnt an invaluable lesson and are now extremely scrupulous and cautious in business, ensuring that we have a meticulous understanding of our employee's actions and every element of our business. Our trust must be earned now and we don't allow friendships to cloud working relationships.

That isn't to say that you can't be friends with your workmates, after all, my fellow Director Matt isn't just my best friend... he's also my husband. Many people find the fact that I run a business with my husband bewildering, but it's all we've ever known. We met when we were working together on the paper and we've always been a strong partnership at work and home.

Our close relationship is an asset in our pitches and meetings, because we can read each other's subtle body language to ensure we're both on the same page in front of clients. We don't talk over each other and we know each other's strengths and weaknesses when pitching. We both have different roles and skills, which complement each other and avoids power struggles. And since we both have exactly the same Director roles, it's a perfectly equal relationship, which definitely helps - I suspect that it would be difficult to work with a partner if one had a more senior role than the other.

Due to the nature of our jobs, with bulging days and regular evening events, we'd never see each other if we worked separately. And the shared triumphs and sticky situations we've encountered building the business, as well as the extraordinary experiences and colourful characters we've met along the way have made us even closer and stronger as a married couple and as fellow Directors.

We do make sure that we keep work and home separate and many of our clients have no idea we're a couple. We prefer not to draw attention to our relationship status to maintain professionalism with clients and we also make sure we're Directors in the office, because we never want our workmates to feel like gooseberries or worry that they are in the middle of a domestic. The strong trust and mutual support in a marriage is also a powerful and vital element in a working relationship, which has proved invaluable to us.

We did make an error by forming a partnership of the business variety though, rather than becoming a limited company when we launched. We were advised to become a partnership at the beginning, for greater tax efficiency and flexibility. However, as we grew, we realised we'd enjoy greater credibility and trust from clients as a limited company as well as better tax benefits. And we became limited just in the nick of time, because - in what would have set a legal precedent, had she won - a Hollywood actress sued us over a story which ran in a host of papers and websites, involving one of our clients.

The journalists stood by the story, as many of them witnessed it themselves. And it was such an inoffensive detail in an overwhelmingly positive story, that their lawyers were baffled by her lawsuit and insisted that she didn't have a legal leg to stand on.

However, possibly knowing The Cult was a small agency, which had encouraged the story, her lawyers decided to sue us, in an unprecedented move. They appeared to be aware that unlike the papers, we lacked expensive legal support, which they hoped would mean we couldn't afford to fight their expensive lawyers, meaning that we'd fold and they'd win the case against all of the titles as a result.

The lawyers claimed she risked losing a multi-million pound deal, because of the story and sued us for an eye-watering sum. Had we still been a partnership, we would have personally been liable and if by some miracle, she'd won, we would have personally gone bankrupt. Fortunately, her lawyers backed down, so peace - and a decent night's sleep - were restored. Our company also became limited just in time, but the experience made us appreciate the importance of having a separate legal identity from your company, something we'd always pass on to start-ups.

One of our best business moves was to make a conscious decision not to limit ourselves by focussing solely on one area of PR, because this results in a narrow-minded and dull campaign, missing out on a wealth of PR opportunities and using the same, tired pool of contacts.

Instead, we represent a diverse and exciting roster of celebrities, brands, charities, fashion labels, events, theatre, art, films and venues.

Our clients complement and strengthen each other's campaigns and broaden our opportunities. Because we are dealing with a wide variety of contacts, so are privy to exciting, mutually beneficial opportunities, which we'd be unaware of if we were dealing with just one client speciality alone.

It also means that we approach each client in a more creative and open-minded way. And it's another reason why we have grown so quickly, since happy clients recommend us to their contacts, who are often in different industries.

Another large part of our journalism careers involved covering PR events, so this experience was invaluable to our agency. We remember how many events the world-weary and cynical journalists are invited to and ensure that ours are fun, newsworthy and original with strong media, celebrity and influencer guestlists; new or exciting venues; newsworthy entertainment; the right sponsors and media partners and carefully selected dates.

Our previous roles have provided us with invaluable insight into the delicate factors which can make or break a press event. For example, February is the worst month for media events, because the year's biggest bashes - the BAFTAS, London Fashion Week, Oscars, BRIT Awards etc - are crammed into the shortest month. So even if your event's date doesn't compete with one of these, if it's during this month, the papers will be saturated with pre or post-event press about them and the journalists/celebs will either be attending or recovering from them.

We also value the importance of applying your trade to your own business - who wants to book a web designer with a rubbish holding page or a hairdresser with split ends? Your company is the best advert for the skills of your business, so we ensure that we don't neglect our own PR needs.

We build case studies; put ourselves forward for awards; bolster our credibility and show our knowledge by putting ourselves forward to provide expert comment and opinion on relevant topics in the press; share trade stories about our wins and successes and enlist celebrities to endorse us.

This has led to significant, business-boosting coverage in titles like The Sun, which branded The Cult "one of the UK's top Three Event planners" in an interview spread exploring our events, like the two official end-of-tour parties we threw for Muse; or shutting Regent Street down for the London leg of our client Gumball 3000's rally; our Wireless Festival's VIP area; taking over the Thames for our Emmy-winning client Sea Shepherd's vast party across two ships or Lamborghini's star-studded phone launch.

As showbiz columnists, we spent our time earning the trust of celebrities, who are understandably wary of the media. This has proved invaluable for our current business and we consequently have an enviable network of celebrities and agents, who are far easier to work with as PRs than as journalists.

Celebrity endorsement is obviously a powerful and often essential tool for clients and ours have reaped the rewards from the diverse range of celebrities we have used for cross-promotional opportunities, from Cara Delevingne, Rihanna, Miley Cyrus and Benedict Cumberbatch (who we made regulars at our venue, Cirque le Soir) to Kate Moss (who we dressed in our client Jess Eaton's Roadkill Couture range) Sir Sean Connery, Pierce Brosnan, Sir Mick Jagger, Pamela Anderson and Daryl Hannah (our Sea Shepherd ambassadors) Elle MacPherson and Vanessa Hudgens (who promoted and designed Hot Tuna collections) and Jonathan Ross, who has supported a host of our projects, from Gumball to our Lamborghini launch and The Library member's club opening, among many other personalities over the years.

Your own business really is your baby, with endless sacrifices, sleepless nights, responsibilities and hard work. Nobody will ever love your baby as much as you do, so I always remind myself not to have unfair and unrealistic expectations of my employees. They can hand the baby back at the end of the day, while I must take it home.

But they will also never understand the tremendous sense of reward, pride, achievement and fulfilment that you have from your own baby... even if you have to clean up its unsavoury mess from time-to-time.

Charli Morgan

Charli Morgan, 33, co-founded multi-award-winning agency The Cult PR nearly six years ago, after a decade on the other side of the media fence, which saw her secure her own national newspaper column by the age of 24; become OK! TV's launch presenter and write for Britain's biggest titles, including The Times, Telegraph, Daily Express and Daily Star.

The Cult's diverse roster of brands, celebrities, venues, films, charities and events has yielded greater opportunities and seen them work with some of the world's biggest names from Cara Delevingne, Kate Moss, Benedict Cumberbatch and Miley Cyrus to Simon Cowell, Princesses Beatrice and Stephen Fry.

The agency has also worked on ambitious campaigns for some of the world's biggest brands including Cadbury's, Ikea, Stella Artois, Honda, Lamborghini Antares, ShortList, Stylist, 888 and Isak.

The Making of a True Entrepreneur: From Scratch to Success
Mike O'Hagan - MiniMovers

"Necessity is the mother of invention, but the birth of an entrepreneur requires more than necessity; it requires a great dream, unwaivering determination to survive, and an unquenchable thirst for improvement. From an almost empty pocket and a dream of being my own boss, I have managed to learn a lot of things about entrepreneurship including the fact that when one decides to be his own boss, scaling up should be a part of your plan starting day one."

At the age of 28, because I wanted to "be my own boss", with a few hundred dollars I started my first "real" business: buying and selling secondhand furniture. I have watched dealers at an auction and simply thought it that looked like an easy way to make a buck. I had no idea what I was doing. A friend in the industry gave me guiding advice: "You work on 100% mark up. You buy it for less than it's worth and you sell it for what it's worth". Move on stale stock. His final word – if you don't know, go low. That was my entire education on how the industry works.

I started by buying at auctions and selling by advertising. Although I discovered this was not highly profitable, within a few months I managed to generate enough cash and confidence for me to rent a shop and stock it. The shop has been empty for over a year so the owner freely agreed to a 3-month rent free period in exchange for a longer rent. This effectively funded my start-up. Start from where you are "at" – avoid borrowing and work a win-win solution.

The shop was located on a corner and was exposed to a very high traffic volume. I figured selling would be dependent on attracting the passing traffic. I had no budget for signage so I cut the letters for my signs "Cheap Secondhand Furniture" out of polyurethane foam, painted them fluorescent orange and glued them high up in full view on a frontage that I had painted jet black. To say it was tacky is an understatement, but it really stood out. From the moment we opened the doors we were inundated in customers, nearly all passed comments about the signage. A shop full of customers commenting about your terrible looking signage is better than an empty shop with no comments. STAND OUT – Be noticed.

Later, when we had other shops, this first shop on the very busy road always turned over at least 4 times than our other shops, at double the rent. I will always pay double the price for exposure to traffic that gives me 4 times the turnover anytime.

I was a great secondhand dealer. I quickly discovered poor people had to get as much as they could from the items so they were a bad source of buying for me, and rich people just wanted to get rid of it and they really didn't care. Mixed into these two markets were a lot of people who simply didn't know the value of their stuff, so they accept any price I offered them. A few individuals were negotiators who would argue at any price, while the rest accepted what I offered. I became skillful at chatting and assessing their "type" before offering them my price. *Understand how the people you are dealing with "think".*

The secret to secondhand dealing was in buying. You make your profit when you buy. The cheaper you could get it, the more you were assured of a good profit. I became really focused on how to buy lots of easy to sell things. We discovered that good buying came from small lineage adverts we placed in newspapers. A typical advert read like this: "Cash paid on the spot for furniture Ph. XXXXXX 7 days". We started with one advert and it worked. It didn't take me long to work out that I could run multiple adverts in the same section with different phone numbers. We used this method to dominate the "wanted to buy" section of nearly every newspaper in our city. Understand where your profit comes from. *Find something that works and do it more.* Today, we are doing the same with different websites.

In the belief that the one call you missed was always the biggest opportunity, we answered the phones 24 hours a day. We ended up with a row of 4 different colored phones. As a seller, we called each one of the leads and every time, we would change our voice and the type of questions. We could both judge how desperate they were to sell and sometimes even get the opportunity to "quote against ourselves" as some phoned every advert in the paper. Interestingly, we also learned what words worked and what didn't. We kept careful counts of both call volumes and outcomes for each type of advertisement we ran. We applied this same thinking to the Yellow Pages book later - multiple adverts in the same section with different wording and different phone numbers etc.
 NEVER miss an opportunity. *Today, we treat email and live chat as we treat phone calls. Build a machine that feeds the profit component of your business – systemise and duplicate to scale it up. OWN your market.*

We also fairly quickly worked out that some things sell and some do not. For example, in those days, wardrobes were bad sellers. They were big so they took up valuable space and simply sat there and were never sold. This led to us to perfecting on the phone assessing of the quality of the "buy". We looked for the type of seller and the saleability of the goods. *Target what has profit.*

Later, when our success was noticed, many started setting up similar shops very close to us. There was a prevailing theory that "as we were not selling the same goods, we were not directly competing". There was a degree of logic to this, however, they all over looked the secret to the Secondhand business "how to buy enough saleable things – at the right price". New dealers were a pain because they came in and started paying too much for things. This, in turn, really rocked our profit. We overcame this by sending them to any sellers we came across who had either unsaleable goods or clearly knew the value of the item and wanted too much for their things. It was amazing to watch this strategy at play. The new shop owner, acting all friendly, would boldly come into our shop and introduce themselves – they always gave their spiel around not competing with us. They would even ask where we bought things from, often saying they used the auctions – a buying source we learned was not good. We would say that we are always being offered lots of stuff and if they liked, we could send some buying their way. Then, every time a bad buy came in on the phones, we would be all helpful, explaining we were "full" and giving them the new shop's number. We watched trader after trader come in and buy all the stuff that doesn't sell, fill up their shops and use up their buying cash, then go broke. Time after time, they would come back, all friendly, and explain how bad their sales were and ask if we would buy their stock. We sent them to the auctions. They never twigged that we had "out-competed" them in business. *Beware of the helping hand and understand how a business works before competing with someone. Copying is competing, and unless you really know your stuff, you are heading for a train crash.*

Of course, at the start, I had no idea what things were worth so I applied the "don't know, go low" rule. I would arrive back at my shop with all sorts of neat things that I had paid very little for. My two helpers did the selling. They would argue between themselves and often agree my price was silly and sell the item for many times what I paid for it. I learned to separate buying from the selling. I figured out how to assess the type of sellers, as well as the probable knowledge of the seller about value of the items, and apply that to what I paid. *See the big picture of how it all works.*

My helpers worked the retail tricks. Put the best out front, based on in either attractiveness or price, to lure them in. Always display the prices and never ever give discount or lower a price if asked. If it's worth that, that's what it's worth. The exception was when we had decided an item wasn't selling, so we would heavily discount it to clear it out and make room for something that was going to give us profit. Move on from bad deals.

Over a period of 6 years, I grew this business to 3 shops. I had become involved in getting the government to change the legislation that regulated the industry. I had a nice leased car and had started paying off a house. I belonged to the local Chamber of Commerce. To everyone, I was "successful". Certainly, we made a profit every year and it has increased incrementally every year.

The problem was the fact that I was personally working 7 days a week and earning pretty well what my employees were earning for their 40 hour week's work. This has to be close to the definition of "stupidity". *What you "see" is hardly ever what it really is.*

So many of us today are trapped into "work hard" thinking and end up in this space. We proudly work hard in our businesses, not letting anyone near "what we do" as we want it done perfectly. *Learn to delegate – it's an acquired skill.*

At the age of 34, for the first time in my life, I started to think about what I really want in life. I, Mike O'Hagan, the individual. Sure, I understand I have my family and all other big things to think about – but here I was, working 90+ hours a week, earning pretty much the same as my employees who were working just 40 hours a week. This wasn't really helping anyone. *Think about where you really want to be in life.*

One night, while watching TV, I suddenly realised my "desires". I was yearning for a big house, a fast car and a big boat, with the jet-setting lifestyle to go with it.

As I thought this through, I realised that I need to feed the lifestyle I dreamed of. I needed two things:

1. A bucket load of cash coming in every week. Like $20,000 to $40,000 a WEEK.

AND

2. The freedom to select HOW I SPEND MY TIME.

Many of us understand the money thing, while very few focus on the "time" issue.

I realised that employment on wages was never going to fund my desires, nor allow me to enjoy the life I wanted. I needed a bigger business. I became very focused on the outcome – my lifestyle.

I increased my learning about business. I attended every business convention, listened motivational speakers and read all the business books I can get my hands on. One day, one speaker said, "You can own a job or a business. If you have to, it's a job – if it works for you, it's a business". It's was then I realised the power of scaling up. *It's in your "mindset".*

I had read the McDonald's stories and was intrigued by systemising and duplicating.

I had tried, many times, to get an employee to be a buyer. However, since it's not their money they were using to buy items for the company's stocks, they were never as "mean" or as assertive as I was. I realised this would stop me from duplicating this business. In short, I could teach people how to sell, but could not teach them how to buy. Funny thing is they were essentially the same skill. Selling was all about stroking an item and telling people why it was wonderful, buying was about kicking something and saying it's not worth much.

I came to a decision to find another business. Something lots of people wanted, products that there was a demand for (so it's easy to sell), something I could develop as a competitive advantage around that wasn't under threat from technology or society changes, and that something should have the potential of being systemised and duplicated. I actually developed an "assessment list" and used it to consider each of the opportunities I noticed. Sometimes the "use by date" is up, and you need to move on.

On a 1 to 2-year period, I concocted all sorts of ideas. Most of those ideas are things I was able to convince myself wouldn't work. I once even did a course in building a business plan, only to convince myself on paper that the idea was unviable.

One day, by accident, a secondhand business customer had been let down by a traditional moving company and needed to move to a new house - right then. I used a truck and two mates to address her problem. Out of this fell an idea that the home moving services during those days (30 years ago), that usually involved big companies sending a salesperson out and giving a fixed price quotation even if the customer was just moving next door, were not the best solution for the customers. I realised that it was much cheaper to get rid of the salespeople, offer the services on the phone, and give price quotations based on hourly rate charges. Booking on the phone also meant I could do lots of moves anywhere.

It's important to understand that this business started from day one with the sole intention to grow me into a lifestyle. Every thought and plan was around scaling it up. I mentor lots of business owners today - rarely do I find anyone with the determination needed to really ramp up the business.

Initially, I played with the market demand by running advertisements. We were inundated with calls. A demand existed. *Test test test.*

We had the truck and communication system – we had the basics needed for a moving business. It was that simple. Not into risk, I kept the secondhand shops. They feed my family. We took no profit from the moving business for a few years, pouring everything back into the business to feed growth.

Later, we sold the second hand business, but only after viability and profitability of the moving business was well proven.

Developing my moving business became a matter of trial and error. Again, I was starting from next to nothing, with no idea of how the industry worked. In hindsight, this became a major advantage. Because we didn't know how it all worked, we used every experience (mostly bad) to learn from. We used common-sense for solutions, often inventing new ways – very disruptive ways - to service people wanting to move a short distance. *Try lots of things – most don't work – do more of what works.*

The first employees were "experienced" and they taught us the workmanship skills we needed.

After the business grew to owning about 2-3 trucks, it was apparent we had something in what we were doing. Customers were starting to rave about the simplicity and quality of our services. Word of mouth referral started driving more work.

At this point, I came across some university students doing MBAs who needed real projects to conduct market research. They liked my ideas and their services were free.

This suited my needs. Their market research showed a massive opportunity. The traditional services marketed to longer distance, interstate, overseas, and the corporate markets. 95% of the people relocating moved less than 15 kilometres.
In short, the "industry" targeted 5% of the market and there was no specialised solution (at that stage) for the needs of the 95%. Of this market segment, 78% moved themselves with the industry servicing 12%. The missing 10% fell between the research cracks. To me, my competitor became "people moving themselves". *Avoid assuming – try to work with facts.*

With this in mind, we developed marketing strategies that grew the work. We hired more people and then got more trucks. Over and over. There was never a shortage of work.

Buying trucks became an interesting problem. I was concerned with borrowing money. By accident, I met a guy who owned a truck but was personally in financial trouble. He owed more on the truck than what it was worth and he had no work for it. No income and unable to sell, he was in trouble. I hired the truck (only no workers) on an hourly rate – we had a second truck. Without borrowing a cent, without risking much, we built this business to 18 trucks WITHOUT buying any equipment. I sought out little operators in trouble and hired their equipment. The cashflow from this allowed them to meet their payments and all was happy. Yes you can start with very little money – you just need to think outside the box.

Workers to service the customers was another issue. The early employees kept telling me that we were doing lots of things wrong. My focus of building a growth model was clashing with the way they were used to this industry working. Avoid the nay-sayers.

We did flaunt with subcontracting for a bit but discovered these guys really wanted to own their own business. So, after we taught them, they left us and became competitors. We also discovered hiring "experienced" movers has issues, as many were not with their previous employer for a reason – which we usually discovered a few months after starting with us. When we targeted inexperienced people and developed an effective training, the business literally took off.

I'm often asked how we find such great people working for us. My answer is "we create them". Today, we will hire no one from the industry, we will not even hire anyone with a truck driver's license. We speed train and license every mover we have.

My approach to the systemising processes was also creative. From day one, I was aware we needed to know exactly what our people were up to. Well before we needed, we started building our own computerised operating system. This have been a continuous project for nearly 20 years. It's all done in-house. From the moment a customer contacts us by phone or through the internet and from the moment a potential employee contacts us through all the booking and training process, to arriving and completing the services; every aspect is recorded including workmanship quality. The result is: we can instantly see our best and worst employees, also the best performing depots and areas. Problems are highlighted and actions can be taken very quickly. *Don't lose sight of the end goal.*

Our focus is to lead the industry. We don't look at others, we benchmark against our past performances continually improving.

My role is to find new better ideas. We were the first to put our prices online. We introduced an iron clad workmanship guarantee and some amazing processes to ensure we stand by this. *Innovators lead the market – copycats follow.*

To me, the growth journey have been about balancing among the following: marketing for new customers, hiring and retraining better workers, and adding service upgrades as well as innovative solutions to add further value.

Like most service businesses, the key to growth comes from doing a great job. Wowed customers rave about you and tell others. 78% (we always counted) of our work comes from our previous customers and referrals. Any competitor who copied our advertising quickly discovered it didn't work as well in the service sector. In fact, most of the 78% didn't call anyone else – just us. Try competing with that – many copycats have and failed.

Missing from this is financial control. I have to admit I suck in this area. I rely on others to take care of the compliance stuff. The actual steering of the business comes from weekly management reports. We use graphs to show performance and trends. The monthly P&Ls are useless as a management tool. Same with budgets. I've never been good at guessing the future, but I know exactly how a stack of indicators historically has been. We set these indicators as the benchmarks and target improving continuously. You cannot count money until - a customers has been found, a service provided and the customer has paid.

As our business peak, we moved over 1000 moves A WEEK in our founding city. We had 500 employees and today operate in 6 Australian cities.

We find planning and executing to the plan does NOT work for us. My strategy is to try lots of things (often at the same time) in an affordable way, carefully measure the results, be relaxed with the fact most of which don't work; but when we discover something that works, we adopt, systemise and duplicate.

Today, the shareholding remains in my family. Whilst still deriving a good income from it, I have moved on and diversified. We now own 6 businesses in 4 countries – but that's another story. I have a passion for giving back. It comes from an absolute belief I have that the future of my home country can only come from the entrepreneurs it develops. And it's doing a bad job at developing entrepreneurs. It does a great job at developing "managers" who work in their business like I was: working 90+ hours a week achieving the goal I had set "to be my own boss".

What's holding most of you back are your beliefs. You have convinced yourself that all the common thought obstacles are real - like you need money to make money, business is too risky, or if you are in a business, you either won't let go and delegate, or your business model is flawed and you refuse to change. You end up where you aim. I mentor many. In my opinion, MOST AIM TOO LOW.

Mike O'Hagan' today lives in Manila where he teaches potential and existing entrepreneurs where the new opportunities are and how to offshore office processes via www.MikesManilaTours.com

Mike O'Hagan

Mike O'Hagan is a Serial Entrepreneur with over 30 years of experience in bootstrapping start-ups. With $200 and a Ute, he started a unique short distance furniture removal business called MiniMovers. Today, MiniMovers operates in 6 Australian cities and employs over 400 people. He remains the founder/owner and is now involved in 6 other businesses operating in 4 countries.

In 2007, Mike completed a 3-year Masters Program in Entrepreneurship at MIT Boston USA. He also sits on several boards in 3 Countries. Mike also served a term as a Commissioner on the FairPay Commission, charged with the responsibility of setting all Australia's minimum pays. Mike can be contacted via www.ohagan.com.au or LinkedIn

LEARN THE BEST WAY TO FIND, ENGAGE, AND MANAGE
$100 A-WEEK WORKERS
3-Day Business Learning and Global Sourcing Tour
with Mike O'Hagan
MikesManilaTours.com
Getting business right in the Philippines

Houston We Have a Product

Melissa Reed - Packable Pails

Growing up I always thought I would be a school teacher. The profession ran in my family and I liked that my mom was home for holidays, summer breaks etc. Fast forward 20 some years and I am thrilled to be known as the mother inventor, momentrpreneur or whatever the fad title is to have created Packable Pails. How do you take a sketch on a napkin to an actual product that sits on the shelves of national retailers? Well I didn't know the answer either and never intended to go down that career path. As a healthcare administrator I had no knowledge or experience on how to design and manufacturer consumer products. However, I did have some limited experience with website and logo design and marketing. My journey was one filled with failures and success, but also support and determination to step out of the box and invent, manufacturer, distribute and market an idea inspired by a little boy I am proud to call my son.

I grew up in a small Iowa town that my parents still live in today. It is one of those towns that you are not from regardless of how long you live there if you can't attach the phrase born and raised. I give my parents all the credit for instilling in me that I was able to do anything that I wanted growing up, there were no glass ceilings and working hard leads to success. Both of my parents got up early, always went to work, gave above and beyond performances and 100% company loyalty.

In my childhood unlike the kids today, you didn't take trips to Europe, Mexico or other places we saw in the National Geographic magazines. Vacations typically included the family loading up in the "nice" vehicle and traveling within a 4 hour radius to a water or adventure park. As an adult I had a real desire to see the United States, go on cruises, and take a weekend trip to Vegas etc. My parents always comment how lucky my son is having by age 5 traveled to New York City, Martha's Vineyard, Florida several times, Disney cruise etc. However, I really just saw it as instilling that sense of adventure and seeing the United States. It was on one of these trips that the idea for Packable Pails was conceived.

Anytime I talk to my parents about Packable Pails, my mom brings up the story of my early invention years. When I was in 3rd grade it was protocol to participate in the school Invention Convention. In 1985, as a 3rd grader consumed by the trends of small town popularity contests it did not interest me! However, as a prideful student and the heavily weighted grade attached to the assignment, I submitted a product I named Little Drippers. The product was a plate you could insert a Popsicle into to avoid getting your hands sticky when it melted. Interestingly enough a better version of my product is actually available in retail today. Who knew at such a young age I had a practical solution to a real life problem! (See the picture of me at the Invention Convention in 3rd Grade).

The Wonderful World Wide Web

Fast forward a few years later, getting married and becoming a mother and I had settled into a routine of work, dinner and going to bed by 8 pm. One night while surfing the internet I found a deal I couldn't resist! Our family never really planned going to Myrtle Beach, however the inspiration for my product and company resulted of this impromptu trip.
My husband, young son and I thoroughly enjoyed going to the beach. Living in Iowa, the seashells, salt water and sand in your feet is hard to resist. We had prepared to hit the beach right after our flight. One bag was packed with towels, sunscreen, my swim cap and everything else we would need for a fun day at the beach. When we arrived, I laid out my beach towel, took off my tank top and was ready to relax. Within minutes my son after looking around and observing the other kids asked for some toys to play in the sand. I sat up and looked around to see nothing but kids playing with beach pails and rakes. I for the first time in my life was speechless. How did I forget this item?
Later in the trip walking along the boardwalk there are many large beach stores offering anything from a giant seashell to a bikini declaring your membership as a part of the Myrtle Beach Lifeguard crew. However

everywhere I looked, all the retailers offered a large plastic beach pail that hung disorganized from the racks and had no way of making it from your vacation spot to your home. What a waste!

When it was time to head home, my son was sad that he has to leave his beach pail behind. However, there was no way it would fit in the suitcase and I certainly wasn't going to claim it as my carry on! After struggling to get my son to agree to leave it behind. The beach pail represented a waste of money and time. On the plane ride home I thought about all the trips we had been on, all the times we could have and will in the future be able to use a product like Packable Pails.

The First Step
I had worked in the arena of long term care for 15 plus years and worked with several companies that were opening new buildings. One of the first tasks was to come up with a name and secure the website domain. After playing with the words, I came up with the product name. I was thrilled when searching for available domains that www.packablepails.com was available. Selecting a product name with an available domain is inexpensive. However, it is not something you want to wait and try to obtain later. The cost of purchasing registered domains can be astronomical. I remember working for a company in the past and searching for a company name on a website that allowed you to purchase domains. I decided not to go ahead with the purchase and research a few days later. That domain was no longer available, but was available for sale for the mere price of $10,000! The entire name of the project, logos etc. had to be changed. A costly mistake for a rookie.

My background had also given some limited experience with logo development. Growing up I have always liked starfish. When we would visit an aquarium the seahorses and starfish were always my favorite. Developing a logo can be very expensive or very inexpensive depending on the route you go. Many companies online offer logo development for less than $100.00. Initially I was unsure I would even be able to get the product made and opted for an inexpensive route that I eventually sought Trademark protection for. The online logo design company I chose had a stock image of a starfish, I added the company name I had chosen and downloaded the logo.

Confidentiality Agreements, Provisional Patent, Design and Utility Patents
The next step was to find a factory that could make my product, but in small numbers to start with. Many companies required initial product orders of 10,000 or more. Financially it was not feasible for me to order this many at one time, nor did I want to send up with a lifetime supply of a product that didn't sell. I knew I need a mould and initially kept spelling it mold, that is how unschooled I was in the arena of product development. I was concerned about describing my product idea to companies to get a bid. After obtaining a confidential non-disclosure agreement merely off the internet and having all potential manufacturers sign it I sent my hand sketched product design along with several actual product pictures that I cut and pasted. I wanted to make sure that my idea was protected at least to the extent possible in the development stage.

Not Made in the USA
I had ever intention to get my product manufactured in the United States. Several estimates from US manufacturers as well as the required initial quantities made it unrealistic to pursue. Alibaba, which is an online list of overseas manufacturers, connected me with several companies that were willing to attempt the project on my small scale.
In the time I was establishing the relationships with possible manufacturers, I did a lot of online research on provisional patents, design and utility patents. I needed to protect my idea, but yet was unsure of the ability to take my design from a scrap of paper to reality. I opted for the less expensive provisional patent, giving me essentially one year to make a decision and purse a design patent

Initial quotes estimated the mould to cost between $1,500 to $10,000. Unfortunately, I had not spent the last 5 years saving my money to start my own company nor wanted to put this idea on the shelf and wait. With the unknown reality of actually making a product that worked, fear of being ripped off and other unknowns, I agreed on a mould fee of $2,000 with half of it being paid via Paypal. Although the protection is limited, utilizing Paypal gave me a small feeling of security. I told myself that I had done my homework but I had to be okay to lose the money, there were no guarantees.

Anyone that knows me in my professional or personal life is aware that patient is a virtue I was simply do not possess. I paid my deposit and anticipated waiting a few days to see the end product. However, unlike a Jell-O mold that takes a few hours, a product mould takes considerable time. From a CAD drawing, making the mould and testing it along with the unknown holiday schedule of the Chinese culture to me including the Chinese New Year which unlike the United States is just not a one day holiday and the Dragon Boat Festival, a few days turned into a few months.

The next obstacle was selecting the colors for the product. Silicone and plastic products are manufactured in colors from a Pantone chart consisting of more than 3,000 options. Did you know each year trending Pantone colors and even the Pantone color of the year are selected? After choosing more than a dozen colors the manufacturer was contacted with our selections. Unfortunately, they required a minimum of 1000 pails per color choice. Our initial budget had been set to purchase 500 to1000 products in total, eliminating our choices to just one color. Orange was selected for the first product run to match our company logo and as sales grew the additional colors yellow, blue and pink were added.

Houston We Have a Product
The first few samples were presented via Skype and amounted to a pail that would not collapse. After many attempts the product finally appeared to work and samples were sent for my review. Again disappointment was felt when the samples either did not function properly or were so thin the silicone would split. Further insult was added when I looked at the manufacturer's website to see my product being advertised as available for purchase! After several harsh emails to the manufacturer it was removed.

The final samples sent several months later. The first person I showed my product to asked why the company name wasn't imprinted on the product somewhere. I had not even thought of that, but they were right. After you removed my cardboard tag, the identity of the product was gone. Another change to the mould and additional time and money, I had our company name imprinted on the product.

Up to this point shipping consisted of one or two samples and all transactions had been done via air. To pay for my first 1000 pails, air shipping was much more than I anticipated. To ship via seas is more affordable, but the timeframe is much longer. The dilemma quickly became fast shipping vs. the cost of shipping. I needed samples to show companies and agreed to shipping via air 100 products and the other 900 shipping via sea cargo and arriving approximately 45 days later!

With my product in hand, I needed to get it in front of buyers and get the purchase orders streaming in. Contacting a buyer for any companies, but especially a large box store retailer is not as simple as sending out a quick email or picking up the phone. A mixture of attending trade shows, sending out emails, flyers and making phone calls eventually paid off when an email was received from a buyer with 1800 stores! The biggest break was after only a few months of launching the product to have it featured on a National Television show. After the quick free 30 second National spotlight all inventory was sold out. This attention was followed by other national media, every local media outlet and buyers contacting us directly to purchase our product. Companies like HARO-Help a Reporter Out, Sourcebottle and Pitchrate will actually connect you with media outlets looking for your product type and give you a free platform to pitch your product.

Don't underestimate the value of virtual networking. With the ever popular social media outlets the ability to contact potential customers and companies is easier than ever. Many of our vendor contacts came from social networking and led to large volume accounts. Cross market and collaborate with other vendors by offering contests, discounts, freebies or other promotions to create awareness about your brand and piggyback off other products. Another option is to market directly to industry organizations such as the Zoo and Aquarium Group (ZAG), Hospital Gift Shop Associations etc. that allow you to connect to large markets cost effectively with one effort.

 My journey is nowhere close to being over. My experience has only given me the drive to continue and make my one product into a product line. Additional products are under development and I can honestly say my life is now a dream come true.

Melissa Reed

Success Coach for New Coaches
Jessica Nazarali - jessicanazarali.com

Back when I was working in the corporate world, I day-dreamed of quitting my job and creating my own company. I knew I wasn't cut out for the corporate grind forever. Although working in HR recruiting gave me valuable experience, I wanted to travel, I wanted to have a family eventually, I wanted to work at four in the morning when I needed to, and I wanted to take long lunches with girl friends when I could.

So in 2011, while still working nine to five, I started a blog on healthy living and eating. I was blogging on nights and weekends and I was completely clueless for a while. I didn't even tell anyone about it for three months!

I thought that surely, if I produced good content and was consistent, I'd somehow work out a way to get paid and be able to quit my job. I really didn't give revenue generating any thought and hoped it would all just work itself out.

Despite my lack of a business plan, within a year, I had built a huge following and I absolutely loved connecting with my readers, writing, and photo documenting. I also loved the freedom of getting to make every major decision, as well as choose every little detail. It was a taste of what I wanted full time, but the reality was I worked night and day, and I knew I couldn't do it forever. In addition to being headed toward burnout, my head wasn't fully in either game.

Worst of all, I was working two jobs, and one of them paid nothing.

Truthfully, I would daydream far too often that I would be discovered by Kim Kardashian just like Mastin Kipp from The Daily Love was.

I mean, surely, it wouldn't take that long to be discovered by someone who could crown me as an authority, right?

Surprise, surprise...I'm still waiting on the day for that to happen, so it's a good thing I stopped waiting for someone else to choose me, because being discovered by Kim Kardashian isn't a business plan.

Since my blog had become popular, I had a few other bloggers approach me, asking for advice on how to do the same with their blogs. In the process of helping them, I realised blogging wasn't going to be the solution to my desire to quit my job. It was merely the catalyst.

What I discovered was that I loved the process of coaching these women, plus the satisfaction from knowing I was making a difference in their lives. Moreover, I realised my true passion and calling was coaching, not blogging.

At first, I thought I would become a health coach. After all, that was the focus of my blog, which was still thriving, and I had even opened an online health food store, so it all seemed very synergistic. But after working with a couple of clients, I realised quickly that while I loved health and wellness, coaching on those specialties wasn't my gift or desire.

Thinking back to what I had found so gratifying about working with women trying to be successful as bloggers, I realised it was seeing them make the same mistakes I had made when I started out and being able to guide them to a place where they understood a better path – without feeling like a failure for doing so.

Like them, I had frequently felt as though I wasn't good enough. With my blog, I had thought, surely, it was not good enough to get as many fans as more established blogs. Then I saw how wrong that was. I did grow a list of thousands, just like many blogs that had been around for twice as long.

Even after that, surely, I was not good enough as an entrepreneur to make my blog truly profitable. Surely, I was not good enough to quit my day job, make it on my own, and replace my current salary.

When I started working with clients, surely, I was not good enough to make it as a coach. This was especially true when I started comparing myself to other coaches who had been coaching for longer. It was a vicious cycle because I could in no way compete with coaches who had years and years of experience when I was just starting out.

It wasn't until I saw my clients in the same vicious cycle that I decided we no longer needed to compete and compare. All we needed was to be ourselves. That's the mode in which we can best attract the right clients and opportunities.

Looking back, it's easy to see now that I was the only thing standing in my way each time I thought that, surely, I wasn't good enough. Fortunately, I didn't let that stop me for long.

At eight in the evening on New Year's Eve 2013, after months of tossing and turning over whether or not I was ready, I invested in my own business in a way I never had before. I hired a coach I had admired for a while. I was nervous. It seemed too expensive. I wasn't sure I needed another program or more training. I was already a qualified coach who was gaining more experience everyday, after all.

However, something told me to take the plunge. So I put my credit card down and prayed that I made the right decision.

I knew immediately when the program started that I had. My business coach was instrumental in providing clarity about my value. Without her, I might still be trading beauty therapies for my coaching services, as well as feeling not good enough for every new opportunity that came along.

Over the next two months, I learned not only about how to become a masterful coach and businesswoman but also how to replace my current salary.

First, that meant getting really clear on my business model. If I learned one thing during that time, it was that the more specific I was about who I am and what I do best, the more success that would bring me. I perfected my brand, built a team to support the business, and started developing my products.

At the same time that I honed my business model and branding, I didn't wait to start getting clients. Not holding out for perfection, I told as many people as possible about my business. I learned that lesson the first time around with my blog, and yet it was still surprising how well it worked. Potential clients came out of the woodwork to start working with me.

Doing so brought out another lesson I needed to learn. Being a public figure, even on a small scale, means putting yourself out there on all levels. I was doing photo shoots, writing a lot of new content, and seeing my personality reflected in my branding and website. I had to come to terms with the fact that I would be judged. Working past that insecurity was freeing. As long as my business was a true reflection of who I am, I no longer cared what others thought.

That proved challenging for a few friends and family members who tried giving me advice. While they thought they were being helpful, their advice would have held me back. Looking back though, I know they were only reflecting my own lack of confidence. Once I projected self assurance about the actions I was taking toward my thoroughly thought out business plans, they were fully supportive.

So by the end of that February, only two months after hiring a coach, I finally achieved my long-held dream. I quit my day job and was working on my own full time with an achievable plan to replace my salary (and then some).

After many months of juggling both the corporate world and my increasingly successful coaching business, focusing on only the latter was liberating and exhilarating.

Of course, I was still working incredibly hard, but it was that much more rewarding being the captain of my own ship.

My love of writing had shifted subject matter since my blogger days, but if anything, as a coach I had more writing to do than ever before. I also discovered a new love – recording radio shows and training calls. I never would have known I was even interested in it if I hadn't gone all in on my dream.

Perhaps the best part was that once I quit my day job, I had the freedom to travel the world and work from anywhere. In my first year of working for myself full time, I traveled a total of two full months to beautiful and exotic locations around the world including Paris, Bali, and Miami.

At the same time, I earned $257,234 from selling high end coaching services and working with a limited number of select clients. I love that I can serve as a living example for my clients that coaching can be a full-time business and replace the salary from their careers. *Who needs Kim Kardashian?*

If you had told me back while I was tossing and turning that this would be my life now, I wouldn't have believed you. Back then, I still had a lot of work to do; not only on my business but also on myself. Looking back, I know all of my fears about money, my resume, and putting myself out there were holding me back, but not one of them was accurate.

Instead, I took on a new mantra… No matter what.

Instead of waiting around for things to happen to me, I dropped all of the excuses. I decided I was going to make it happen, no matter what. It's too easy to believe that a perceived lack of money, education, time, experience, or qualifications is justification for not following dreams. Once I stopped limiting myself when it came to money and success, it changed everything.

No matter what, I decided I would stay out of my own way. I would no longer let insecurities about putting myself out there, and even sharing vulnerabilities like my Kim Kardashian business plan, stop me from going after what I wanted. In fact, sharing vulnerabilities has been one of the pieces of feedback that women consistently give me about why they decided to work with me.

No matter what, I would be me. I built a business that no one else could ever build because it's so uniquely personal. I stopped doubting that I was good enough and I embraced the fact that I have made just about every mistake when it comes to finding coaching clients because now that I'm out on the other end, I know what works and what doesn't. I can prevent my clients from making those mistakes and fast track their success.

No matter what, I would take the driver's seat on all business decisions. In fact, once my friends and family saw what I am capable of, everyone, including those who were trying to temper my success at first, is on board with my no matter what attitude.

This year, I've set a new goal. And for once, I haven't created a false limitation on my own success. I'm working toward making a million dollars in 2015… no matter what. That's nearly ten times what I made in 2014.

The thrilling thing about that goal is this… By setting such a lofty goal for myself, even if I fail at achieving it, I'm not actually failing at all. Coming just shy of a million-dollar goal would still be worth far more than succeeding at a quarter of a million-dollar goal.

Back in 2011, when I started a blog I was too shy to even share with my friends and I spent my time hoping Kim Kardashian would discovery me, I could never have imagined that would have been the start of a journey toward a completely thrilling coaching business where I am honored to work with amazing women all around the world and be on pace to earn seven figures this year. I've come an unbelievably long way, and now my only question is this: If I've come this far in four short years, how far will I have come in four more?

Jessica Nazarali

Jessica Nazarali is the success coach who inspires women create coaching businesses and build beautiful, personal brands. In her first year of working full time as a coach, she went from trading beauty therapy for her coaching services to earning $257,234, selling high end, one on one coaching services and working with a limited number of select clients. She's a living example that coaching can be a full-time business and replace the salary from your career. Find out the three steps to consistent clients - an exclusive video series for new women coaches - at JessicaNazarali.com.

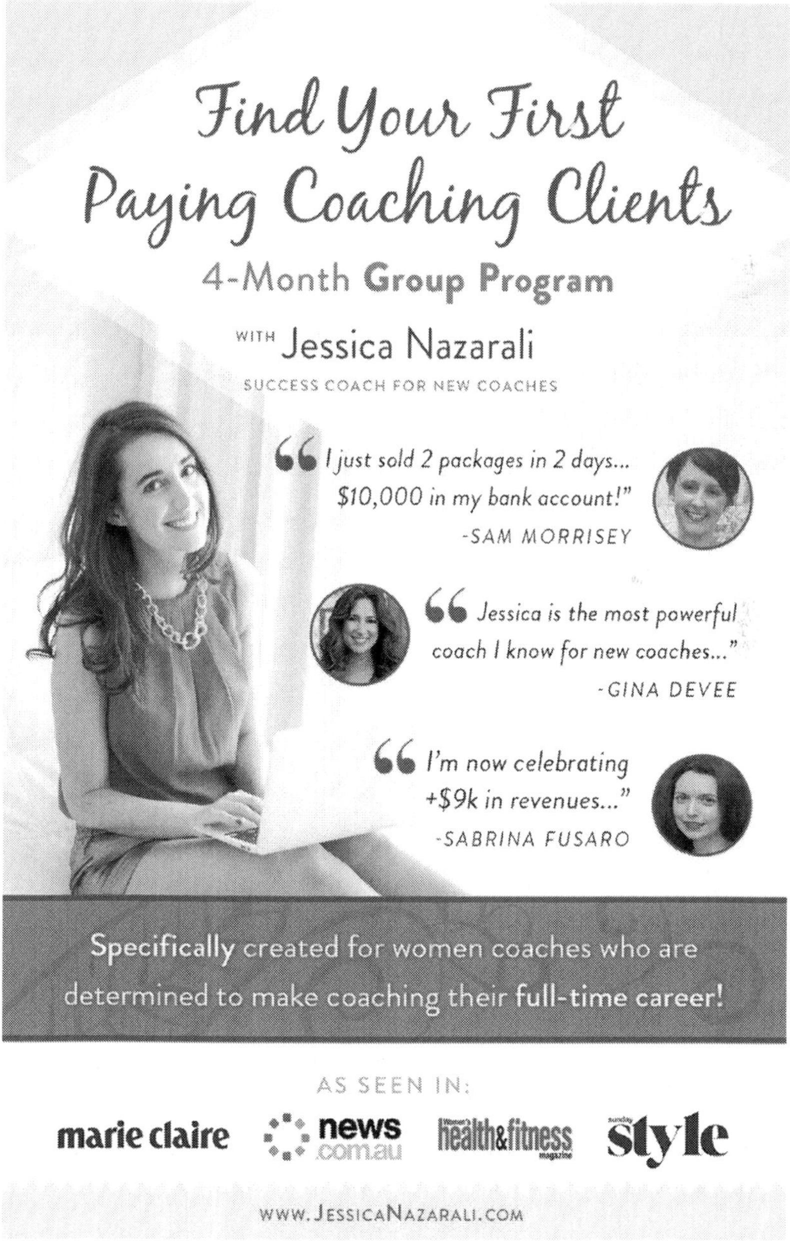
Find Your First
Paying Coaching Clients
4-Month Group Program
WITH Jessica Nazarali
SUCCESS COACH FOR NEW COACHES
“I just sold 2 packages in 2 days... $10,000 in my bank account!”
-SAM MORRISEY
“Jessica is the most powerful coach I know for new coaches...”
-GINA DEVEE
“I'm now celebrating +$9k in revenues...”
-SABRINA FUSARO
Specifically created for women coaches who are determined to make coaching their full-time career!
AS SEEN IN:
marie claire
news.com.au
health&fitness
style
WWW.JESSICANAZARALI.COM

Clarity Consultant & Dream Business Builder
Nicky Leonti - nickyleonti.com

Being an entrepreneur is one of the most intense personal development journeys I have ever been on.

My entrepreneurial journey began when my husband and I took over the managing rights for a small sporting facility. Our dream was to have this business and create the ultimate lifestyle for our young family by being able to work together and bring in a great income whilst doing something that we loved.

The dream was shattered within months of starting when we realised that the reputation of the owner was terrible and his reputation spread across town. Numbers were low in getting new enrolments but we were hopeful for the prime season during summer. Summer came and the entire city flooded which meant that our prime season was getting washed away too. All of our families that we rely on for bookings had their houses flooded and a lot of people lost their jobs when their workplaces washed away too.

This was the biggest challenge we had ever faced as we had to speak with solicitors and get out of the management contract as we had run out of money. We lost nearly everything financially but also we were physically drained. We had a four month old baby and had to start all over again in a city where a lot of people were looking for work. My husband ended up going back to University to retrain and I had to get a full time job. This was the hardest challenge of our lives and it took a huge toll on our mental health.

We both spent a couple of years working in jobs and living 'safe' but after a while we realised that we just weren't meant to be working for someone else. It had been 2 years since the business had closed and I was ready to start my own again. With another newborn baby in my arms I started a blog. This blog was focused on my skills as an Early Childhood Teacher and my passion for good food and gardening for kids. I enjoyed seeing it grow and I started speaking at industry conferences and hosting workshops for Kindergartens. I was having fun but I wasn't making the money I had wanted.

Over the next two years I tried many different ideas but I failed fast and failed forward. I realised when an idea wasn't working I learnt from it and moved on. Below I share with you my five lessons that I learnt throughout my entrepreneurial journey.

Lesson 1: Define success and what it means to you

As an entrepreneur there are so many people to look up to; Richard Branson, Oprah Winfrey and Steve Jobs are top of the list. We see them and imagine our lives with such a level of success. We imagine the people we could hire, the impact we could make and the lifestyle we could live. We have unconsciously defined success as having a multi-million (even multi-billion) dollar company and having an international reputation.

When starting up as an entrepreneur money is tight, lessons haven't been learnt and your reputation is minimal. How on earth am I going to have such a level of success as those who I have been looking up to?

Since becoming an entrepreneur I have constantly pegged myself against the conventional idea of what success looks like. After several years of striving for that and sacrificing time with family and my health I realised that the level of success I was aiming for was not my own idea of success.

Defining what success meant to me was a huge turning point for my business and for me personally. Success to me meant that I could have an income doing what I want to do each day. Success also meant that I could stop and spend as much time with my children that I wanted and was able to always put my health first.

It was such a turning point as I realised I was already successful.

I was already earning a decent income to support my family doing something that I absolutely love. I was already able to drop my kids off to school and pick them up. I was already able to get up early for my morning routine of exercise and meditation to put my health as a top priority.

Since that particular point in my business of defining success and what it meant to me, I have continually grown and my reputation has grown with me. By defining what success means to you doesn't mean you are 'settling' for less. It doesn't mean you have to 'aim low'. It helps you identify what your values are and create a business that is fully aligned to your values. When your business and personal life are aligned amazing things will happen.

If you are striving for someone else' definition for success you may never make it as it does not take into account what your values are and the lifestyle that you truly want.

Lesson 2: Choose a niche

This has been one of the biggest lessons in business and this doesn't just apply to business. It applies to life too. You can't be everything to everyone. If you try and please everyone then you won't truly be connecting with anyone.

When it comes to choosing a niche you must do your research and have a plan. You want to research;
the size of the niche you are choosing to ensure that it is big enough to generate the income you want
the demographics of that niche to ensure they have the money to sustain your business
do you have the ability to serve this niche in the best way possible

Choosing a niche is a very strategic process and the earlier in your business process that you do it, the better.

The benefits of choosing a niche is that you are able to design your product or service to their specific needs. Not only are you able to tailor your product or service but you are able to tailor all of your marketing. By truly understanding your niche customer you will be able to understand the problems they have, solve those problems with your amazing product or service as well as create the most appealing branding to attract your niche customer.

If I was to give you an example of a clothing designer. If they don't niche their product or service they may bring out a pretty plain top for people to wear. As they don't want to 'miss out' on any of the market they make the top to fit both male and female, it's not too colourful so more people would like it, it's not too expensive so more people can afford it. How many people would buy this plain top? Not many.

What if that clothing designer chose a specific niche of luxury female corporate clothing. They would be able to know exactly what their customer wants because they are able to research this niche and understand the problems that this type of customer would have.

The customer wouldn't be overly concerned with price and they would be looking for high quality. The number of people who purchase may not be a huge number but the profit from this kind of product would be worthwhile as long as you truly understood the customer.

Even if you have an existing business but your niche isn't truly defined then I suggest you take some time now to work this out. You also need to align this with who you truly want to serve as this will support you in the sustainability of your business. If you don't enjoy this particular niche, regardless of how well you do then you just aren't going to be putting your heart into it.

Lesson 3: Be confident in what you have to offer

If you are really struggling to grow your business or even get it off the ground one of the common problems may be that you aren't confident with what you have to offer.

If you aren't truly confident in your ability to deliver the product or service you are offering then you need to stop. Now. You need to reevaluate why you aren't confident with what you have to offer. Do you feel like you aren't good enough to deliver? Do you feel that you haven't got the product or service to the level that would you like to have it? What ever the problem is you need to address it before you continue.

Have you ever bought a product from someone who was so enthusiastic about their product that you were really relaxed and excited about your purchase? This is the ultimate feeling you want for your customers. You want them to feel confident during the purchase process as this is the beginning of them loving your product.

In my first two years as an entrepreneur I rarely told people what I did as I didn't feel like I was good enough to promote myself as an expert just yet. I also struggled to ask for testimonials from my clients even though they were so happy. My confidence in my own service and products was so low. Once my confidence increased I started telling everyone about what I did and implemented a system to request testimonials from clients.

As an entrepreneur there are going to be a lot of mindset barriers that will come up that impacts on your level of confidence. Working on any mental barriers you have is one of the best investments of time and money you can spend on building a solid foundation for your business. There are many different methods that you can use to work through your mental barriers including Emotional Freedom Technique (EFT), counselling, mentor programs, hypnotherapy or journaling are just a few.

Some of the most common mental barriers that you could face as an entrepreneur are fear of success or fear of failure (or both). These fears may seem irrational but they are very real. I have had a deep fear of success as when you are successful more people will see you and therefore more people will judge what you are doing. A fear of failure can be just as limiting as you struggle to really give it your all in case you might fail. Spending time daily to work through your mindset barriers is a great place to start.

The most effective strategy I used was joining a paid mentoring group where I was completely surrounded by amazing and supportive entrepreneurs in the same situation as me. Being surrounded by these people and hearing the stories of their journey was so motivating as I was able to see exactly where they started from and how they have got to where they are. Learning that all entrepreneurs start from the beginning was refreshing and helpful in times where I felt like I wasn't getting anywhere.

Lesson 4: Your health is the biggest investment

As an entrepreneur you are your biggest investment. Most importantly your health is your biggest investment. Your success can only get to the same level as your health. If you don't have the same level of health to maintain the energy you need to put into your business then you can't ever achieve the big dreams that you have set.

Some of the most amazing entrepreneurs dedicate time each day to ensure that their bodies are in the best shape in order to achieve their goals. They ensure there are non-negotiable time slots each day for exercise, meditation and eating well. When your body is thriving you have more energy to put into what you love; your business, your life and your family.

This was a big lesson for me and I learnt it the hard way. I was putting so much time into my business that I felt guilty to spend any more time on myself by going to the gym or yoga as I wanted to spend the rest of my time with my family and friends. By not scheduling any time in for my health and fitness I got completely exhausted and burnt out. It took me months to get back into shape and from that point I haven't taken my health for granted. I have non-negotiable time slots in each day from 5.30-6.30am where I do my morning exercise and meditate.

By having dedicated time slots in your day for your health you are making a huge investment into your business. As the leader of your business you need to ensure you are in the best shape and leading by example for those in your team and for those who you are serving through your business.

Lesson 5: Having a life can increase business

When starting as a new entrepreneur all of my time was dedicated to my business and I rarely went out and enjoyed my life as I was just so engrossed in websites, marketing, working with new clients and growing my business. I was becoming a bit of an entrepreneur hermit.

As most of my interactions were online or via Skype I started organising times to meet up with others in my mentoring group at a local cafe. This made such a difference and got me out of the house. I then realised that I needed to start having fun again that wasn't business related.

Spending quality time with my family was a big thing but also reconnecting with my friends helped me to see what I was missing out on. I started to understand my potential clients better as I got out of my little entrepreneur bubble.
In this bubble everyone is an entrepreneur and understands everything you say when you start talking about optins and mailing lists. Outside of the bubble not many people understand those things including my potential clients. This certainly helped me pinpoint how to improve the language I was using in my marketing material.

I highly suggest you get out of your bubble and enjoy life. This is going to help you in your business.

Over the last 12 months I have created a business that focuses on mothers who want to create their own business from home.
This has been such a rewarding journey since my first business attempt with my husband. I now have an online school for mothers who are looking for the lifestyle I had dreamt for my life all those years ago.

I now work in my business full time and spend my days doing what I love being able to spend my time with my kids.

Nicky Leonti

Nicky Leonti is a clarity consultant for creative mothers looking to create and grow a business. The School of Holistic Learning (SOHL) is the virtual hub for women to come together and be supported throughout their journey to identify their passion and create a business that they truly love.

A mother of two who has created a range of online courses that focus on helping other mothers to build a business so that they can have the lifestyle to be able to care for their child and make change in the world at the same time.

Nicky's passion is getting women to uncover their real gifts and see them shine into the world.

OUT NOW: HOW TO START A BUSINESS WITH LITTLE OR NO CASH

Available from Amazon and Mithra Publishing

Small Beginnings – Big Ambitions
Amber Daines -Bespoke Communications

In many ways I am an accidental entrepreneur. It does not run in my family so was never in my DNA or overtly encouraged, to be honest.

My Baby Boomer generation father is a PhD graduate in town planning whose 50-year career in property development and as a CEO for other people's businesses has taken him from Sydney to Los Angeles and back again to Melbourne. He has asked me many times since I began my business "why consult when you always have to worry about your next contract or client while you are madly working on the current one?" My dad is a wise but overtly cautious character, who is not big on taking professional risks.

On the other side, my mother was typical of her generation, one where career was largely defined by your station in life and marital status. Though retired now, mum worked by and large in administration and support roles for government or private businesses but never as a self-employed person. She worked hard but had a definite break of around eight years at home all up.

That is something I have not been able to do when I had my two sons, aged two and six years old. It was a different time in the 70s and 80s, where not working as a married woman was the social custom of a conservative place like suburban Australia. Now it's hardly a choice for many families purely financially speaking, though I have consciously made one to remain working in a business I love, with my own family in the mix, though I am realistic about how much I can work and grow my practice with my home life also front and centre.

So my own business story is maybe rather unremarkable in many ways but it has certainly been adventurous and continues to evolve. If I can teach anyone anything from my entrepreneurial experience, I will be more than satisfied. As Oscar Wilde famously said: "The only thing to do with good advice is pass it on. It is never any use to oneself." How true.

Small beginnings, big ambitions

I officially started Bespoke Communications on 2 December 2007 with one client and $1000 in the bank. It's interesting how I recall the date so clearly. I had worked in corporate for 12 years, having earned my early career stripes as a 20-year-old print journalist cadet for a major daily newspaper, fresh out of three years of university and ready to learn. In the mid-1990s, these newspaper cadetships were rare and highly competitive – the money was dismal but I was keen to take the opportunity to work with some of the biggest and best editors in Australia and make my mark. After a year or so there I was restless. Australia is small but our media saturation at the time was staggeringly high and remains so. Australia has one of the highest consumption levels of magazines per capita in the world, spending $894m buying 172 million copies of magazines a year. It is also particularly female-friendly, with 78 per cent of women saying they read magazines.

All well and good except my specific areas of reporting was more business focused, hard news related and male dominated., I knew at aged 22 I was either going to wait for a senior editor to retire at Fairfax to get a serious promotion or leave town. A chance to move to Hong Kong came up and I was on a plane six weeks later.

Beige a senior Asian correspondent covering the 1998 Asian financial crisis was exhilarating and terrifying in equal measure. Global reach and the rush of being in amongst the action was a journalist's dream ride. I moved to London in 1999 to be the European derivatives writer for a weekly magazines and found myself enticed by the decadence and thrill of that first dotcom boom. Apart from the USA, the online dot commerce fever was no greater than in London at the time.

The first leap of faith
Having decided to leave the challenging but narrow beat of derivatives reporting, I was presented with a choice. In a heaving, suit-filled pub in the heart of the City of London, I made a choice. Take the prestigious job as an analyst with Goldman Sachs that one of my regular banking interviewees had put on the table, or take a major pay cut to join a dotcom in the online arts world as an Assistant Editor for a start-up. No prizes for guessing where I ended up. It was here perhaps that I got my first genuine taste of entrepreneurism.

In the cramped confines of a west London building, I was able to witness the highs, the lows and the realities of a new small business in a relatively infant sector. It was just the variety I needed. The 20 or so staff, from the PA to the developers to the sales team and us in the editorial team were offered shares or sweat equity – one week valued at $70 million by none other than Goldman Sachs who was keen to secure the web site Cloudband but less than six months later the dotcom bubble burst. The party was over. I have the fondest memories of my two years at Cloudband; learning much about the history of East Asian art, the market forces of a new economy and how a company in its early days can't always offer the big bucks in the war for talent, but it can create an amazing culture. That was without a doubt what kept of us there until the end.

Changing my career gear
Back home in Australia by 2002, my communications career became predictable and I almost picked up where I left off four years earlier. I could hardly stomach the prospect of hustling my way back into a no-so-senior journalism career, though I did a stint in SKY news TV but soon moved into public relations (PR). The pay was better and the challenges news. I admit it was not an easy transition. Agency PR life is more grunt than glam. The never-ending administration certainly not my forte – as a reporter I would use a phone, a computer and a note pad and pen to write up to four 1,000 word stories a day.

My PR world was suddenly all about billable hours, weekly WIPs (work in progress updates), new business pitches and long-winded discussions with clients on whether they should say "shall or should" in their two-line quote for a media release.

However, I did quickly learn the ropes and saw the value of what I was able to generate for business leaders and brands. I was a strong writer and could nail a deadline, given my former years spent as a journalist, and could communicate complex or unusual ideas to media and clients alike (thank you *Derivatives Week*).

After experiencing my first redundancy at one PR agency, I decided to just take some time away from a single employer and freelance. This engaged my arts knowledge from Cloudband, and having just finished part time study of a Masters at the College of Fine Arts, focus on major arts festivals like the Biennale of Sydney and Sydney Writers Festival to be a publicist in the spaces I enjoyed in my down time. It was a highlight in my job life so far. The pay was fickle as arts events don't happen every day in Sydney, and the expectation to be at openings and do 5am radio calls to media ahead of launch or prize announcement was hectic but it such a rich experience. I met some talented souls, and learnt how to be creative on a shoe-string budget; something that was a far cry from the $100,000 event budgets I was able to play with in corporate PR but perfect for what was to lie ahead when I starting my own business just three years later.

The end of work as I knew it
I landed a job in Sponsorship and Marketing inside an art gallery who was a former freelance client. I enjoyed the change and steady income for 14 months. It was to be my last job working for somebody else, but at the time I was not to know that. I kept being approached by people while working in this job asking me if would do some media release writing for them, or update their web site copy or devise a media list. One of them became a friend and said "just start a PR business of your own, I would happily be your first client – three months campaign guaranteed."

I resigned from the job a week later. I had not set out to become an entrepreneur, or business leader, and the first year was hard yards, long days and nights and not much cash flow – the way one man bands always are. Even today business remains lean on staff – we use freelancers and contract out parts of bigger jobs sometimes – but it has certainly survived the magical "five year mark" when only two thirds of small businesses remain open for business. I am grateful mine was a stayer.

Finally: Learning to lead

Below are my top six take outs for you to ponder, no matter where you are in your entrepreneurial journey.

1. **Embrace the numbers**

Money and cash flow can be king or the killer for many small business owners. I started by own PR business with just one small client and $1,000 in the bank some seven years ago. I won't lie, it was scary times. But it was more than lady luck and being good at what I do that has helped me stay in business and bring in a six-figure sales turnover while having two kids, noting that in Australia 1 in 3 start-ups fail within the first five years.

So with the benefit of hindsight, how can you also succeed in making your business not just survive but thrive?

As a wordsmith by trade, even five wonderful years as a business reporter didn't make me love spreadsheets let alone understand them as much as I should. But the facts remain, if you don't understand how to read a profit and loss sheet, to create a business plan with a growth trajectory, or plan for down time, you are really undertaking a hobby not a serious business. It took me a few years to find a fantastic, pro-active accountant and business advisor who took the time to explain the nitty gritty to me. It was daunting but it also changed my life. So if it's not your forte, hire a book keeper or accountant that does more than just "tick and flick" processing of your annual tax return.

2. **Start small**

Very rarely do you need a fancy office in the inner city or a company structure to get going and have more than $50,000 a year in revenue. A company structure is ideal if you are operating a high risk business and needed the limited liability protection a company structure offers or if there are a number of different people in the business.

3. **Find and keep the good eggs**

Keep on speed dial a stable of reliable, casual labour to ensure that the business is not burdened with overheads we can ill afford should a client take a break, or I am on leave for a month with no work to do for staff. I manage these resources myself and at the end of the day. The client always has a direct line to me.

4. **Be nimble**

Hire slowly, fire quickly. That goes for clients, suppliers and employees.

5. **Work with like-minded folk**

Strive to work with only the most suitable clients that share similar values, profile and service capability. For me that is mid-sized firms or project of larger corporates doing new campaigns that demand an agile and experienced communications agent. One man bands, no matter how edgy, exciting or personally engaging that don't have the experience with a PR agency, limited budget and a need for too much "hand holding" are more energy than reward.

6. **Reassess and walk away**

Once you go from start up to a more long-term business, always find new ways of working smarter, but certainly not harder. I rarely do weekend work and late night sessions compared to even two years ago, thankfully due to implementing new systems and streamlined processes.
The take out here is, be prepared to have a business achieving year on year success will mean whole new level of tough decisions every day.

Be true to what you value and have courage to make the big and small changes. Any business you run has to make money but has to be more rewarding, exciting and fun than working for someone else.

Amber Daines

Amber Daines has spent almost 20 years of her career devoted to all things communications including print and TV journalism, PR, sponsorship and marketing working in her native Australia as well as in Asia, the UK and Europe.

Launching Bespoke Communications in 2007, Amber combined all her expertise to form a boutique agency servicing the corporate, small business, creative and charitable sectors. These days her practice is focused delivering media training workshops, developing corporate communications strategies, giving key note talks to other business types and professional writing services.

While Amber has contributed to scores of blogs, articles and books over the years, in May 2013 launched her first self-published title '*Well Spun: Big PR and Social Media Ideas for Small Business*'.

In 2015, her second non-fiction book will be released entitle '*Well Said: How to be heard in Business and Generate Real Influence*'. It will share insider tips, methods for writing and delivering stand out talks, and over 20 case studies for all modern business leaders wanting to make online, seminar and small group speaking their secret weapon.

Amber is passionate about the power of communications to change your business and your profile. With two children under five years old, Amber also thrives on the financial and mental flexibility that being self-employed allows.

Academically, Amber has obtained a BA in Communications (Journalism major), a MA in Arts Management and a Graduate Certificate in East Asian Art. She has been a nominee in the 2013 and 2014 Telstra Business Women's Awards.

Bespoke Communications also chooses to support a range of not-for-profit groups, and Amber and her husband David helped found the First Seeds Funds http://firstseedsfund.com.au/ in 2013. This scholarship, awarded annually in Australia, directly supports disadvantaged youth seeking to improve future via higher education opportunities.

Please contact Amber on her web site www.bespokecomms.com.au

# The secret to being a great entrepreneur? Love what you do

David J. Bradley - Primal Digital Marketing

The Journey Begins

Month after month past and I was working on a new slew of business ideas. Dozens of different projects, ready to go at any point. Some in the pure concept stage, others fleshed out with financials, products, and delivery defined.

Yet, I hadn't actually started on any of them. I was still working my job while studying for my MBA. It wasn't what I wanted, but that's where I found myself.

What was the limiting factor that stopped me from starting one of these projects? It's surely the money. You need upfront cash to invest. And, you can't assume you will start a business and be profitable the next week. Research might be it, too. I needed to do more research before it would make sense to begin, right?

Actually, I had a typical entrepreneurial issue. It wasn't money or research. I wanted to do so many things and could never decide on which to focus on.

I could have started multiple projects, but I knew that wasn't the smart way to approach jumping into entrepreneurship. Choosing just one ripped me apart mentally and emotionally. It's so far from my philosophy to choose just one thing to do, even though I know it's important.

My final decision to enter entrepreneurship was made by combining a few key factors: being sick of working for someone else, conviction that I could run my own business, confidence in delivering value to others, and an idea that ignited my passions, interests, and needs.

Let me explain that last part. That's the real driving factor that helped me decide on what exactly to pursue.

I decided to start consulting with growing companies in digital marketing strategy. Let's break this down to why it works for me.

First, consulting means you work with a variety of companies over time. That isn't the same job day after day. It's new projects constantly, and potentially, multiple projects at once. That eases my entrepreneurial spirit that doesn't like monotony.

Second, I love companies that embrace growth. I knew that's who my clients would be. Through combining what I can offer companies, what companies needed, and what mindset the company executives need to have to find success, it only made sense to work with these types of businesses.

Finally, digital marketing *strategy* was my offering. Digital marketing itself is a large subject that covers many areas, all of which I love. But, I could never be an expert in every area. The idea of focusing on a specific element, like web design, online advertising, or content marketing, still felt too confining, commoditized, and unaligned to what I love.

I love helping companies grow. At the core of business growth is strategy. With my expertise in understanding the complete digital marketing landscape, I found my focus on digital strategy. I love doing it and businesses desperately need it. It took a long time to discover this, but it was a worthwhile wait. In retrospect, however; I'd start sooner because you learn a lot more once you begin.

As a bonus to all of this, the business combined many passions and interests. This was another element that was vital to starting. You often hear, "follow your passion", but there isn't a clear path to doing so.

Instead, I realized that a grouping of interests and passions collided with what I can do each day. They aren't direct, but they are all relevant. The intersection that combined bits of each interest made it something I would find fulfilling. For me, these interests were psychology, communication, neuroscience, emotional intelligence, growth, strategy, and, of course, digital marketing.

So with that, I decided to officially start my own business and set out on my own.

The Challenge of Customer #1
I think optimism is prevalent in most young entrepreneurs, and I say young in years of self-employment rather than age. I started out thinking of how in just a few weeks, I'm going to have my big clients rolling in, pouring tens of thousands of dollars into my business in no time.

Weeks later, my sales pipeline grew stagnant and I was struggling to figure out why. I set up my website professionally, I got my business name under an LLC, and I started my cold outreach campaign to top prospects.

The main issue was that I was new. It wasn't that I didn't know how to market or sell myself, or that I wasn't as good, if not better, than competitors in the market. But, agencies, consultants, and freelancers were in business for decades already. Then there I was, a few weeks after opening. They had all the proof that they had experience, while I didn't have a large portfolio of clients.

The best way to communicate that you can deliver on what you promise is case studies. This short report is testament to one's ability to deliver real, quantifiable results that matter. Unfortunately, again, I had no customers. No customers means no case studies.

So, I tried to think of the best ways to start getting new clients. I could do deep discounts and hope someone bites, but that would leave me with the type of clients and business I never wanted. I could offer my services on barter, in exchange for referrals and promotion. Better, but there's still the hurdle of convincing someone I can get the job done.

That's when I realized, I started my new business and got everything ready, yet I barely told anyone. I had a network of hundreds of business connections and loving friends and family. They were all left in the dark.

I immediately laid out a plan. I would go through all my email, LinkedIn, and Facebook contacts. That meant about 800, 700, and 300 contacts respectively. A lot of work, but much easier to reach out to someone who knew me than the cold outreach that I was attempting.

The biggest mistake anyone makes in reaching out to their contacts is that they don't personalize the outreach. Blanket emails are *not* worth it! You want to nurture these relationships, and you should genuinely care about connecting with these individuals. That means personalizing each and every message you send out. It takes time and effort, but it pays off for your short and long-term success.

Very simply, I started with a personal note between myself and that contact, mentioned how excited I am that I just started my own business, and then made the ask. Making the ask is vital!

Keep it simple and to the point: "it would be a tremendous help if you could connect me with one or two people who you think would benefit from speaking with me." Never ask for referrals without specifying how many, but also don't ask for too many. You want to give that low expectation of one or two contacts to reduce friction.

Close out the email with another thank you, and a P.S. that explains who your ideal customer is. Be as specific as possible so that your contact knows the type of person and business to refer to you. This is an incredibly important step that many forget in the referral request process.

Don't expect referrals to pile up now. You're still new to the business, so even friends and family may not be completely confident in referring your new company to their contacts. Some contacts may not have anyone they can refer. But still, this will result in warm connections and begin word-of-mouth.

In my opinion, your personal network is the best tool you have to starting your marketing. It requires no financial investment and will likely teach you quite a bit about *how* you communicate who you are, what you do, and who you serve. Now, set time aside to plan this out and work on a rough script to use for your contacts.

You Have To Love What You Do
No matter what your plan is and how well thought-out it may be, it's never easy. You can be the best person out there to help your target market, and yet, gain no traction after months of tireless days. There's a tremendous learning curve for most entrepreneurs.

If you don't embrace marketing and sales, you're going to struggle even longer. We all are salespeople in life, but it's even more true when we are running our own business. When you identify what value you bring and who exactly would benefit from it the most, marketing and sales becomes a virtuous activity. Remember that.

But regardless of the hours you put into building your business and your energy spent on marketing and sales, there's one ruling factor: you must love what you do. You must love being an entrepreneur!

You really need to take the time to consider whether you love the business you're getting into *and* what you will be doing each day. Those two things are often not the same, but we often get blinded by a passion and excitement and fail to realize that.

For example, you can be an amazing baker who loves nothing more than creating delicious pastries. You want to reach more people and share the amazing recipes you've created while freeing yourself from having to work within the creative confines of someone else's bakery or restaurant. So, it seems to make sense that you would strike out on your own and open a bakery.

You punch the numbers, scout out some locations, and get a logo designed. You know that part of running a business includes these factors in getting going. What you forget is the daily grind of being a business owner and not a baker.

You'll have a business to maintain and market. Employees need to be managed. Accounting and financing needs to be taken care of. Sales and partnerships need to be made.

All of a sudden, all your energy goes into running the business and you aren't behind the oven nearly as much as you can ever be working for someone else. This isn't necessarily a bad thing and I'm not trying to scare you. Risk may be part of entrepreneurship and glamorized by magazines and the media. But, successful entrepreneurship is about calculated risks. As long as you calculate the risks and seriously consider whether or not you will enjoy the aspect of your life that is being a business owner, you'll be okay. Just love all that you will do.

Work ON Your Business Not IN It
You may have heard this before. What does it mean exactly?

Let's look at the last example with our baker friend. With the warning I gave, the new business owner was working in their business more than on.

This is rather common, especially for new entrepreneurs. To some degree, it is for the best early on when you have a lot to learn about your business.

However, when you want to grow your business and build a lifestyle around being a business owner you really love, you need to work on your business. That's when you can restructure the operations and get back behind the oven!

So, we do that by working on systemizing the business and continually improving. It takes an investment of time and energy to do this, but it will produce a return-on-investment. The result will be more time, energy, and money from systemizing.

Most refer to systemized processes as SOPs, Standard Operating Procedures. The SOP is a document outlining the specific way to do a certain thing in your business. It allows anyone to pick up the document and get to work immediately. It's one of the main reasons that McDonald's became the successful organization it is today.

Don't seek to overcomplicate things now with how to develop an SOP. Just go through a process you do each day in your business and write down each step as if you were writing an email to a friend, instructing them how to do it all. But be meticulous about detail.

The result is a step-by-step guide. It isn't final, though! This guide outlines a process that can likely be improved, so seek out opportunities to do that. Every time you do, update the SOP.

With this, you can outsource work you don't want to do yourself to others. It frees you to focus on what matters to you, makes training easier, and gives you confidence in the job getting done the right way.

This is what I used to help me prospecting for new clients. It's helping me complete the more basic functions for client projects and hire an assistant to take care of public relations opportunities. It takes away the minutiae that goes along with work and lets me focus on the things I love.

That's where I am today. Expanding my team and freeing myself through standard operating procedures. It is one of the most beneficial times for my business and personal growth. I highly recommend it to all entrepreneurs.

Advice For The Aspiring Entrepreneur
There are three aspects of my life I nurtured throughout my teens and early twenties that prepared me for entrepreneurship. They are things anyone can work on in any point of their life. You don't need an established company, large bank account, or any experience at all. You just need commitment to your own personal growth.

The first aspect is being comfortable being uncomfortable; or comfort in discomfort. When I was growing up, I was always incredibly shy, reserved, and easily embarrassed. It was part of who I was. For the most part, this attitude ran my life. There was just a miniscule threshold for discomfort before I was overwhelmed.

Eventually, I realized this was holding me back from growth and happiness. I decided I needed to do something about this, so I began noticing all the times I was uncomfortable. When I found myself uncomfortable, I would explore it further. It wasn't easy and definitely not an overnight change, but it was drastic.

At my prom in high school, I wouldn't dance. I was terrified. So, in college, I joined the ballroom and Latin dance club. I never went to parties in fear of having to actually communicate with others! In my senior year of high school, I got involved in nightclub promotions. I was always awful at sports, athletically paralyzed by fear of embarrassment. So, around sixteen years old, I joined mixed martial arts and stuck with the sport until my early twenties.

The point is none of these things directly have to do with being an entrepreneur. Instead, I found different areas I was uncomfortable and pushed myself into changing that. As an entrepreneur, every day will bring discomfort. To be able to perform and persist, you need to be okay with that. Start today being comfortable being uncomfortable.

The second key to becoming a great entrepreneur was *hustle*. Simply, look for every opportunity you can. When you are actively seeking out opportunities, getting involved in different projects, and meeting new people, more growth occurs. It's guaranteed.

Fortunately, this places you in a position of abundance. It is far better to have several opportunities to choose among than waiting for that one perfect opportunity. You need to create the opportunity by keeping your eyes open, but it's there for you.

In my first two years of college, I was involved with 23 different jobs, projects, and internships. I was never fired from anything. Rather, most were temporary gigs that helped me explore different areas and meet new people. One opportunity would open the door to more.

It's also fair to point out that I was a workaholic in college. There were weeks as a full-time student with the maximum allowed course load of six, I worked full-time as well. In fact, I remember two weeks in my senior year that aside from the six classes, I worked 63 hours. There was a "shift" I recall also in which I ran between three different jobs, allotting 27-hours of continuous work. (Needless to say, I slept well over 12-hours after that shift.)

I don't give these stats and accomplishments to brag. There's a part of me that is proud, as they are times I can look back to and recall what I've invested and been capable of. But most importantly for you, the lesson is simple: get out there and hustle.

Finally, I have one last key that's been helpful to me more recently. It's something I wish I had a more intellectual understanding of when I was younger, as I believe it would have helped me grow more effectively and efficiently as an entrepreneur. I call this concept "structured flexibility".

In structured flexibility, you want to have an idea of the ideal outcome you wish for. You can think about the vision for yourself in three or six months. You can also think of it as your vision in one to five years. The point is to understand intellectually and emotionally what you want in your future and who you want to be.

Now, before you start mapping out every step to get there, I want you to embrace a mindset. Getting that vision gives you a framework to function within to get there, your map. This is structure. It's flexibility that will give you the power to fuel yourself to that ideal future, or the power to change directions for your betterment.

Flexibility requires discipline and self-awareness. The purpose and mindset of this is that you do not need to take a single, direct path towards that ideal future. In fact, that ideal future can, and will, change as you go. However, you need to be flexible to understand when that does need to change and when you need to persist in your current direction.

Additionally, I find it helpful to focus more on what I want to *do* in my future than what I want to *be*. For example, there was a time I wanted to be a talent agent. Focusing strictly on who to be, I would study film history and spend time learning about different agencies.

Instead, I could have focused on what I wanted to do: build a personal network, understand the art of promotion, and identify and nurture talent both in the entertainment and business fields.
You can see the latter would serve me in any area, whether as a talent agent or a consultant. What I focused on at the time, while helpful and fun, hasn't been as impactful, however.

Give yourself structure with a vision going forward, but keep the plans loose and exciting with flexibility.

David J. Bradley

David J. Bradley is an entrepreneur from Providence, Rhode Island. He is the Managing Director and founder of Primal Digital Marketing, where he puts the digital marketing skills he started developing at 12 years old to use.

At Primal, David helps businesses create strategies and build digital sales funnels to generate more sales online. He wrote a book to teach others how he helps businesses in this way, Getting Digital Marketing Right.

David studied Marketing and Operations Management at Rhode Island College and pursued his MBA in Marketing at Providence College. Outside of his business, he encourages entrepreneurship and personal growth in others through speaking and coaching.

Driven by growth for his personal self, his business, and in others, David is happy to connect with aspiring entrepreneurs and professionals. You can reach out by visiting him at DavidJBradley.com

A Leap of Faith
Manel Daetz - Henry Corbett & Co

Henry Corbett & Co. Flagship boutique showroom Woollahra, Sydney, Australia

Taking a leap of faith and creating Henry Corbett & Co. is something I will never forget. The journey has been the most exciting adventure I have ever embarked on and the scariest.

My love for all things creative started when I was a child and playing with interiors was where I had the most fun. Even at a young age my interiors were built to last, with pegs and bed sheets as bricks and mortar. Spatial planning was a hobby and my lifelong love of interiors began.

As a teenager I was constantly changing my bedroom around and rearranging furniture. Fabrics and woven items grew my passion for interiors anything with a natural fibre caught my eye. I loved layering fabrics and using colour tones to create interest in the room.

As well as rearranging existing pieces and collecting new ones I would design and build pieces for my room.

Henry Corbett & Co. Signature Sofa designed by Manel Daetz

The first large scale piece I built was my bed which was inspired by a Japanese bamboo hanging lantern. I used earthy taupe colours as opposed to the traditional black as even back then I believed in pushing design boundaries.

Creating a furniture item that was functional was so inspiring for me. It took up all of my weekends for months and finally after sanding timber beams and learning about how to use tools as well as hand painting with fine brushes so that I could achieve the desired effect the bed was finished. It was an absolute success and I was hooked on creating beautiful interiors. The next step that I took was gaining work experience with an Interior Designer who was such an inspiration for me. She opened my mind to different design styles as well as introducing me to the business side of Interior Design and from that moment on it was my dream to start a design business.

Then at 17 years old I part timed my higher school certificate and started at the International School of Colour and Design. I studied Business, Colour Consulting, Surface, Textile Design and Interior Design. During that time I kept a library of amazing ideas using notebooks, visual diaries and scraps of paper, just in case I was ever able to use them. I even jotted down an idea on a piece of gum wrapper so I wouldn't forget it.

I continued to write and draw down ideas even after my schooling had finished but it was 13 years later that I felt I had gained enough knowledge to start a business of my own.
The best part is that in having waited so long all the books of creative ideas and concepts eventually evolved into the final vision for the business and boutique showroom along with the experience I had gain while being in my industry.

Ethically sourced timber hanging rail custom made at Henry Corbett & Co.

During my time working in Interior Styling, kitchen and bathroom design, interior styling and commercial design in Sydney, I identified a gap in the market and an opportunity to offer a whole vision service for clients so that they did not have to go from store to store to pick and match something that worked.
My vision was that Henry Corbett & Co. could be an experience where a client could be guided through their journey of creating a dream build whilst having consistency in design and concept.
I had a vision of being able to create a business from Architectural planning through to interior styling, where all aspects of design were considered and there was seamless integration from one design phase to the next.
I must admit that in the early stages I was unsure if my vision would work. Solution finding was a challenge from the get go and there were a number of challenges that all happened in quick succession.
The first one was the pursuit of Hand Crafted, Ethically Sourced, and Sustainable products and coming up with a business plan which could easily be transferable to market.

Hand crafted ethically sourced bone bracelets with hand casted silver links.

I truly believed that there was a way that I could create interiors and use local and international artisans with ethically sourced, sustainable products that would represent the core values I had for my business.
We had many conversations with creators, designers, our building networks as well as collaborators to find out where to source the right products that were able to fit the ideals we had.
Much of the conversations where about explaining the philosophy of holistic design and of transfusing luxury with authenticity to create, elegant designs that move the soul, which took some work.
It was a hard concept to get people to embrace as it required a lot of research.

Building a strong network of reliable people from the start was critical to me. I wanted to make sure that if I created a viable business that the right people would be in place to support it.

At times I felt like may be this was not what I was supposed to be doing, it was hard work with a lot of leads that turned out to be dead ends.

It was in these times that I heard my inner voice saying "That this dream was a long time coming and it was possible." So I would pick myself up and continue on.

Solving puzzles and being a detective is a core ingredient of all interiors. Seeking out possibilities and finding resolve where there may not be an obvious answer is the challenge.

I think that because of the way I thought in times where all the roads seemed to lead to nowhere I was able to look at the situation as another interior design puzzle.

Henry Corbett & Co. Signature Sofas with the bases made from 80 year old recycled timber beams wire brushed by hand.

The next challenge I faced was nutting out the details of a business plan as I had already identified the gap in the market and found the type of people I wanted to work with and who wanted to work with me. All I needed now was to plan it all out.

My business plan was to provide a holistic service whether it was a commercial build or creating a home. I wanted Henry Corbett & Co. to be able to for fill the brief and give people an oasis away from mass product. I wanted to also achieve a business which was able to reconnect with the client easily if they wanted to add to their collection or go to the next step in their design journey. I found that the simplest way that I could give this to people was to integrate a high end boutique showroom into the Architectural and Interior Design side of the business.

The concept was to house furniture décor and even carefully selected jewellery items and fashion. I knew that in a world of duplication and replication people hungered for products that move the soul and by seeking out unique pieces of clothing, jewellery, home wares and art clients and customer could do that.

Hand Crafted 100% organic and chemical free skincare range by Henry Corbett & Co.

This also allowed the everyday shopper who wanted to indulge in luxury pieces, though was not necessarily ready for a full scale renovation or new build, to come in a select items that reflected their own style.
I found that a lot of Architecture and Interior Design companies didn't offer this approach to design. Identifying this and being able to implement these missing pieces from the market into my business at the start was a great way to set Henry Corbett & Co. aside from the completion.
It also allowed me to market the business in a way that was a completely unique.
Marketing a holistic design service where clients could receive guidance from floor plans at the start to being able to finish their project with soft furnishings was an easy way to create interest as it had never been done before.
I believed that the ability to receive design assistance at every stage of a project whether it was Interior Design, Interior Styling, fashion advice or Architecture was key to holistic design and I knew that in creating this in a business plan Henry Corbett & Co. would be the most unique retail and design experience in Sydney. So I put together the business plan and went about setting up the business.

I also think that if I had not set the bar so high the chance of success would have been much less. My mantra "Aim for the moon at least if you don't make it you will fall among the stars." Motivates me to realise my dreams and acknowledges all the challenges we face as individuals setting out on our own journeys to create something new in the world.
The next challenge that I found was creating a point of difference in service and I found that in my research across many fields this was one of the easiest ways to set Henry Corbett & Co. aside from other similar businesses. For me creating great customer service standards was a key part in growing and maintaining Henry Corbett & Co.

Listening to our clients and customers' needs and imbedding that into our service standards has been the most important part of our business and I was very lucky to have identified this as I was setting up the retail boutique.

Focusing on service really allowed us to create the ideal space for our clients and pinpointed everything that we were about which is in essence 'lifestyle'.

Custom Kitchens by Henry Corbett & Co. Featuring Sawkille & Co. Benchtops in solid American Oak.

Looking after their needs and listening to the desires of the people who are putting their trust in our expertise is the first point that we educate anyone in who joins the Henry Corbett & Co. team.
Our belief is that great design is able to transcend and elevate lifestyles and that great customer service sets the bar of what to except when having your project designed by our team.
I also believe that customer service is not only about an instant with a client in a retail situation or if they purchase through our e-boutique it is the future of keeping our clients.

If I can create a great experience for my clients then they will walk or click away with that gift and they will tell everyone about what they got from being involved with our business.

As each client goes on to build their next home or commercial space I know that they will be back to Henry Corbett & Co. because of what we offer, a boutique service with a world class experience to each person who we engage with.

Our boutique showroom in Woollahra Sydney, Australia

I believe that this has been the biggest and most valuable asset to our businesses and it is the one that you can't see.

I wanted every person to walk in feeling welcomed and I wanted them to feel that they had stepped into something special.

The great part about mastering high service standards is that people gravitate towards us and become loyal repeat customers and because of this, sales increased and our company has been able to grow.

It has been a long journey from having an interest and love for design into creating a successful business.

There are so many challenges that I faced on the way though I believe that when you choose to follow your passion and create something that you really believe in through hard work it can come true and be successful.

Somehow at every road block I faced, sooner rather than later a door would open and things fell into the right place. I also think that this happens when you have done the research, taken the time, put the work in and given it your all. For me sourcing ethical products that are hand crafted and made from the heart is the most important part of Henry Corbett & Co. it was the driving force that inspired me throughout all the challenges.

Keeping this philosophy across the Architecture and Interior Design aspects of the business as well as the boutique showroom has allowed me to purse my ideals and given our clients an experience quite unlike any other.

The 3 most useful things I found out on my journey of creating Henry Corbett & Co. was researching and finding out all the information I could about design and design businesses. Also knowing what made me different from everyone else and capturing that uniqueness so that I could make it into a successful business.

I also think that surrounding myself with people who supported and believed in my ideas even before I had started out on the journey was extremely useful.

I found they always gave me helpful, honest advice and as they were people who were either in a similar industry or benefited from Henry Corbett & Co. being successful they were always willing to help me when things got tough.

The last thing that I found that helped me the most was focusing on the reason why I started a business and that for me was my love of design.

Creating a beautiful boutique showroom and making sure that all the visual elements come together in a way that completely captures what Henry Corbett & Co. is about is what keeps me inspired. As well as continually sourcing and featuring new designers who make pieces that are irresistible, luxurious, earthy and unique also gives me focus for the future.

My quote for people who ask me about my design style is:

"I believe in using organic elements and creating designs which purely consider my client's needs.

I create designs from an intricate understanding of each individual and then bring those elements to life."

Manel Daetz

Manel Daetz is Creative Director of Henry Corbett & Co, a luxury boutique retail business that offers a range of services from Architecture, Interior Design, Lifestyle and Culture as well as an exclusive collection of jewellery fashion and decor. Manel's philosophy is to infuse luxury with authenticity to create elegant natural designs that focus on premium quality and unique style.

Manel Daetz passion is for flawless design with a holistic approach to architectural planning through to unique styling, designing beautiful furniture, fabulous kitchens and interiors. Manel says her most exciting project to date was the design of the Henry Corbett & Co. boutique in Woollahra, Sydney Australia. .

Manel has over 14 years industry experience from forecasting design trends in Milan Eurocucina, Paris and London trade fairs to designing both for commercial and residential interiors. She says that her years spent at the International School of Colour and Design was the foundation of her creative journey. "The knowledge gained there was invaluable and has fundamentally formed my organic design style."

As creative director at Henry Corbett & Co our focus is on seeking out designers who are leaders in their field who are inspiring and whose collections enhance the luxury and originality of the Henry Corbett & Co. showroom. My goal is also to create bespoke pieces that give meaning, stand the test of time and add value to our lives.

Lessons from Sticks

Kevin May - Sticks

Some people are born to be entrepreneurs. These are the few who knew from their early years that they would always be running their own show long before they even had any idea what that show might be. This rare breed never even considers being anyone else's employee.

And then there are the rest of us, the ones whose main aspiration on entering the workforce is for something that we can enjoy, be good at, and find rewarding.

Some of this group also go on to start their own businesses, but a lot of what's involved doesn't come naturally to them. Just like writing a book, the only chance they have of doing it really well is if they start with something they know inside out and care deeply about.

For me, it was the advertising industry. It's not unusual for those who have had a bit of success in that business to start their own agency, but I was never interested in doing just another one of those. The intention behind Sticks was to build a new resource that didn't mimic a thousand companies that had been started before.

Sticks: The Concept

The original idea was to provide something that could help agencies in their strategic endeavours. My background was in account service and planning, and it felt that the whole area of strategy within agencies had been losing traction for some time. The planners were being used primarily to retrofit rationale to what the agency most wanted to do, or were wheeled out whenever a client fire got out of control and the only way to douse the flames was with the semblance of intellectual rigour. Apart from that, they were just left to look after managing research and writing briefs, neither of which many other people in the agency cared much about or paid a lot of attention to.

It wasn't so much that I was disgruntled or bitter about any of this. Shameful waste as it seemed, I could kind of understand it. The changing market had made clients far more promiscuous than they previously were, and the increased tenuousness of accounts had made agencies fearful to the point of struggling to function properly. A confident agency has bold points of view about many issues surrounding its clients' businesses, but a fearful agency can only focus on doing what it thinks its clients want. Almost by definition, planning has very little role in an organization that is in perpetual react mode.

The Foundations

And there were other general observations about the state of planning within the broader industry that signaled an opportunity to build something better. These were to form the foundation stones that helped shape what Sticks would become.

1. **Variable workload**

The first was how variable the need for strategy was within an agency. The other key functions – account service, creative, production, media – all enjoyed a much steadier workflow. The amount of client business determined how many of each were needed, and they could be kept consistently busy through a year-long cycle. Not so the planners, who live much more of a Goldilocks life. There are periods of intense activity when the demands are so hot and the timelines so tight it's almost impossible to do anything properly. Then come periods of chilly abeyance, when planners find themselves casting about for anything even vaguely meaningful to do. The amount of the year when the balance of planning work and capacity is just right amounts to probably less than 50% in most agencies, and that's clearly something that needed to be addressed both for the people doing the job and for those employing them.

2. **Consistency in terms and understanding**

The second was to do with terminology. When you are heading up a department outside of a major market, you have little choice but to be perpetually recruiting. If you wait until the job opening is there, you'll take months to fill it without an already-stocked pipeline of warm candidates. Throughout my first three years in Seattle, I spoke with at least one potential recruit each week, and I had noticed that the word "strategy" was being used on resumes by people whose work was quite some way removed from the day-to-day of the standard agency planner. I found many of these people to be fascinating and sometimes brilliant but, much as I would have loved to have been able to access what they had to offer, there was no way that I'd ever have been able to keep them busy on an ongoing permanent employee basis. So it started to dawn on me how limited the static model of a full-time workforce was, and how the thinking of an agency could be significantly galvanized by the injection of a greater diversity of perspectives.

3. Structure impacts on success

The third observation was something that had been bugging me since long before I left London. It is often said that agencies are valued by their clients for their thinking and their creativity. If this is the case, it seemed odd that while the agency machine is geared around the creative department, planning tends to be an adjunct to account management. Creative departments are structured around people working in pairs and extended teams, with junior and senior partnerships all doing in principle the same sort of work across an ever-changing variety of accounts. The ethos involves a significant emphasis on ideation and "percolation" time, a dogged pursuit of ground-breaking output, and extremely rigorous quality filters. Planners tend to work by themselves, with the senior folk doing the big stuff and the juniors the grunt work, and value is attached to tenure within category and the ability to get stuff out quickly. There are no formal quality filters to interrogate output before it goes off to client beyond those instigated by the author of the work. Given how masterfully agencies had built their creative departments, it seemed there was a great opportunity to mirror that in the construction of a new sort of planning operation.

So, armed with these thoughts, I left my last agency job in June 2009 to make a go of doing something about it. The plan was straightforward enough: assemble a diverse array of strategic thinkers that could be deployed in a turn-on/turn-off fashion to provide much more textured planning input for agencies, and organize them to work in a fashion much more akin to a traditional agency creative department.

Scoping out the opportunity

At the beginning of any entrepreneurial endeavour, it is important to have a clear sense of what you are prepared to invest, in terms of both time and money. I reckoned I was in a position to go at least 12 months without having to earn money, and the business plan called for minimal up-front cost (certainly in our pre-revenue phase). But I wanted to find out sooner whether I really thought there were legs in the idea, so I gave myself the rest of the summer to stand the idea up. I booked for the family to go back to England for the whole of September, with a view to returning in October knowing more fully whether there was a business to be built or the need to start searching for a job quickly.

I thought my biggest problem would be finding the people, especially given that our location wasn't one of the main advertising markets. On the day I started – June 8th 2009 – I had a list of five people I could call. Fortunately, each of them also had lists of people they could recommend, and so there was only one day in that first three months that I didn't meet with anybody. Most days I saw two or three people, and some days as many as five or six. And all those people had others they could suggest, and so the pool just kept on growing. Of course, not everyone was suitable or necessarily interested, but by the time we went back to England that September, I had a list of about 45 potential participants.

I had seen enough to believe that the talent was there and deployable, and that there was at least enough interest from potential clients to suggest this business could be a success. I'd also been able to figure out what the real challenges were going to be. It was clearly going to be difficult operationalizing this workforce: the strength of the group lay in its significant diversity of viewpoints, but we were going to have to find a way of creating just enough glue to hold them together and be able to hit the ground running without squeezing all that difference of perspective out of the equation.

Monetizing was also going to be a thorny issue. With a business this unstructured and volatile, there was never going to be enough margin in charging by the hour to sustain it, and I didn't want to do that in any case. Charging time for thinking seemed inappropriate; if anything I believe you should be able to charge more for delivering quality quickly, rather than dragging work out unnecessarily just to rack up fees. The principle of wanting to charge based on value rather than cost was straightforward enough, but it becomes decidedly more elusive when your business has little in the way of repeatable output, deals mainly in intangibles, and represents an entirely new paradigm for the clients who are going to be paying its invoices. After all, precisely how much cleverness does a few thousand bucks of good thinking amount to?

Vetting/challenging myself

The final major challenge that I found myself contemplating that September was whether or not I personally had the entrepreneurial balls to pull this off. For all its cutting-edge chutzpah, the advertising industry has a track record of breeding fairly risk-averse conservative types who like to do their adventurous thinking within the safety of familiar, established parameters. I knew myself well enough to recognize that I was not one of the natural-born entrepreneurs mentioned at the opening of this chapter (after all, I had waited until I was in my forties to abandon the sanctuary of paid employment). If there were a word to describe me more accurately, it was probably something like "baronial". I was comfortable within my own fiefdom, with the license to push some boundaries without any of the exposure of real business disaster. I knew that the best days of running my own business would far outstrip the best days of being an employee, but I also knew the worst days would be much darker than anything I had previously experienced. I knew that I would inevitably find myself staring into the abyss at times, but I had no idea how often that would be and how much stomach I would have for it.

All this had to be weighed against the huge enthusiasm the idea had been met with by both potential clients and participants, and my own deepening conviction about what Sticks would have to offer. Of course, figuring out how to make the business function was only a part of the challenge. Even if that could happen, we needed to find a way of getting some actual clients to hire us. Here I felt particularly vulnerable. I had only been in the US for three years, and in that time only worked at one agency. I was very poorly connected within the client community, with no real reputation to speak of. But I did know a lot of people who worked at advertising agencies, in Seattle and in other major markets across the country.

The call to arms begins

When I returned from England in October, I assembled the dozen or so most enthusiastic of the participants I had met and told them that I was going to go out and drum up some initial projects for us to work on. I warned them that I would neither be charging the clients any money for this work, nor paying any of the people who did it. I made it clear that I neither expected nor wanted anyone to pass up proper paid opportunities to help out Sticks, but that if they believed in the idea and were prepared to offer some of their unused capacity, then we might just get the show on the road.

Between then and the end of 2009, we undertook a total of eleven assignments and used 21 different people. We learned quickly from things we did wrongly. The first was that when it comes to intense brainwork, people start to spin their wheels well within two hours. We were making more progress on the work where we devoted a succession of 90 minute sessions than to the assignments where we'd hole up for complete days at a time. The second was that too many people in the room quickly became counter-productive. We figured out that four was the ideal number, but that it needed to be at least three and certainly never more than five. During this period we also devised our basic view of the anatomy of a modern brand, the core tools that would form the framework for how we went about our unstructured work, and the central conviction that the most interesting thinking comes from asking better questions rather than trying to rush to conclusive solutions.

We also developed some values. We intentionally put a significant premium on the way we treated our people. I already had an acute sense of gratitude to those early participants who were trying to help realize my dream at the expense of their own free labour. And while I intended to pay them as soon as we started making money, it was clear from early on that our model would offer dependable income only to a very limited number of them. For the majority, it would be a peppering of work here and there but they would still need to maintain a livelihood elsewhere. So it was certain that our business would not work without the significant goodwill of this diaspora of contributors.

Being selective to encourage/retain support

From the outset, we have always gone out of our way to make the work we do both interesting and enjoyable. We pass on assignments that hold little promise for anything but a thankless grind (however well-remunerated they might be), and we have nurtured an environment that is friendly and energized. While we don't hold to the ridiculous notion that there is no such thing as a bad idea – quite obviously there is – we don't belittle anyone for chancing their arm and missing the mark.

We practise what we refer to as "courteous confrontation", where we call out fragile thinking without scoring points off each other. And, very importantly, we always pay our people within 24 hours of receiving their invoices.

As we entered 2010, I realized that we needed to start charging for our services, and I felt those eleven assignments had sharpened our game sufficiently to justify it. We continued to focus on advertising agencies, believing there was significant potential in helping out big agencies at times of intense burn – major client crises or new business pitches – and also for smaller agencies who wanted to be able to punch above their weight strategically from time to time, but who could never practically build a robust planning function into their permanent infrastructure.

The basic pitch was to go up against the idea of a standard freelancer, who would represent a static level of experience regardless of whether the job called for desk research or grand strategy, who would cost the same on days the workflow was slower than others, and who would move forward in linear fashion through the time of the engagement. Sticks offered a potent counterpoint to all these frailties.

Learning on the job

Our early negotiations were comical, and amounted to little more than asking how much the prospective client had available and then agreeing to it, however risible the sum. The first time we were asked to submit a formal proposal to a major corporation – a leading national insurance company – my first draft was akin to a high school essay on the whys and wherefores of remunerated activity (fortunately one of our senior marketing participants forced me to make some concrete calls, and our proposed numbers and terms ended up being accepted). Somehow we secured enough of a succession of tiny assignments to enable us to stay afloat. We were lent space at a downtown advertising agency with "rent" coming in the shape of consultative projects on their clients, and I was finally able to pay people for their work (though I remained some way off making any income from the business myself).

Even allowing for the limitations of our starting position, I was surprised by how difficult it was proving to gain any sort of momentum. I had naively assumed that people would just get that we offered everything a planning department could do, but with the significant benefit of thinking fueled by a high degree of diversity of perspective. Unfortunately, the harsh truth was that nowhere near enough people understood what a planning department really did in the first place, and they were all broadly ambivalent to the idea that what we offered was done in a completely different and fresh way. The most common response we met was along the lines of "It sounds good, but what the hell is it that you actually do?"

We were not helped by refusing to offer up case histories. This shortfall was not down to an absence of examples, but really fell out of some of the other values that were intrinsic to our operation. Even if the most interesting facets of our work had not been protected by non-disclosure agreements, we felt it was completely inappropriate to compromise (even potentially) the commercial interests of our clients just to serve our own ends. On top of this, there was a significant discomfort with the post-rationalized fiction that lies at the heart of so many (if not all) case histories, and the absurdity of trying to glorify a strategic play as if it were an end in its own right.

Challenging the status quo

At this stage we were not even publicly identifying the agencies we were helping, let alone shouting details about that work from the rooftops. But even as early as the summer of 2010, we were already starting to move away from our original mission of providing planning support to advertising agencies. We were learning with every new assignment, and it was becoming painfully clear that we weren't very good at just populating somebody else's pre-existing process with content. We never quite got it right, but this problem was compounded by the extent to which agencies never really wanted our brains.

They are closed architectures which want to own their thinking, and are not looking for external provocation. We would often go in and challenge some of the fundamental premises at the heart of the problem as it had been articulated, only to be told to get back in our place and just focus on the question that had been asked of us.

Not only were agencies ill-equipped culturally to embrace what we had to offer, they weren't very good from our point of view either. They didn't own any of the stuff that really mattered: the problem, the budget, the timeline, or the decision. And they obstructed access to the relationship wherein lay the prospect of continued engagement on the business.

Dealing directly with the end-clients removed all that drag from the equation. They are perfectly acclimatized to bringing in external perspectives that they don't pretend are available within their own standing resources. They put a value on smart thinking that can advance commercial interests, and have both an ability and willingness to pay for it. And, if the work is good, they will keep coming back for more.

Six years on challenges remain

As Sticks approaches its sixth birthday, some of those early challenges remain for the business. While we have smoothed out many of the operationalizing issues, we're still grappling with the two main canards of how to describe what we do to prospective clients, and how to scope accurately so the deal ends up being fair to both sides. As with our attitude towards paying our people well and promptly, we want clients to feel they are getting a good return for what we cost.

It's our express intent not to make money an issue for anyone who touches Sticks. We have become better at charging appropriately as our experience and confidence has grown, but our model means that this will never be perfect: when the deliverable is often ill-defined at the outset, and by design the value of the work doesn't become apparent until quite some time after the assignment is done, then there will always be room for some significant miscalculations. Thankfully we have tended to gravitate to working with decent and reasonable clients, and usually we are able to adjust along the way if things get too out of kilter.

The problem of describing what we do will not go away. We have tried to create a framework to productize our main activities, spanning brand positioning, single issue business diagnostics, and enquiry-driven research. We have a philosophy that is geared around driving to simplicity and creating attractiveness rather than interruption. And we have a methodology that is anchored in an elemental toolbox, a commitment to diversity of perspective over skill-set, the use of concentrated face-to-face salons, and a search for better questions at the heart of the situation.

But none of that alters the fact that barely any two assignments in the history of Sticks resemble one another, except in the most general sense of being commissioned by clients who recognized they needed something other than an off-the-shelf solution. Probably the most effective tag-line we have come up with for ourselves is *Where to go when you don't know quite where to go*.

Our offering is less about knowledge/expertise and more about stuff that requires brainpower, and our niche arises from the change in business environment that means the challenges facing many companies are becoming less and less standardized than a couple of decades ago. I believe this is our real legacy from the advertising industry. The creative executions that came out of the ad business were simply the best manifestations for the time of what that talented pool of people had to contribute to the world of business.

But it was always about much more than slick TV commercials and clever posters; it was the application of collaborative imagination to intractable problems where no formula existed to develop a solution.

Advertising dealt with the area of business that wasn't reducible to a defined way of doing things, and the best work didn't always come from the oldest, wisest or most practiced. It put instinct and emotion at least on a par with analysis and rationale.

The best agencies tended to be the most unstructured ones that were driven by beliefs and passions rather than process and discipline.

Sticking to our guns

Perhaps the over-productization of its output – those bits of advertising execution – is one of the factors that now lies at the root of so many of that industry's problems. It is certainly a trap that we are keen not to fall into at Sticks. Some of our clients have asked us why we don't build on an execution back-end and make ourselves into a full-service shop, but that would belie everything that we are about. We don't want to be approaching every assignment with a mindset that the answer is something we can make, learn to make, or profitably get someone else to make, regardless of the question. We want to be able to take every situation on its merits and go from there.

This has probably cost us business and most certainly money. Clients don't want to pay big bucks even for ideas, let alone strategy. The fortunes are to be made in execution, at least for the meantime. How viable it will remain to make money out of content-creation into the future may be moot, but at present it remains the key deliverable that clients look at and realize they can't do themselves. Unfortunately for us, that is not always the sentiment when it comes to strategy.

Despite this, we have been able to build a stable business – albeit on top of a highly volatile model – that has never had any debt (except to me personally). In the end, it took 21 months before I was able to start making a living out of the business, and my first draw took place in April 2011. By 2013, I was back to earning the same sort of money as my last salary at an agency, but to this day I continue to pay myself last depending upon what we have left. And from time to time, I still have to subsidize our cash-flow in order for us to be able to pay our Sticks people within that 24 hour window. Our clients may all be from the more pleasant end of the spectrum, but most of them still operate on 30-60 day terms of payment.

Strategy doesn't need to be "strategic"

Although our continued inability to express with concise precision what exactly it is we do hampers us, that only really presents an issue for the first date. Once they hire us for one thing, most clients are able to realize quite quickly how we can be useful to them. It may seem a little passive – ironically non-strategic perhaps – but our entire business has been built on a combination of relationships, repeats, and referrals. It is a low-volume high-value model, and our flexible talent pool is not a hugely hungry machine that needs constant feeding. On the few occasions that we have agreed to do something solely for financial reasons, we've usually ended up regretting it. The work we do is an important part of who we are and why people hire us.

The Sticks community is now just over 250 people, and surprisingly few of them have traditional agency planning backgrounds. The rest fall into a number of buckets: some researchers, some management consultants, some "digital" folk, some local entrepreneurs, some marketing clients. The biggest group is the rest: a collection of interesting business thinkers that have been attracted to Sticks along the way, spanning attorneys, accountants, academics, architects, a chef, a neurologist, an educator, a non-profit fund-raiser, and a host of other jobs beginning with letters from the back end of the alphabet. What unifies them all is that each has an interesting lens through which they view business situations, they enjoy working collaboratively and having their opinions changed by the questions of others, they can all think foundationally and deconstruct issues, and none of them are unpleasant people.

Moving in the right direction

These are express recruitment criteria that we talk openly about, both to clients and prospective participants. Most of our people are still deployed only occasionally, and virtually all as freelance consultants. We do have a handful of full-time employees at the core, and recently I have brought two partners into the business as we attempt to take things to the next level of scale. Sticks has always done well on repeat business – of the 250+ assignments that we have now undertaken, there have only been three occasions that have not resulted in follow-up work. Within the past nine months we have achieved official vendor status with five different multi-national corporations, and so we're moving in the right direction.

When I reflect on these initial years of Sticks, there are several things that make me feel proud. We launched into one of the toughest periods in recent economic history, and have been able to stay afloat despite some choppy waters at times. The quality of our output has been consistently high: at least eight of the ten best bits of work that I have been associated with in my career have happened in the time since I started Sticks. And we've not just built a functioning business, we've built a brand that has its own narrative arc that people who encounter us can believe in.

Culture is key

At the pinnacle of all this is our culture, which is all the more pleasing given how few full-time people we have. Everyone entering our offices is immediately able to snap into Sticks mode, a combination of restless enquiry, honest analysis, blunt articulation, and understated bonhomie. It is not only the thing that allows us to do the work we do, it is the thing that keeps those participants coming back to us. We make that open commitment to ensure the work is always interesting and enjoyable, and this is something we don't just say but actually mean. Without it, we'd have no people so we'd have no business. We have made many mistakes along the way, and fortunately have been able to learn from them, but there are two things that we have got right from very early on that I believe lie at the heart of why we've been able to survive long past the point where many start-ups fail.

Articulating the story

Most businesses arise from the combination of a passion and competency meeting a monetizeable model. But this is rarely enough. In order to catch fire, you need to do these two other things well. Your business needs a story that exceeds just an explanation of what you do. It has to be a thing that people can believe in. This is more than just a marketing ploy: arguably the most important audience for this "brand" is the people you have inside the company. Get that right, and the business will follow.

Ground the business to be flexible

And you need to start with a plan that is grounded in something you know very well, but you have to build in the flexibility to change direction. You need the vision to identify a potential destination, but your ability to turn the wheel as you drive down the road will be the main factor determining whether you ever get there.

As Dwight Eisenhower once noted, "Plans are nothing. Planning is everything."

Kevin May

Kevin May, founding partner of Sticks, is a veteran of the UK and US advertising industries. The first 20 years of his career were spent in London, at agencies such as J Walter Thompson, TBWA, CDP, BBDO and Y&R, as well as time working as a journalist and independent strategist. He came to the USA at the end of 2005 to head up the planning department at Publicis in Seattle, before leaving to start Sticks in 2009. He has provided the strategic smarts behind numerous campaigns that have won awards for both creativity and effectiveness in market, including Nestle (confectionary, ice cream), RAF (recruitment), Telegraph (newspapers), Gallaher (tobacco), Virgin (financial services), Canon (cameras), T-Mobile (cellular), and Washington Lottery (lottery).

Sticks was founded to provide a more flexible and circumspect strategic resource for both agencies and marketing clients. It comprises a community of over 250 ideas professionals from the worlds of agency strategy, management consultancy, market research, digital specialization, client marketing, and entrepreneurialism, as well as from more diverse fields such as law, industrial design, teaching, architecture, neurology, and restaurants. The central promise is a fresh and independent perspective on anything from single issue challenges through to full-blown business plans and positioning's. We organize ourselves like a creative department, and our output is actionable, simple and expressed in plain English.

To date, our clients include major corporations such as Microsoft, T-Mobile, Starbucks, Expedia, Moet Hennessy, and Virgin, through to more local companies and start-ups such as Mutual of Enumclaw, Lagunitas, BroVo Spirits, HomeAway, Everspring, Group Health, Medamonitor, LearnBIG, and Front Desk. We have also worked with agencies such as BBDO, Dentsu, Publicis, Cole & Weber, Razorfish, Creature, Wunderman, Inferno London, and Wexley School for Girls.

More details and client recommendations are available upon request.

Printed in Great Britain
by Amazon.co.uk, Ltd.,
Marston Gate.